AFGHANISTAN
AID, ARMIES AND EMPIRES

Peter Marsden was Coordinator for the British Agencies Afghanistan Group from 1989 to 2005. He is the author of *The Taliban: War, Religion and the New Order in Afghanistan.*

AFGHANISTAN
AID, ARMIES AND EMPIRES

PETER MARSDEN

I.B. TAURIS
LONDON · NEW YORK

Published in 2009 by I.B.Tauris & Co Ltd
6 Salem Road, London W2 4BU
175 Fifth Avenue, New York NY 10010
www.ibtauris.com

Distributed in the United States and Canada Exclusively by Palgrave Macmillan
175 Fifth Avenue, New York NY 10010

ISBN: 978 1 84511 751 1

A full CIP record for this book is available from the British Library
A full CIP record is available from the Library of Congress

Library of Congress Catalog Card Number: available

Printed and bound in India by Thomson Press India Ltd
from camera-ready copy edited and supplied by the author

CONTENTS

1

INTRODUCTION

It is hard to reflect on the outcome of the US-led military intervention in Afghanistan of October 2001 without also referencing the previous military interventions of Britain and the Soviet Union. However, while these are regarded as absolute failures, the US-led intervention is presented as a relative success, albeit facing multiple challenges.

US and other Western politicians often cite, as key indicators of this success, the creation of a democratic process, the return of refugees, in large numbers, from Pakistan and Iran and a substantial increase in the number of children in school. Yet the democratic process was seriously flawed and the return of refugees from Pakistan and Iran has been followed by a reverse flow, on a similar scale, of Afghans to both countries, in search of work that cannot be found in Afghanistan. Further, the increase in the number of children in school has not been accompanied by a commensurate increase in quality, given a reluctance by donors to inject a sufficient level of funds.

At the same time, the efforts of the international community to effectively counter the insurgency launched by the Taliban and Hisb-e-Islami have been far from successful. We are, therefore, led to question whether the US-led intervention in Afghanistan has achieved significantly better outcomes than those of Britain and the Soviet Union.

Leaving aside the question of the relative benefits of each intervention to the population of Afghanistan, it is important to establish to what extent each of the intervening powers achieved the strategic objectives that it set itself. This is inevitably a complex question as the objectives of each were very different. Yet there are similarities in the strategies adopted which it is important to explore. Among these is the provision of resources, not only by the intervening powers but also by other actors, to influence outcomes on the ground.

A key purpose of this book is to analyse the extent to which this provision of resources was effective in enabling each intervening power to achieve its strategic objectives, or if it undermined them. Alongside this is a consideration of the roles of human dignity and religious identity in generating and strengthening resistance movements. Was the much-vaunted Afghan resistance to invaders no more than the normal human response to the feeling of humiliation that invasions bring about? To what extent did the level of brutality that accompanied each invasion enable the resistance to build a support base within the population? Was the centrality of Islamic identity to each of the resistance movements a consequence of historical factors within Afghanistan and its immediate hinterland or was pan-Islamic solidarity a key determinant?

This inevitably leads to a consideration of the importance of material benefits, relative to human dignity or Islamic identity, in determining the response of the Afghan population to the invader. How important is it that the intervening power has serious regard to the actual needs of the population, as opposed to its own strategic interests? An equally important consideration is whether the intervening power actually believes that it is delivering some benefit, even though its own interests predominate.

It would therefore be of interest to speculate what the outcome would have been if the intervening powers had been guided purely by the perceived greater interests of the Afghan population. Thus, if the US, in sitting around the table with the Afghan Government and other members of the international community, had reflected on how the needs of the population could most effectively be addressed, without other objectives intruding on the process of reflection, would it have delivered more significant benefits on the reconstruction front? If the US had not, simultaneously, been engaged in a 'war on terror', involving a search for high value targets such as Osama bin Laden, would it have given earlier priority to the reconstruction process? If it had given aid to Afghanistan on a par with that given in the Balkans or East Timor, would it have created livelihoods in Afghanistan on a sufficient level to reduce the subsequent support for the Taliban insurgency? Has the US, in building up a network of military bases in Afghanistan, simply been mindful of the need to prevent Afghanistan becoming a centre for terrorist training or has it also been concerned to counter possible regional threats to its interests from China, Iran, Pakistan or Russia? Has the investment in the US military infrastructure been disproportionate to investment in the reconstruction process?

The history of Afghanistan over the past two centuries thus presents a useful opportunity to explore the various issues relating to the use of aid in pursuit of strategic goals. The three British interventions of the nineteenth and early twentieth centuries, the Soviet intervention of 1979 and the US-led intervention of 2001 therefore create a lens through which we can look at the effectiveness of aid as an element in great power politics? What lessons can be learned in comparing the interventions of the three major powers? What parallels were there? What were the key differences?

A linked question, in relation to the US-led intervention, is to assess the degree to which the actions of the US and other international forces, in delivering aid in pursuit of military objectives, undermined the work of the humanitarian agencies which had been responsible for much of the health care, education, agricultural support and other benefits received by the Afghan population over the previous decade or so.

In considering these many issues, we will first focus on the British military interventions of the nineteenth century to reflect, among other things, on the circumstances which led to the horrific massacre of virtually the entire British contingent. The influence of colonial attitudes is of particular interest in relation to these interventions.

This will lead on to a consideration of the complex dynamics, both within Afghanistan and internationally, which led to the Soviet military intervention of December 1979. The use of brutality in pursuit of utopian visions is of considerable relevance here in relation to the actions of the People's Democratic Party of Afghanistan (PDPA) Government. Also of interest are the complex factors which led to the Soviet intervention.

The period of the Soviet military occupation will be considered next, with a particular focus on the efforts of the Soviet Union to rein in the PDPA Government to make it more acceptable to the population. In this section, the balance between the Soviet Union's recognition that the PDPA regime had seriously alienated the population and its simultaneous recognition of its own strategic interests will be explored.

The following chapter will assess the complex politics of the resistance movement and the resources which influenced its internal dynamics. Of particular significance is the relationship between the development of this resistance and the emergence of the Taliban movement and, ultimately, the US-led intervention.

The period which followed the US-led intervention will be considered in particular depth in looking, first, at the factors that were used by the US to lend legitimacy to the intervention. This will link to an analysis of the possible relationship between the stated objectives of the neo-conservatives in the US and their interests in Afghanistan. Also to be considered is whether the US achieved the strategic objectives that it set itself.

The next chapter will analyse the relationship between US strategy and the aid process and will look, particularly, at how the level of attention given to influencing the US public, the Afghan public or the wider Islamic world significantly affected outcomes. A key area of focus will be the radicalization of the political environment, both within the US and within the Islamic world, and the impact of this radicalization on the level of acceptance of the international presence.

We will next look at the specific impact of the development and humanitarian assistance provided by the USA and other donors, both in meeting the needs of the population and in terms of the state-building process.

The related question of the continued ability of development and humanitarian agencies to operate in the midst of a counter-insurgency war will then be considered. The efforts of NGOs to achieve changes in the policies of the international military will be reflected on, in this context.

The final chapter will draw comparisons between the British, Soviet and US interventions on the basis of a range of criteria. These will include the influence of colonial attitudes and value systems, the effectiveness of aid in pursuit of strategic interests, human rights and the impact of the interventions on the ability of the population to survive.

2

THE GREAT GAME

The three British military interventions in Afghanistan of the nineteenth and early twentieth centuries can usefully be seen in the context of the mutual paranoia which Russia and British India felt, to an intense degree, as each suspected the other of seeking to expand at its expense.

Britain had been successful in building up a significant presence in India from 1599, through the British East India Company (which was dissolved in 1858), but its hold on the country was extremely tenuous. As a result, it was concerned that Russia would either invade from the north or seek to sow unrest amongst the population of India so as to cause an insurrection.

Russia had suffered from successive waves of invasion from Mongolia and Central Asia over the centuries. It feared that Britain would establish a presence in Central Asia and so thwart its own efforts to gain control of the Caucasus, Central Asia and eastern Siberia, whether through deals with local power holders or through conquest.

Each empire eyed the other nervously, often overreacting to every move which might be deemed to be expansionist. To protect their positions, a succession of emissaries and under-cover intelligence personnel were sent to test the water with the major and minor power holders along the routes that invading armies might take, and to take note of the likely operating conditions on the ground. Persia was in a particularly important position, providing a potential route to India through Afghanistan, or offering access to the Persian Gulf, where British naval supremacy could be threatened.

Also targeted were the various khanates or principalities of Central

Asia, along with the succession of power holders who controlled one or other area of Afghanistan. Many of these were in remote areas where extreme desert or mountain conditions would put armies at risk. Their willingness to facilitate or impede the progress of armies passing through their territories was therefore crucial. The British saw it as particularly important to build alliances with the multiple power holders who controlled the various routes across the Hindu Kush, the Pamirs and the Himalayas.

Britain was also fearful that Russia would build influence with the Ottoman Empire, based in Constantinople, and so dispatch its ships to the Mediterranean through the Black Sea. However, it estimated that China could be relied upon to protect its northern and western reaches from encroachment by Russia, even though it was, for part of the period, weakened by expansionist activity from Britain and other European powers. Japan took action to ensure that Russia's conquests in eastern Siberia did not threaten its own interests.

Over the course of the nineteenth century, Russia was successful in taking territory, from Persia, within the Caucasus and in capturing the khanates of Central Asia and large areas of eastern Siberia. However, this was not without setbacks and many thousands of Russian soldiers lost their lives in the process. Britain embarked on three military interventions in Afghanistan to pre-empt possible invasions by Russia and also suffered significant casualties.

The most catastrophic of these interventions was in 1839, which resulted in the massacre, in January 1842, of almost the entire British garrison of troops, camp followers and families, as they fled a situation which had become untenable. The stated rationale for Britain's military involvement was the restoration of the former Afghan ruler, Shah Shuja, to power in Kabul. However, it was prompted by a failed Persian siege of Herat and the arrival of a Russian delegate to hold talks with the then ruler, Dost Muhammed. Britain was concerned to strengthen its position in Afghanistan by placing its own protégé in power over Afghanistan.

The British army had entered from the south and passed through Kandahar and Ghazni, where it overcame fierce resistance, before reaching Kabul. Assuming that it had established a reasonable hold on the country, the army then imported wives and children and the colonial lifestyle which had been enjoyed in India. Regrettably, the

British contingent failed to pick up on signs of growing resentment around them so that, when an armed insurrection occurred in Kabul only two years later, they were both ill-prepared and ill-equipped to deal with it. A negotiated deal with Dost Muhammed failed to protect the departing British colony from armed attacks, along the length of their route, as they attempted the journey from Kabul to the Khyber Pass on foot. Only one person made it to Jalalabad, just over halfway to the Pass.

The following spring, two other British forces were sent to Kabul, entering via Kandahar and the Khyber Pass and exacting retribution against populations en route. The British then withdrew, leaving a power struggle behind them that resulted in Dost Muhammed returning to power. Their final act was to blow up the ancient Kabul bazaar, on which much of the commerce depended.

Britain then left Afghanistan alone for over 30 years, reaching tacit agreement with Russia in 1872 that the Amu Darya would be the northern frontier of Afghanistan and, in 1873, that Russia and British India would be separated by a finger of land, in the extreme north east of Afghanistan, which touched on China.

However, Russia's success in extending its domains to the edge of Afghanistan, with the capture of Khiva and Merv in 1878, led it to send a mission to Afghanistan in that year. The British insisted, in response, that they should also be permitted a mission but when the then ruler, Sher Ali, refused to allow the mission to proceed, Britain opted to send an intervention force in November 1978, again entering via Kandahar and the Khyber Pass as well as by another route between the two. In order to forestall an advance on Kabul, Sher Ali's son and successor, Yaqub Khan, signed the Treaty of Gandamak with Britain in May 1979. This provided that Britain would control Afghanistan's foreign affairs and that it could also place a resident mission in Kabul.

However, the first British representative was assassinated in September 1979, within only two months of his arrival. In response, General Roberts, one of the three British Generals who had led forces into Afghanistan the previous year, marched on Kabul. Yaqub Khan abdicated and General Roberts became the de facto ruler of Kabul. One of his first acts was to order the hanging, from gallows especially constructed, of nearly one hundred Afghan suspects.

Whether for this or other reasons, the British again faced resistance and, finally, accepted, as ruler of Afghanistan, Abdur-Rahman, a nephew of Sher Ali, after he had built up a sufficient support base to challenge the British hold. The British nonetheless faced a military defeat, at the battle of Maiwand, to the west of Kandahar, in July 1880. This prompted General Roberts to head a punitive force to Kandahar to avenge the defeat. After a successful military offensive, Britain withdrew from Afghanistan again.

Over ten years later, definitive agreements were drawn up between Britain and Russia, in 1891 and 1895–6, to delineate the border between Russia and Afghanistan. This brought to an end the major tensions between the two empires. At the same time, the Durand Line was drawn by Britain to indicate the boundary between its domain and Afghanistan, cutting through the territory of the Pushtun population. Britain finally gave up its ambitions in India in 1947, resulting in the creation of India and the two separate states of West and East Pakistan. However, the Durand Line remained as the border between Afghanistan and West Pakistan. It continues to be disputed by the Afghan Government and to be a source of tension between Afghanistan and Pakistan.

The rulers of Afghanistan acquiesced in British control of their foreign policy until May 1919, when the then ruler, Amanullah, took advantage of Britain's weakness at the time, and declared war, setting in motion the Third Anglo-Afghan War. However, following military victories on both sides, the two parties agreed to cease hostilities after only a month and to sign the Treaty of Rawalpindi, under which Afghanistan recovered its right to conduct its own foreign affairs.

An interesting insight into the thinking of the British Government over this period is given in a confidential memorandum[1] written by a British official in 1878, when Britain was considering how to respond to the arrival of the Russian mission but preceding the departure of Britain's own mission.

The anonymous author of the memorandum thus noted:

> A mission, under the charge of General Sir Neville Chamberlain, is about to proceed to Cabul to confer with the Ameer; thus affording our first, and possibly last, opportunity of entering into personal explanations with

the ruler of Afghanistan, in his own capital, regarding the relations between his own country and the British empire.

Resulting, as the mission does, from Russia's recent action in Central Asia, it cannot but raise the whole question of the relative positions of Russia and England in those regions, and may not improbably lead to a final settlement of that long vexed question. It is, therefore, desirable that we should very carefully examine, in the light of recent events and disclosures, the problem of our future with Asia, with a view to arriving at such broad and definite lines of policy as may serve to guide our Envoys in their difficult task, and to direct our efforts for the consolidation of our dominion and due influence in the East.

The author then analyses the imperial advances of Russia and British India over the previous 150 years as follows:

At the beginning of the last century, Russia's most advanced posts, at Orenburg and Petropaulovsk, were nearly 2,500 miles distant from the insignificant British settlements in India. Our only rivals there were the French. The advance of Russia southwards seemed practically bounded by the vast and almost impassable deserts of the Kirghiz Steppes. For a century past, her progress and conquests had been entirely in an easterly direction; and no-one could, at that time, foresee that England and Russia would ever come into collision in Asia.

About 1730, Russia commenced the absorption of the hordes of the Kirghiz Steppes, and the gradual occupation of those arid deserts – a task which occupied her for more than a hundred years; and her outposts began to draw nearer to India. England, meanwhile, had not been idle. Bengal had been conquered, or ceded to us, the Madras Presidency established, and Bombay became an important settlement; and, at the close of the last century, less than 2,000 miles intervened between English and Russian possessions.

In the beginning of this century, the more rapid progress was made on our side; while Russia was laboriously crossing the great Desert, and slowly consolidating her power in the Kirghiz Steppes, England was advancing with great strides over India. The North-Western Provinces, the Carnatic, the territories of the Peishwa, Sind and the Punjab successively came under our rule; and, by 1850, we had extended our dominion to the foot of the mountains beyond the Indus. Thus, during the first half of this century, the distance between the outposts of England and Russia had been reduced, almost entirely by advances on our side, from 2,000 to less than 1,000 miles.

In 1854–56, the Crimean War temporarily checked the design of Russia in Europe; but this seems rather to have stimulated her progress in Asia. The great Desert once crossed, Russia found herself in presence of fertile and settled countries, whose provinces fell under control as rapidly as those of India had fallen under ours. Twenty-five years have not yet elapsed since that war; and, during this period, the distance between England and Russia in the East has been reduced, this time entirely by advances on Russia's side, from 1,000 to less than 400 miles.

It is noteworthy that the author speaks in stereotypical and pejorative terms of the population of Central Asia, describing them as 'hordes', and also that he talks of English and Russian 'possessions'. The attitude of imperial arrogance is also evident when he refers to provinces falling under Russian and British control. The paranoia felt towards Russia is manifest when the author comments:

It might well seem unnecessary to recall such well known facts; were it not that there are those who argue, even now, that there is no imminent risk of contact with Russia in Asia; that we have no reason to anticipate further advance on her part; and that the dread of such advance is groundless, since we are still separated from her by vast distances and almost impassable obstacles...

But along our existing frontier, every pass is in the hands of tribes independent, if not hostile; and who, if we elect to remain permanently within our present border, must ultimately become allies and subjects of our great rival...

I conceive, then, that it would be simply suicidal to allow Russia to establish herself peaceably and securely at Cabul, and extend her authority to our present borders and over the passes leading to India...

Thus, it appears that both Russia and England have, now, weak frontiers, at which they cannot willingly accept contact with a great rival power; and are both equally urged forward by considerations of military and political expediency, and by the instinct of self-preservation, towards the Hindu Kush, the great natural boundary between India and Central Asia...

I pointed out that Russia was too farseeing and wary to shipwreck her cause by a premature invasion; that she would first appear at Cabul in friendly guise; and that what we had really to fear was the gradual establishment there, by friendly means and by a policy more active than our own, of an influence hostile to us. This is precisely what happened. While British officers have been rigorously excluded from all parts of Afghanistan, Russian officers have been permitted to visit Maimana and other points on the northern frontier; a Russian mission has been received and hospitably entertained at Cabul, where it still remains; and proposals have been openly made to the Ameer to receive Russian workmen to aid in the improvement of his manufactures, among which arms and soldiers would doubtless be included.

The author then proposes that efforts should be made to persuade the Amir, Sher Ali, to order the withdrawal of the Russian mission, to consult with Britain before entering into diplomatic relations with foreign powers and to permit the establishment of a British representative at his court. He suggests that a show of force would help persuade the Amir but stresses that an invasion should only be embarked upon as a last resort. In detailing how the Amir should be persuaded, he comments:

> If this course is established, we should, in the first place, endeavour to establish our influence in Afghanistan through the present Ameer... Whether we can win him to our side is questionable. He has become estranged; he has learnt thoroughly to mistrust us; and all recent information confirms the belief that, of his two great neighbours, he hates the Russians least. On the other hand, he knows that we are nearer and more powerful for good or harm, than is Russia; and that no assistance from her could preserve his country or his throne against us.

> But if we wish to bind the Ameer to us, we must appeal to something beside his fears; we must hold out hope of advantage to him as well. He will probably demand a subsidy; though he seems latterly to have extracted from his subjects a revenue sufficient for his wants, and to be comparatively indifferent to money...

> If the Ameer proves hopelessly estranged, and we fail in our efforts to win him; or if the Envoy considers that, from any cause, it is not desirable to involve ourselves in engagements with him, we must take immediate steps to neutralize his hostility, and to secure our interests. The best course of action then open to us would probably be to aim at dethroning him, and replacing him by a candidate more favourable to ourselves.

As an alternative, the author suggests 'entering into negotiations with all the tribes and parties in Afghanistan who are unfriendly to him', adding that 'there is little doubt that his kingdom would fall to pieces by itself'. In arguing against an invasion, he comments that such a measure would at once 'rekindle the animosities' of the people, 'uniting the whole nation against us'. He further states:

...I view an invasion of Afghanistan, like a war with Russia, as a measure which may become unavoidable and must, therefore, be taken into consideration in our forecast; but which is only to be resorted to in case of absolute necessity, when all others have failed. Our immediate object should be to apply such pressure only as may be necessary, either to bring the Ameer to a truer sense of his interests, or to dethrone him and give an opportunity to the party which still remains favourable to us at Cabul. And such pressure should be applied in the directions, and in the manner, which seem least likely to bring us into collision with the Afghans, or arouse their fanatical spirit of independence.

The desire for independence is thus presented as 'fanatical' rather than normal. The arrogance of the imperial power is again manifest in the closing paragraph of the memorandum when he states:

I earnestly hope and trust that we shall be able to attain, by peaceful means, a settlement of the questions considered in this Minute which shall be alike becoming to the dignity of the great British Empire, conducive to the security of that part of it specially committed to our charge and beneficial to the neighbouring States concerned.

A letter sent by a British soldier[2] to his family during the British intervention of 1839 also includes an interesting example of the attitude of the colonizer. In this, he states: 'A few years of good government and regular payments to the Afghan forces, like ours, will, however, do wonders.'

These extracts are of considerable interest in presenting, in very stark terms, the attitudes of the colonizer. There is, in the first instance, a perception that it absolutely fine for a country to conquer the territory of others. This assumed right is seen to justify any actions which prevent others from threatening the process of expansion or which help secure the captured territories. There is, therefore, a pattern of total disregard for the interests of the people of the territory which the colonizer seeks to control.

Further, there is a tendency to objectify and negatively stereotype these people, using words such as 'hordes' and 'fanatical'. This leads to a view that they would benefit from the 'civilizing' influence of the colonizer, to achieve 'good government'. It further generates a momentum in which action is taken to impose the 'civilized' values on the colonized. This, in turn, creates the illusion for the colonizing force that it is 'a force for good', that it is bringing benefit to the territory to be conquered.

These attitudes lead the colonizer, once arrived in the country to be conquered, to become complacent and to import the colonial lifestyle and values. A consequent reluctance, based on cultural arrogance, to engage, listen, learn and show due respect leads to both an ignorance of cultural norms and values, and a failure to pick up on signals that the population is increasingly restive. The cultural insensitivity that is thus generated inevitably results in actions which cause insult, particularly if they offend religious sentiments or are seen to dishonour women.

When popular anger over such offences leads to violence, the colonizer will often opt for further violence, rather than dialogue, but with a brutality which arises from a fear of the colonized, based on a perception that they are 'fanatics', and from a contempt for them.

This brutality removes, from the colonized, any sense that the colonizer has any right to claim that he is more 'civilized'. It also further alienates the population, not only because of the deaths and injuries that are caused but also because of the humiliation that is felt, so that repeated cycles of violence ensue. If torture is practiced on the colonized, as is frequently the case, the humiliation is all the greater.

As the cycles progress, so the colonized become radicalized and moderate voices give way to more extreme ones, thus creating a people whom the colonized have good reason to fear. However, the colonizers fail to pick up the signals or rising discontent because, in their arrogance, they assume that the people can easily be put down by force. At the same time, the colonized increasingly objectify the colonizers, thus justifying levels of brutality which cause horror to the colonizers and are seen to warrant punitive action. Thus did the British garrison create the conditions for the massacre of 1842 and the subsequent retaliatory action. Thus also did the British generate the mistrust which Sher Ali manifested towards them in 1878.

The extracts are also of interest in demonstrating the oft-repeated pattern of the colonizer seeking to overthrow the government of a country in order to impose a ruler who will be compliant to its interests, to therefore create a 'puppet' government. They are of further interest in arguing strongly against military intervention, except as a last resort, lest it unite 'the whole nation against us'. Yet, at the same time, there is a willingness to use overwhelming force in order to take control of key strategic locations and so establish a sufficient hold on the country.

These extracts also demonstrate that Britain felt no need to justify its military interventions in Afghanistan to the wider international community. There was an assumed right for Britain to pursue its imperial ambitions. There was, therefore, little attempt to present the interventions in altruistic terms, as being aimed to provide benefits to the population. For the British public, there was an acceptance that it was important to thwart Russia's imperial ambitions and to defend Britain's own empire. There was, nonetheless, an implied assumption that the British presence would bring about 'good government' and an improvement in the capacity of the Afghan army.

The extract is, in addition, noteworthy in referring to the possible use of financial inducements in support of Britain's strategic objectives. In this case, there is a reference to a likely demand, by the ruler, for a subsidy. However, there are many indications, over the imperial histories of Russia and Britain over the eighteenth and nineteenth centuries, of an assumption that rulers, in particular, but also populations can be won over, or bought, through the provision of material incentives.

Four key forms of inducement were in evidence over this period: the provision of luxurious gifts, the delivery of military training, the suggestion that beneficial trade links might follow and the offer of protection from feared adversaries.

Thus, in 1717, Peter the Great decided to take up an offer, made some years earlier by the Khan of Khiva, that, in return for Russian assistance in suppressing unruly tribes, the Khan would become his vassal. He hoped, thereby, to establish a base or staging post to facilitate Russian trade with India and to also search for gold. To this end, he sent a heavily armed expedition to Khiva. As they approached the city, the expedition leader, Prince Alexander Bekovich, sent couriers ahead bearing lavish gifts for the Khan and these couriers were mandated to give assurances that the mission was a friendly one. However, the Khan suggested that, because of the difficulties of accommodating Bekovich's army within the city, they should be split up and provided with hospitality in the various villages around. Taking advantage of their dispersal, he then ordered that Bekovich and his forces should be slaughtered.

This example is an important one in demonstrating that, in spite of the provision of luxurious gifts, the suspicion that the Khan felt towards a foreign army prevailed over any tendency to feel well disposed towards the bearers of these gifts. It is not clear whether the Khan had an accurate understanding of the power of Russia or of its potential to launch a punitive attack. However, he would have been aware of the considerable obstacles that the desert terrain and harsh climate would have placed in the way of any invading army. The experience was instrumental in generating an even greater mistrust, within the Russian establishment, of the populations of Central Asia, leading to a brutal approach to conquest in that region and in the Caucasus and Afghanistan.

A further example can be seen when, from 1798 to 1805, the Governor-General of India, Lord Wellesley, was able to expand the dominions controlled by the British East India Company from the three coastal presidencies of Calcutta, Madras and Bombay to include the greater part of the area contained within present-day India. This prompted the Russian Tsar to propose to Napoleon that their two armies launch a combined attack on India. Part of the Russian strategy included recruiting the Turkmen tribes with offers of plunder if they helped drive the British from India. Napoleon declined the offer and the Russian Tsar decided to launch a purely Russian invasion. However, this was aborted, following the death of the Tsar, when the invading army was still north of the Caspian.

Lord Wellesley was unaware of this Russian initiative but remained suspicious of Napoleon's possible ambition to invade India. He was particularly concerned that Napoleon might build an alliance with the Shah of Persia with a view to using this as a possible invasion route. Wellesley sought to pre-empt this by sending his own diplomatic mission to Tehran in 1800, bringing extravagant gifts. These included 'richly chased guns and pistols, jewelled watches and other instruments, powerful telescopes and huge gilded mirrors'. These were sufficient to persuade the Shah to sign two treaties, one political and one commercial. The former included an undertaking that he would prevent any French entry onto Persian territory and a further agreement that he should declare war on Afghanistan, with which there was a long-standing enmity, if it attacked British India. In return, the British would protect him from any invasion by either country.

However, when the Shah subsequently appealed for help from the British in response to Russian advances in the Caucasus, which Persia regarded as within its sphere of influence, the British ignored his plea, both because aggressive acts by Russia were not part of the treaty and also because Britain was now allied with Russia against Napoleon. However, this alliance was soon undermined by Napoleon's defeat of Russia in 1807 and by a deal struck between Napoleon and Tsar Alexander to jointly attack India. To this end, they persuaded the Shah of Persia to abandon his treaty with Britain in favour of an agreement with them. The Shah then reflected on whether this would result in a Russian withdrawal from the Caucasus. He concluded that it would not, which made him susceptible to British overtures to expel the French emissaries from Tehran. This susceptibility was greatly enhanced by the delivery of the largest diamond that he had ever seen, as a gift from George III. As part of the new treaty, which included defensive arrangements against Russia, Britain agreed to provide an annual subsidy of £120,000 to the Shah, together with the services of British officers to train and modernize his army.

In another episode, in 1819, Russia sent an emissary to the Khan of Khiva, in the hope of encouraging him to form an alliance. The strategy involved the delivery of impressive gifts and offers of commerce that would provide luxury goods from Europe and the latest technology from Russia. It also included the use of flattery.

En route to Khiva, the emissary overcame the suspicions of local chieftains on the eastern shore of the Caspian, also through gifts. Having subsequently delivered the earmarked gifts to the Khan of Khiva, he offered him the opportunity of commerce through a new harbour that Russia was planning to build on the Caspian's eastern shore, suggesting that Russian luxury goods would be available to Khivan merchants there. He also indicated that Russia could help protect caravans, travelling to the new port, from plunder by Turkmen tribes controlling the route.

The Khan, in this case, was suitably impressed and agreed to send his own emissaries to Russia to conduct further negotiations. These met with a Russian General after travelling across the Caspian but little of significance came out of the discussions. In the meantime, the attentions of the Tsar had become focused on threats to his own position.

This example is significant in demonstrating how, because of the fluidity of international relations and of power dynamics within states, the attentions of governments can quickly turn elsewhere, leading to a failure to honour verbal undertakings given to other states.

The tenuousness of relations was also in evidence when, in 1820, Russia sent an emissary to the Emir of Bokhara, offering trade with Russia. He agreed to receive it, through intermediaries, and was rewarded with expensive gifts. These included guns, furs, watches and European porcelain. In return, the Emir allowed Russian goods to enter Bokhara's market. However, the Russian mission's intelligence operations aroused local suspicions and they had to leave after a year.

The Sikh ruler of the Punjab, Ranjit Singh, was courted by both Russia and Britain. In 1820, Russia dispatched an emissary to Ranjit Singh, in the hope of persuading him to trade with Russian merchants and, at the same time, distance himself from his good relations with the British. The emissary carried with him a considerable sum of money, together with rubies and emeralds, some of great size and value. However, the emissary died en route.

In 1831, in support of their friendship with Ranjit Singh and in return for his gift of Kashmiri shawls to the British King, Britain sent five massive dray horses and a gilded state coach to him. These travelled by boat for 700 miles up the Indus to Lahore and were well received by Ranjit Singh. Gifts were also provided to rulers en route so as not to incite envy or attacks.

Aid, in the form of military assistance, was used in 1837 when Persia invaded Herat. A British intelligence officer, who happened to be in the city, was able to play an instrumental role in advising the ruler's Vizir on techniques for resisting the siege.

The British invasion of Afghanistan in 1839 demonstrates, very vividly, the limited potential of aid to win hearts and minds if the invading army is, at the same time, behaving in a manner which seriously alienates the population. Thus, when Britain invaded Afghanistan from the south and entered Kandahar with Shah Shuja, their nominee to rule Afghanistan, they quickly became aware of his lack of popularity with the tribes en route as they advanced towards Kabul. They sought to buy the allegiance of these tribes through the distribution of gold. However, they faced resistance in Ghazni and had to storm its huge fortress. Any possibility of winning support from the population was further undermined by the brutality with which Shah Shuja dealt with prisoners, most of whom were hacked to pieces. Having taken Kabul, punitive action was taken against tribes who refused to submit to Shah Shuja's rule while others were persuaded through supplies of gold.

The British Government subsequently sought to reduce the cost of the military occupation of Afghanistan by building up the forces of Shah Shuja and phasing out those of Britain. Britain also decided to end the distribution of gold to the tribes. Those deprived of these gifts were among the first to rise up against the British. Once the momentum of the resistance had gathered strength, the efforts of the British leadership to win over key Afghan leaders through further disbursements (or promises of them) were of no avail.

In contrast, a successful Russian attack on Tashkent in 1865 was followed by a clear effort to win hearts and minds by allowing the city's elders to run its affairs and by not interfering in its religious life. Russia also opted not to levy any taxes. The Russian General who led the siege was reported to have ridden alone through the streets, talking to ordinary people.

There were many other examples over this period of efforts, both successful and unsuccessful, to win the support of leaders and populations through material inducements. A key factor in the success of these was the degree of power the targeted power holders believed the potential benefactors to have. There were instances in which the receipt of luxury goods was followed by treachery. In some cases, emissaries offering benefits were killed when it appeared that the power holder they represented was losing power relative to its principal adversary. The actual or threatened use of force could also be variable in its outcome, in that it could both persuade and alienate.

Although most of these examples do not relate directly to Afghanistan, they provide an indication of the attitudes of the colonial powers to the rulers and populations of the territories they sought to control or influence. There was clearly mixed success in persuading rulers through the provision of luxury goods. However, the provision of gold to the Afghan tribes was closely linked to the use of force. Those who were not persuadable through the supply of gold were to be dealt with punitively through the maximum use of force. This was certainly the case in relation to Sher Ali, who was said, in the extract above, to be 'comparatively indifferent to money'. There was no apparent attempt to engage with the population, to listen to them, to demonstrate respect.

This failure to engage constructively with the population, as part of the process of delivering material benefits, meant that there was little understanding of popular attitudes or concerns. As a result, the British contingent in Kabul failed to pick up signals of growing public discontent over their continued presence.

They also actively aroused popular anger through specific abuses of human rights. Notable among these was the murder of large numbers of civilians, when the British army entered Afghanistan in 1842, to avenge the massacre of the British contingent the previous year. The destruction of the Kabul bazaar, during the same expedition, would have had a major impact on the economy of an already impoverished country and, thereby, on the livelihoods of the population.

The public hanging of around 100 Afghan suspects, carried out by General Roberts in response to the assassination of the first British representative in September 1879, would, in combination with his own assumption of absolute power, have also aroused both fear and antipathy.

In both cases, the use of force to punish the population was a key characteristic of the British interventions. A further characteristic pattern of behaviour was threatening force in order to secure compliance, based on the assumption that the population would be aware of Britain's superior military capacity. There was also an assumption that Britain would be able to successfully negotiate with the Afghan tribes, in order to progressively erode the support base of the ruler.

The human rights abuses of Afghan rulers who were perceived as 'puppets' of Britain provoked further antipathy. Thus, the brutality with which Shah Shuja dealt with prisoners during the storming of Ghazni in 1839 seriously undermined the efforts of Britain to win the support of tribal leaders through the provision of gold.

A key question, in relation to massacre of 1841, is how much the failure of the British contingent to show respect for Afghan values, and for Islam, was a factor in their fate. It would appear that the decision to withdraw subsidies from tribal leaders contributed to the outcome but this is unlikely to have constituted a sufficient reason on its own. It was also the case that there were British intelligence officers within the contingent who had a good understanding of the political and cultural environment, but it would appear that they chose to ignore the signals that 'animosity towards the British in Shah Shuja's newly restored capital had been building up for months'. One of them, Sir Alexander Burnes, was to 'describe himself in a letter to a friend as a "highly paid idler" whose advice was never listened to by his chief'". His boss, Sir William Macnaghten was said to have remarked to one of his staff: 'the present tranquillity of this country is, to my mind, perfectly miraculous.'[3] It would certainly appear that offence was caused by the culturally insensitive behaviour of the British contingent. There was said to be 'growing anger, especially in Kabul, over the pursuit and seduction of local women by the troops, particularly the officers'[4] The historian, Sir John Kaye, was reported to have written:

> The Afghans are very jealous of the honour of their women, and there were things done in Caubul which covered them with shame and roused them to revenge... It went on until it became intolerable and the injured then began to see that the only remedy was in their own hands.[5]

The British political agent in Kandahar was said to have warned, in August 1841: 'The feeling against us is daily on the increase and I apprehend a succession of disturbances... Their mullahs are preaching against us from one end of the country to the other.'

It is likely, therefore, that Islam provided a rallying call for an anti-imperialist response to the intervention. It thus provided cohesion to an otherwise fragmented society, to enable it to confront the invader. In defending traditional and Islamic values, the resistance movement was also able to mobilize support over perceived affronts to the honour of women. Thus, while Britain did not actively set out to change the values of the Afghans, it may have hoped that, through limited efforts to improve the process of governance, it might achieve some shift in attitudes. At the same time, it was felt to be importing alien value systems which threatened to undermine, weaken and potentially replace those of Islam and of Afghan rural society.

It could reasonably be argued that the British, in seeking to establish a presence in Afghanistan in order to prevent Russia doing likewise, were able to secure a degree of public acquiescence through the provision of gold and subsidies. In imposing a 'puppet' government, through Shah Shuja, the use of their assistance clearly enabled him to remain in power, albeit for a limited period. However, the benefit to the British of the initial willingness of the population to accept gold or other subsidies was, in due course, offset by public anger over affronts to traditional and Islamic values and over acts of brutality. The assumption that the population could be easily 'bought' led the British to disregard the potential importance of personal honour and dignity in the willingness of Afghans to acquiesce in a foreign occupation.

In the case of the British intervention of 1839–42, therefore, the Afghan population rejected the very presence of the British colony because of its behaviour, even though this meant a potential loss of subsidies and other benefits. There was a similar rejection of the arrival of the British mission in 1879, manifested in the assassination of the British representative. Further, the hangings ordered by General Roberts, later that year, may be assumed to be one of the factors which led the British to conclude that it was better to do a deal with Abdur-Rahman than seek to remain in Afghanistan.

Thus, when the British faced growing manifestations of discontent towards the end of the first Anglo-Afghan War, their efforts to bribe the population through payments to those in leadership positions were of no effect. This clearly demonstrated that the need to assert dignity, in the face of assaults on personal honour and of acts of humiliation, is a more powerful driving force than the desire for material gain.

The British thus proved to be unsuccessful in their pursuit of their strategic goals. Their inability to win the support of the Afghan population was a major factor in their failure to achieve these goals. In fact, their ability to inflame opinion was an important characteristic of their interventions.

3

THE BUILD-UP TO THE
SOVIET INTERVENTION

Reform and backlash

The seeds for the Soviet military intervention can be found in the tentative efforts of King Amanullah, during the 1920s, to introduce some initial reforms relating to the rights of women and girls. These included the removal of the requirement for women to be veiled and the creation of a school for girls which provided for the daughters of the ruling elite.

These initiatives, which followed a tour of European capitals in 1928 and were partly manifested in the Queen and other female members of the royal family appearing unveiled on a public platform, were seen by religious and tribal leaders as being aimed at the imposition of Western value systems onto an Islamic society. As opponents of the reforms marched on Kabul, Amanullah sent his army to confront them but most of them deserted to join the rebellion. He opted to flee rather than await a worse outcome. This powerful backlash demonstrated the strong resistance, within Afghan society, to the imposition of external or non-Islamic values and created a fault line which has dominated the history of Afghanistan up until the present time. It has also served as a warning to subsequent rulers to build any process of reform on existing value systems and to adopt considerable caution. Regrettably, the PDPA Government of 1978–9 ignored this lesson although its immediate predecessors had taken it on board.

The period from 1930 to around 1950 was, in consequence, one of relative stagnation in terms of social change. At this stage, the process of government was highly authoritarian and heavily based on patronage networks, notwithstanding the existence of a constitution and a parliament. The civil service operated at a very basic level, with staff poorly paid and dependent on their ability to demand bribes for bureaucratic services provided. Nadir Shah, who was King in 1929–33, relied to a large extent on Pushtun tribal militia to deal with challenges to his authority, rather than the small regular army, but he lacked the personal security to prevent his assassination in a blood feud. His successor, King Zahir Shah also did not challenge the status quo at this stage. It was not until the 1950s that any serious attempt was made to build up the Afghan army.

The need for external aid to bolster the State was therefore very limited. During the 1930s, Afghanistan's rulers continued to maintain a delicate balancing act between Russia and Britain, accepting aid from both while setting clear limits to their involvement. Thus, King Nadir Shah accepted some limited British aid in 1931 while the government of his son and successor, Zahir Shah, resisted a request by the Soviet Union, in relation to the 1936 Russo-Afghan barter agreements, to establish trade missions in Afghanistan. Instead, Afghanistan accepted aid from Germany, Italy and Japan, on the assumption that these were unlikely to interfere in its internal affairs, and was able to maintain a position of neutrality throughout the Second World War, in spite of this aid.

There was also little external interest in Afghanistan over this period. The Russian revolution of 1917 had resulted in a temporary loss of some of the acquisitions of the previous Tsars, but these were eventually recovered and formed a network of semi-independent republics within the Union of Soviet Socialist Republics. This process of internal consolidation combined with the Second World War to keep the attention of the Soviet Government away from Afghanistan, although it did provide some limited aid to Afghanistan from 1919. The Soviet Union thus sent King Amanullah a gift of thirteen planes in that year, together with pilots, mechanics, transportation specialists and telegraph operators. It followed this up in 1924–5 by laying telephone lines between Herat and Kandahar, and between Kabul and Mazar-e Sharif. By 1928, it had established an air route between Moscow and Kabul, via Tashkent. In response, Britain offered to build a road from Peshawar to Kabul but refused a request that it should provide cash instead. At this stage, Russia had consulates in Herat and Mazar-e Sharif while Britain had consulates in Jalalabad and Kandahar.

Turkey also offered concrete support, in the form of military advisers to help train the Afghan army. This followed the European tour by King Amanullah, during which he was advised by the Turkish leader, Kamal Ataturk, to strengthen his army before he embarked on a programme of social reform. However, the King was impatient to start the reform programme immediately and the Turkish advisers were not able to influence him.

In the meantime, Germany sought to build influence in Afghanistan during the inter-war years in the hope that it could persuade the Afghan Government to help it undermine the British position in India. German engagement was, to a large degree, related to its efforts to achieve its strategic goals during the First and Second World Wars. In 1915 a Turko-German mission had visited Afghanistan in the hope of persuading its then ruler, Amir Habibullah, to join forces with them against Britain. To this end, they agreed to give 100,000 rifles, 300 cannon and the equivalent of £20 million in gold. However, Habibullah insisted that he would only attack British India if German and Turkish armies entered Afghanistan to lead the assault, an offer which neither Germany nor Turkey was disposed to follow up. Habibullah simultaneously sought to negotiate with Britiain for it to relinquish its control of Afghanistan's foreign affairs, in return for keeping Germany and Turkey at bay. As has been noted in the previous chapter, Britain ceded this control to his son and successor, Amanullah, in 1919. In this case, therefore, neither Germany nor Turkey secured the strategic outcome that they sought and their efforts created the conditions for Afghanistan to strengthen its position in relation to Britain.

The German presence was relatively strong during the years running up to the Second World War. Thus, in 1937, Germany began to explore the mineral resources of Paktia, while Lufthansa established an air route from Berlin to Kabul in the same year. The German company, Siemens, established an office in Kabul which permitted it to win bids for several post-war US contracts. During the same period, an Afghan entrepreneur bought machinery from the Soviet Union, Britain and Germany to develop cotton production in Kunduz and Pul-e-Khumri. A group of Afghan students went to Japan in 1936 to study mining. The USA also made a tentative entrance. A US company, the Inland Exploration Company, was granted a 25 year oil concession but, after initial surveys, it gave up its rights in 1939.

However, in an early example of the pitfalls of aid which is not preceded by thorough research and discussion with beneficiaries, small dams and bridges constructed by Germany, Italy and Japan failed to survive the first big spring floods.

Immediately after the war, Afghanistan entered into negotiations with a US company, Morrison-Knudsen, to construct two dams and an extensive canal system on the Helmand River, in southern Afghanistan. Under the contract subsequently drawn up, both parties agreed to carry out specific elements of the project. However, failures on both sides undermined progress from the beginning. These included a tendency by both parties to cut corners, including essential surveys. Capacity problems were also an issue, as were shortcomings on the US side with regard to cultural awareness and sensitivity. The two dams, the Kajaki Dam and the Arghandab Dam, had nonetheless been completed by April 1953.

The tensions created between Afghanistan and the US over the management of this project soured relations between the two countries. This made the Afghan Government of Prime Minister Daoud Khan (1953–63), which was accountable to King Zahir Shah, cautious about too great a reliance on one major donor. It therefore opted to diversify its sources of aid and looked to the Soviet Union as an additional provider. An agreement, in January 1954, for the Soviet Union to provide a loan to construct two silos and bakeries was followed by further measures to facilitate aid, trade and transit measures. Many of the aid projects were small in scale and were of immediate benefit to the urban population in particular.

An additional loan of $100 million was agreed in 1955 to finance the first Five Year Plan, which commenced in 1956. This included two hydroelectric plants, a road from the Soviet border to Kabul, a new airport at Bagram and port facilities at Qizil Qala on the river Oxus border. Soviet advisers were brought in to take the programme forward, much of which failed to be achieved.

Prime Minister Daoud favoured a process of reconstruction but he also sought to bring about a degree of social reform. He recognized the need for external resources to achieve this and gave high priority to building up an army, mindful of the fact that Amanullah's attempts at reform during the 1920s were undermined by his inability to respond to opposition from tribal and religious elements with military force.

In his determination to maintain a position of neutrality between the USA and the Soviet Union, Daoud approached both for arms. The USA rejected his request in response to his refusal to join the Baghdad Pact, which brought together the USA, Britain, Pakistan, Iran, Turkey and Iraq. However, the Soviet Union was willing to oblige and reached an agreement, in 1956, to provide arms to a value of $25 million, along with its partner countries in Eastern Europe. Further arms deals followed so that, between 1960 and 1968, the Soviet Union provided arms worth $120 million. The Soviet Union joined forces with Czechoslovakia to also provide military training from 1961 onwards. By 1970, around 7,000 junior officers had been trained in the two countries, as compared with 600 who had received training in the USA. In addition, West Germany provided training and supplies for the Afghan police force up until 1973.

The strengthened Afghan army and secret police helped Prime Minister Daoud stand up against those tribal and religious elements which opposed a number of social reforms, introduced in 1959, which included the removal of the requirement for women to be veiled. These reforms laid the foundation for a relatively liberal environment to emerge, at least in the cities.

By 1972, Soviet military assistance had reached $300 million, while its non-military aid, from 1957 to 1972, was valued at $900 million. This was almost exclusively in the form of loans. This was in contrast to the USA and Germany, which gave grants as well as loans. A significant proportion of the debts to the Soviet Union were later repaid in the form of gas transported from Afghanistan's gas field, at Shiberghan in northern Afghanistan, to the Soviet Union.

State finances were heavily aid dependent. As much as 65 per cent of investment finance for the Government was provided by foreign aid, between 1953 and 1963, when Daoud was Prime Minister. However, this may have been a consequence of agreements with both the USA and the Soviet Union to construct a major part of Afghanistan's highway system between them. The USA thus built the stretches from Torkham to Kabul, Kabul to Kandahar, Kandahar to Spin Boldak, Kandahar to Herat and from Herat to Torghundi, on the Soviet border, while the Soviet Union was responsible for the sections from Kabul to Jabal es-Seraj, from Jabal es-Seraj to Doshi (including the Salang Tunnel) and from Doshi to Sher Khan Bandar on the Soviet border. The USA had completed its part of the highway by 1965, when US aid to Afghanistan decreased significantly. The Soviet Union had also completed the major part of its sections by the same year. It is noteworthy that the quality of these roads, which were constructed under conditions of relative security, was extremely high.

The political environment was also conducive to the use of external advisers on a significant scale, with Soviet advisers in the majority. Out of a total of 2,000 foreign advisers in 1970, over half were from the Soviet Union. 200 were from China, 152 from West Germany and 105 from the USA. By the time of Daoud's Presidency of 1973–8, following the overthrow of King Zahir Shah in a coup, the number of Soviet civilian and military advisers had reached around 3,000.

The 1950s saw an expansion of education so that, by 1962, there was a professional class of 7,000 administrators and technical staff, most of whom were in State employment, together with several thousand military officers with higher education. However, in 1960, only 10 per cent of eligible children attended school because the resources were simply not there. The number of teachers had nonetheless increased from well under 4,000 in 1956 to 13,200 by 1967. By 1968, 540,000 students were in school, of which 13,000 were in high schools. Girls represented one fifth of high school students. It should, nonetheless, be noted that the number of children in school during the pre-1978 period was less than it is now. Having said that, the quality of education provided at that time may have been greater because the good security conditions that existed then would have been more conducive to the provision of uninterrupted teaching and teacher training. Funding support for educational institutions was provided by a range of donors, including the Soviet Union, the USA and a number of European countries.

The greater availability of education for girls led to the tentative entry of women into the workforce, in what are globally regarded as the more stereotypical roles of teachers, nurses, receptionists, administrators and air hostesses. It was also increasingly common for women to appear unveiled, in Kabul at least, and, to a lesser extent, in other cities.

The expansion in education created the conditions for the emergence of a new intellectual class, most of whom were the first in their families to receive a formal education. This linked with an initiative to create a parliament and draw up a constitution. These developments, in combination, led to a growing vocalization of dissent, with periodic over-reactions by the police and army. As political life became more active during the late 1960s, two movements emerged with highly polarized positions. One of these was socialist, looking predominantly to the Soviet model but with some, a minority, more influenced by China. The other was radical Islamic, drawing on the thinking of the Moslem Brotherhood of Egypt and of the Deobandi School of the Indian subcontinent.

When Daoud took absolute power in 1973, through a coup against King Zahir Shah, he was quick to clamp down on the radical Islamic parties, notably Hisb-e-Islami of Gulbuddin Hekmatyar, and he expelled many of their leaders to Pakistan. Relations with Pakistan at the time were soured by his advocacy of the Pushtunistan cause, based on Afghanistan's continuing contention that the Durand Line, which delineated Afghanistan's border with Pakistan, should not be regarded as the permanent frontier. At the time of Pakistan's creation in 1947, Afghanistan had argued that the Pushtun areas of Pakistan should be autonomous, even an independent state.

However, President Daoud initially cooperated with the socialist parties, particularly the People's Democratic Party of Afghanistan (PDPA). At the same time, he sought to reduce his dependence on the Soviet Union by looking to Iran to provide assistance. Agreements were signed worth hundreds of millions of dollars to finance projects, on a substantial scale, to develop agriculture and the Afghan infrastructure. The second agreement, signed in 1974, involved a potential investment from Iran of $2,000 million. This rapprochement with Iran is often seen as a contributory factor to the drift away from the Soviet Union. However, the overthrow of President Daoud, in April 1978, and the events which led to the Iranian revolution of February 1979 cut short Iran's reconstruction plans.

China was also an important aid provider, particularly following the 1960 split between Moscow and Peking. By 1970, it was the fourth largest donor, having allocated loans to a value of $33.6 million for irrigation in Parwan, the Bagrami textile factory, a carp fishery and attempts to introduce sericulture and tea plantations. In addition, China provided technical and other expertise, as noted above. The assistance provided, alongside that given by Western states, enabled Afghanistan to reduce its dependence on the Soviet Union.

In a final effort by President Daoud to lessen the growing dependence of the Afghan Government on the Soviet Union, he sought aid from other Muslim states. In February and April 1978, he travelled to Kuwait, Libya, India, Pakistan, Saudi Arabia, Egypt and Kuwait to this end. He also used these talks to discuss issues relating to a meeting of non-aligned states which was planned to take place in Kabul in May 1978.

President Daoud had thus taken active steps, as Prime Minister in 1953–63, to build up the Afghan State in order to implement a reform programme which had eluded Amir Amanullah in the 1920s, because the latter had lacked the army that he needed to stand up against religious and tribal opinion. To this end, President Daoud had sought external aid on a massive scale but, in spite of his efforts to draw on as many sources as possible, had found the Soviet Union to be more willing to oblige than the others. By the time he returned to power as President in 1973, the Soviet Union had already established itself as a major influence within the country and Afghanistan was heavily in debt to it. By the late 1970s, he was aware of the challenge to his power that the People's Democratic Party of Afghanistan posed, but he did not want to build an alternative power base in the radical Islamic parties, many of whose leaders he expelled to Pakistan. In desperation, he looked to Iran and other Muslim states for help, but this did not arrive in time to save him from the PDPA coup, and his own death in the course of it.

The PDPA coup

It was the growing tensions between President Daoud and the socialist groups which led to the People's Democratic Party of Afghanistan coup of April 1978. Fearing that Daoud would arrest them, the PDPA leaders brought forward the planned date of the coup and benefited from a significant body of support from within the Afghan army which had, by this stage, built up a reasonable level of strength.

It is not clear to what extent the Soviet Union provided active support to this coup. However, it was the first state to accord recognition to the new government. The fact that the more moderate of the PDPA leaders, Babrak Karmal, was immediately taken under the wing of the Soviet Government in Moscow, suggests that the Soviet Union was uncomfortable with the hard line positions taken by the remaining leaders, Taraki and Amin. However, the Soviet Government kept its distance when the more extreme Khalq faction purged the government of individuals affiliated with the Parcham faction of the PDPA even though it appeared to favour the Parcham element. The Soviet Union was also slow to respond to the growing resistance, within Afghanistan, to the attempts by the Government to impose reforms related to land ownership, literacy, bride price and usury on the highly conservative population. Additional public anger was aroused by a change in the Afghan flag, in June 1978, to denote the new socialist character of the country in the place of the previous Islamic one.

The Soviet Ambassador, Alexander Pusanov, was widely regarded at this stage, 'with having the final word in all important decisions made in Kabul', a view which was compounded by his 'commanding airs', earning him the epithet of the 'little tsar'. However, the Soviet Government initially failed to persuade the PDPA regime to moderate its policies in order to establish a middle ground which might make it more acceptable.

The PDPA regime, at first, assumed that it would have no problems overcoming the emerging resistance and opted for the use of maximum force. However, it soon faced problems within the ranks of the army, with morale suffering heavily from the association of the regime with the Soviet Union. Thus, Anthony Hyman comments:

> Many Afghan officers became alienated through 1979 precisely because of the steady growth of the Soviet presence in the armed forces (with Soviet officers down to company level in many areas by the autumn). Arrogance

towards Afghan officers alienated even Khalqi officers, causing more frictions.[6]

Although the offensives against the resistance forces resulted in heavy casualties a result of Soviet air raids, the overall effectiveness of the combined operations of the Afghan army and Soviet forces was undermined by desertions from the army. Further, it proved difficult to retain control of captured roads and population centres without the ongoing presence of strong forces. As the army moved to new areas, so they lost those that they had previously captured to the Mujahidin.

An early, and significant, manifestation of this resistance was an uprising in Herat in March 1979 when elements of the army joined forces with other groups. The consequent bombing of Herat, with Soviet pilots possibly flying the planes, led to the deaths of over 5,000 civilians and rebel soldiers. In the process, fifty Soviet citizens – military advisers and their families – met horrific deaths at the hands of crowds. Several hundred Khalqi officials were also reported to have been killed. The PDPA Government responded by setting in motion a third purge of professionals and other liberals, building on those already undertaken in the summer and autumn of 1978. The Government also made a series of accusations against Iran which culminated in a rupture in diplomatic relations by April 1979. Foreign technical advisers working on development projects in many regions were withdrawn to Kabul or sent back to their home countries. Wives and children were also sent home. Additional security measures were introduced by the UN and other agencies in Kabul. Travel restrictions were imposed to the provinces.

To help strengthen the regime, the Soviet Union assisted the creation of a paramilitary force of PDPA party loyalists. Forces of tribal volunteers were also raised from particular Pushtun tribes.

An intense climate of paranoia within the Government, which resulted in suspicion of any moderate opinion and consequent arrests of perceived political opponents, generated further opposition to the regime. Tens of thousands of fellow socialists, along with professionals and liberals, found themselves arrested and imprisoned in Pul-e-Charkhi Prison on the edge of Kabul. A high proportion failed to survive the conditions and treatment that they suffered.

According to Amnesty International, writing in September 1979, 'reliable international observers estimate that there are at least 12,000 political prisoners in Kabul's Pul-e-Charchi prison alone'.

The emergence of a spontaneous resistance movement against the PDPA Government, and the subsequent Soviet military intervention, gave the radical Islamic parties that President Daoud had exiled to Pakistan the opportunity to claim leadership of the resistance, which took on the name of the Mujahidin. However, although resistance fighters derived some benefit from links with some parties, they largely relied upon their own resources.

As growing numbers of the army joined the resistance over the following months, the Soviet Government became increasingly concerned that the PDPA Government would not be able to hold the situation. The Soviet Union therefore prevailed upon President Amin to adopt more conciliatory policies towards the population. This resulted in an end to the large-scale purges of perceived opponents, although arrests continued on a smaller scale. He also appointed a committee to draft a new constitution. This was called upon to pay due attention to Islam. In addition, speeches on radio and television were required to begin with the standard Islamic preamble.

In fact, by April 1979, even President Amin was seeking to dissociate himself from actions, carried out by particularly hard-line elements within the party, which had seriously alienated the population. By the summer of 1979, both the Afghan Government and the Soviet Union were already taking active steps to broaden the base of the government.

Although the Soviet Union would appear to have been somewhat equivocal about the nature of the new PDPA regime, on account of its excessive radicalism, the PDPA Government demonstrated a clear willingness to align itself with the Soviet Union, through a series of civil and military contracts signed over the summer of 1978. It also had no hesitation in opting for the model of a centrally-planned economy, to be organized through five-year development plans, in spite of the highly laissez-faire and informal character of the Afghan economy. Further, it opted for an industrialization programme, set out in the five year plan, to be funded and supported by the Soviet Union and its Council for Mutual Economic Assistance (Comecon) partners, particularly Czechoslovakia.

The World Bank, Asian Development Bank, UN agencies and the International Bank for Reconstruction and Development were also investing in Afghanistan at this stage.

By the spring of 1979, the Soviet Union had earmarked over $1,000 million to the five year plan, most of which was to be invested in a development of the natural gas and, possibly, oil industries. This was particularly focused on the natural gas field at Jarquduq, close to Shiberghan in northern Afghanistan, some 30 miles south of the Soviet border. Production from this field started in 1982.[7]

The Soviet Union had previously constructed a 100km pipeline in 1967, to link production at another gas field near Shiberghan, at Kwoja Gugerdak, to the Soviet border.[8] The development of the new gas field was aimed to augment the supply of natural gas to the Soviet Republics of Central Asia, which had just lost an important source of supply from Iran, following a disagreement over price. Although the Soviet Union had its own gas reserves, the use of Afghan supplies, on highly favourable terms, enabled it to export more to Western Europe and benefit from the higher rates paid.

The development, control and management of the gas industry was overseen by Soviet experts and the meters calculating the quantity of gas exported were on the Soviet side of the border. The Soviet Union also determined the price to be paid, at a level considerably below the global market rate.

Further, as has been noted above, the Afghan Government did not benefit, in terms of contributions to its revenues, from the income earned on the gas fields; the Soviet Union offset the income against the debts owed to it by Afghanistan for its investment in the country.

Although gas production increased from 1.68 billion cubic meters in 1968 to 2.8 billion cubic meters in 1980, it failed to exceed the 1980 high in subsequent years. During the mid 1980s, production was averaging around 2.5 to 2.6 billion cubic meters each year. This was due to technical problems.[9]

Czechoslovakia contributed $90 million for the five year plan, in addition to $60.8 million in credit, to cover the development of coal mining and a large cement factory in Herat, among other projects.

Afghanistan's trade with the Soviet Union and the Comecon States also increased over this period but the Soviet Union's trade with Afghanistan only represented 0.59 per cent of its global trade.

Education was an important element, with thousands of Afghans sent to study in the Soviet Union and the Comecon States. It was hoped that young people thus educated would support Soviet interests as they advanced in their careers.

US aid to Afghanistan was at a relatively low level, at $27 million, by 1978 and suffered another dramatic fall, by 80 per cent, when the US Ambassador to Afghanistan, Adolph Dubs, was kidnapped and killed in February 1979, as police stormed the hotel room where he was being held. This led to a withdrawal of US diplomatic relations with Afghanistan and also a substantial reduction in the size of its aid programme. US funding continued, however, for the Helmand-Arghandab Valley authority, which managed the Kajaki and Arghandab dams. The PDPA Government therefore became even more dependent on the Soviet Union to sustain its finances.

However, this was not sufficient to impact significantly on incomes. The broad mass of the population, who were living at the margins, viewed the regime in an increasingly negative light after the initial promises of economic improvement, which led to heightened expectations, failed to materialize and disillusionment set in. Kabul thus continued to experience shortages of both income-earning opportunities and housing. Efforts by the Government to introduce subsidies and coerce traders into keeping prices down were not enough to significantly alleviate the chronic poverty.

The population was also negatively influenced by abuses of power by members of the PDPA, including examples of personal enrichment which contrasted with the publicly declared socialist ideals of the regime. However, as Anthony Hyman comments, 'it was rather the brutality of the new regime which rapidly alienated even early sympathizers'.[10]

By June 1979, the Soviet Union had already supplied the Afghan armed forces with considerable military hardware. In spite of this, or because of resentment over the significant presence of Soviet officers in the Afghan army, the army was continuing to suffer a significant haemorrhaging of its ranks.

In response, Soviet forces were built up in Afghanistan over the autumn of 1979 and Soviet pilots were increasingly flying jet fighters and helicopter gunships. With an increase in the level of dependence on the Soviet Union, 'Soviet influence in the country was now an undeniable force'.[11]

The number of Soviet civilian and military advisers increased significantly following the PDPA coup. In part, this reflected the need to replace the many technically qualified Afghans removed from the ministries by the Government's purges of its perceived opponents. This was particularly the case in the Ministries of Defence, Planning and Finance. Around one third of the Soviet advisers were working with the armed forces.

Soviet advisers were also used to strengthen the organization of the PDPA machinery, together with the recruitment of members and to enhance the use of the media to influence public opinion. The latter was made all the more necessary by the loss of trained Afghan radio staff as a result of the purges instituted by the PDPA Government. However, the support provided to the propaganda process would appear to have been counterproductive. The messages given out in the media were clearly alien to the society at which they were targeted and were also found to be offensive, because of their strongly secular character.

East Germany assisted with the training of party members. In addition, both the Soviet Union and East Germany were heavily involved in the training of the police and the secret police. German-trained officers were largely replaced. This led to both countries being complicit in the human rights abuses committed by the PDPA Government. Anthony Hyman thus comments: 'There is a considerable body of evidence to prove the complicity of Soviet advisers in brutal acts committed in many Afghan interrogation centres and prisons.'[12]

The Soviet Union may therefore have been party to a situation in which the PDPA dealt harshly with those it regarded as opposed to its policies. The torture practiced on prisoners was said to have included electric shocks, using 'devices supplied from the Soviet Union – and apparently West Germany'.[13]

Thus, in spite of massive investment in Afghanistan over 25 years, and a huge upscaling of that investment after 1978, the Soviet Union found itself in a situation in which a regime it was supporting was facing significant opposition in both rural and urban areas. In part, the Soviet Union was responsible because it did not step in early enough to rein in the excesses of the regime and also because it lent active support to the regime on many fronts.

However, the primary cause of its failure was the utopianism of key individuals within the PDPA Government and their unwillingness to accept anything less than an immediate transformation of economic and social relations within Afghan society. Their intolerance of dissent, and their apparent paranoia in relation to those of a liberal persuasion, led to purges in which many thousands died. This alienated the very section of the population which might have been won over by a more moderate approach to change.

Further, their dispatch of young party members to the villages to enforce reforms relating to land reform, marriage and literacy deeply offended the highly conservative rural society and provoked spontaneous resistance. This resistance was reinforced by the dominant messages given out through the media, which indicated that the regime was secular and therefore opposed to Islam.

Efforts to take a more conciliatory approach, including references to Islam in public statements and in the formulation of the new constitution came too late to reverse the process of resistance and the Soviet Union felt that it had no choice but to intervene. If it had not intervened, it would have become increasingly entangled in a civil war of uncertain outcome. However, by intervening, it justified an upscaling of the jihad or insurgency which had already commenced from bases in Pakistan. It also justified a decision by the USA and others, notably Saudi Arabia, to provide overt assistance to the Mujahidin, assistance which led to a radicalization of the political environment in the region.

4

THE SOVIET MILITARY
INTERVENTION

It is very clear that the Soviet military intervention of December 1979 was planned independently of the Afghan Government, particularly as Babrak Karmal was brought in to take over from Hafizullah Amin, Taraki having already died in mysterious circumstances. It is also clear that it was planned some time in advance, with 1,500 Soviet troops first entering through Kabul airport from mid December. An additional 1,500 Soviet special forces flew in on 24th December and seized key strategic positions. At the same time, a massive land force, with tanks, crossed the northern border while a further 5,000 arrived by air over the following three days. These supplemented the 4,000 Soviet military advisers who were already in Afghanistan. The total size of the Soviet intervention force was 85,000.

However, there was no prior attempt to seek international sanction, based, for example, on the need to restore stability. In fact, the military intervention in Afghanistan very much echoed earlier interventions in Hungary in 1956 and Czechoslovakia in 1968, in which the Soviet Government acted to establish control over its sphere of influence. The Soviet Union was therefore very much seen as having imposed itself upon Afghanistan.

It is likely that the decision of the Soviet Union to intervene militarily was influenced by a number of geopolitical developments at the time which made it feel vulnerable along its southern frontier. There were particular fears that the USA would seek to replace the loss of its bases in Iran, following the assumption of power by the Ayatullah Khomeini in Iran in February 1979, by supporting resistance movements in Afghanistan. The Iranian revolution, combined with a possible growth in the power of the radical Islamic movement in Afghanistan, also threatened to create an anti-Soviet Islamic bloc to the south of the Soviet Union and thus re-ignite a rebellion undertaken by Central Asian Muslims in the immediate aftermath of the 1917 revolution. There was an additional risk that this Islamic bloc might encourage the Soviet republics of Central Asia to pursue a radical Islamic direction. A recent rapprochement between China and the USA, combined with the Sino-Japanese Treaty of Peace and Friendship of August 1978, had further reinforced concerns over possible encirclement.

J. Erikson commented that there were:

> ...acute fears within the Soviet establishment as to the vulnerability of their Asian frontiers, vis-à-vis China; 'to allow Afghanistan to slip from their grasp would mean accepting total encirclement running from Japan to Norway – the ring would snap shut'[14]

However, there were important additional factors associated with Afghanistan's status as a socialist state, in that it was now regarded, by the Soviet Union, as part of the progressive states which had espoused Marxism, even though it was not a member of the Warsaw Pact or of Comecon. Further, the emergence of the PDPA government in Afghanistan was consistent with the ambition of the Soviet Union to transport its model to other parts of the world and to support other communist movements to this end. The PDPA government was clearly failing in its efforts to establish itself and needed some military muscle to help sustain it. It had also entered into a variety of agreements with the Soviet Union and other socialist States.

It could be argued that the existence of the People's Democratic Party of Afghanistan was a consequence of the significance influence of the Soviet Union, through the delivery of aid, over the previous 25 years. However, it may also be the case that any process of expanding education would have led to the emergence of a socialist movement, given the nature of global political movements at the time.

To have abandoned the PDPA government after a heavy investment in Soviet advisers, both civilian and military, would have meant a loss of prestige. Many of these had already lost their lives in the civil war and the lives of others were potentially at risk. In addition, the Soviet Union had invested considerable political, military and aid resources in Afghanistan and did not want to see the benefits of these lost. The Soviet Government was also feeling less than sure about the loyalty of President Amin, following recent overtures, by him, to the Afghan opposition, to China and the USA. The intervention was, therefore, a largely defensive move.

In fact, the Soviet Union presented it as such in the international domain. It thus gave three reasons: that it had received a request for military assistance from the Afghan government; that it was committed, under the 1978 Treaty of Friendship and Cooperation, to give that assistance; and that it was acting in self-defence against foreign armed aggression, in accordance with article 51 of the UN Charter.

However, considerable doubt has been expressed over the claim that President Amin made such a request. Some sources suggest that the Soviet Union was drawing on requests made the previous year by President Taraki to justify the intervention. Subsequent statements by the Soviet Union cited the United States, Britain, China and Pakistan as the sources of 'imperial aggression'.[15]

However, Anthony Hyman comments:

> Yet more apt is surely the parallel with Prague in 1948, when an independent country, rather than a member-state of the Warsaw Pact and Comecon, was brought into the Soviet sphere of control, by a communist coup organized from Moscow. By the application of the 'Brezhnev doctrine' into Asia, Soviet troops were trying to ensure that a formally non-aligned and independent state did not slip out of the Soviet sphere of control.[16]

It is thought to be unlikely that the subsequently-manifested interest of the Soviet Union in accessing Afghanistan's gas and other natural resources, at highly concessionary rates, was a significant factor. It was simply a by-product of the intervention.

The new President, Babrak Karmal, thus found himself in a position of profound weakness, with the Soviet military and Soviet advisers playing a major role in determining how the Afghan Government should both seek to impose its vision and respond to the growing resistance. This resistance was not only to be found in the countryside but it was also very strong in the urban areas. By the time of the Soviet intervention, large areas of the country were already outside the effective control of the Government.

At this stage, as Anthony Hyman has noted,[17] 'the effective authority was in Soviet hands, and was to remain there, though the façade of an independent administration and military command was retained'.

Hyman also comments:

> Karmal's undoubted talents and personal qualities could not be divorced from the fact that he presided over a puppet regime set up by and for the Russians, kept in power by a foreign army... Karmal himself was known from the first as Shah Shuja-i-Moscow, from the (unsuccessful) British attempt to place their protégé Shah Shuja in power over the Afghans, 140 years before.[18]

In later years, the PDPA Government proved able to operate with a greater degree of independence from Moscow.

In recognition of the weakness of his position, Babrak Karmal made determined efforts to accommodate the regime to the population by demonstrating due respect to traditional and Islamic values. He also offered to what remained of the intelligentsia an undertaking to introduce a liberal constitution, with a multi-party system and an elected assembly.

He was, in addition, able to hold the prices of basic goods steady for a period, benefiting from Soviet support to this end. With funding and commodity support from the Soviet Union, state employees were provided with coupons, distributed through employee's cooperatives in Kabul and provincial towns, which entitled them to monthly allowances of 28 kilos of flour for single people and 56 kilos for married couples at reduced rates. Vegetable oil was also available on the same terms.[19] This benefited 250,000 people in 1983, of which 140,000 were in Kabul. Resources were also provided to enable Soviet-style housing blocks to be built for key government workers.

In addition, the government, again with Soviet support, provided flour, bread, sugar and vegetable oil at subsidized prices in the open markets of Kabul. However, the limited quantities made available were said to be insufficient to reduce chronic food shortages and keep down prices in a situation of severe inflation, in which the prices of some basic items were nearly doubling each year from 1981–3. The prices of electricity, water and bus transport services were also fixed at below-cost levels.[20] However, supplies of electricity and water were disrupted as a result, in part, of the actions of the resistance forces. The population also faced serious shortages of firewood. While government employees received salary increases to partly compensate for inflationary increases, there was no such cushion for the rest of the population.

Pressures on food supplies were greatly increased by the arrival of 1.5 million people from the rural areas of the Panjshir Valley, Logar and Koh-i-Daman, in the vicinity of Kabul, in response to bombing raids by Soviet aircraft. The scale of the influx accelerated in 1982 after offensives against heavily populated areas near to Kabul.

In 1982, Babrak Karmal acknowledged that there were 'food shortages and malnutrition'. He noted that it had proved necessary to import 200,000 tonnes of wheat, 30,000 tonnes of rice, 70,000 tonnes of sugar, together with vegetable oil, milk and other food items. Most of this had come from the Soviet Union.

The situation was not helped by a deterioration in the security situation within the capital, with bomb attacks by resistance forces on government offices, the Soviet Embassy, the Police Academy and restaurants. The bombing of the Mahipur electric power station on the Kabul river was one of many well-planned attacks carried out by the resistance over the winter of 1982–3.

However, the political environment was not conducive to any process of national reconciliation. The Soviet Union had just intervened militarily in Afghanistan, without any international sanction, and was already embarked upon offensive operations against resistance forces. This far outweighed any possible softening in the opposition to President Karmal's regime as a result of his overtures. Further, he could not escape from the reality that he had no popular legitimacy, having been brought in from Moscow to take over the government. In addition, feelings were running very high after the events of the previous two years. He also faced declining morale amongst party officials, civil servants, diplomats and the armed forces.

In seeking to regain control, the Soviet military, in conjunction with the demoralized Afghan army, largely opted for the use of force during the early period. In so doing, they sought to make maximum use of air power, in the form of helicopter gunships, fighter planes and bombers, to support their ground operations, in order to keep to the minimum the number of casualties among their own troops. Over the first six months of 1980, the Soviet strategy was to undertake retaliatory attacks on villages and towns held by insurgents. However, from the summer of 1980, a scorched earth policy was adopted. Villages were thus bombed and then burned while, at the same time, crops were destroyed. The populations of entire valleys were therefore driven into exile, leaving a barren environment in which insurgents would find few villages left to provide shelter or food. This policy was particularly used in locations of strategic importance such as areas around cities or along key roads. However, resistance forces continued to benefit from support in areas where it was still possible for the population to survive. They also resorted to intimidation in seeking to build support. Thus, for example, religious leaders lending support to the regime were assassinated.

The efforts of Soviet forces were very much undermined by a willingness of members of the Afghan army to collaborate, through the provision of information and arms, with the resistance forces. A call-up of thousands of reservists in September 1981 brought many unwilling conscripts into the army but it also led large numbers to flee the capital and other cities to avoid the call-up. Morale within the army was affected by fears that the two-year tours of duty would be indefinitely renewed because of a shortage of volunteers or conscripts.

By 1981, the Afghan army was only 30,000 strong, a figure which the present Afghan Government regards as too low to provide security to the country. Efforts to increase the numbers by forcibly recruiting young men from the cities led many families to seek exile in Pakistan and elsewhere. However, some progress was gradually made by improving the pay and conditions so that, by 1983, the size of the army had increased to over 50,000, in spite of low morale and the desertion of several thousand conscripts each month. This was partly a consequence of the use of press-gangs, but the granting of special privileges to those who volunteered and a more effective use of propaganda also played a role. This progress may also have been facilitated by growing popular disillusionment with the Mujahidin parties and, after 1989, by the departure of Soviet troops.

Because of the disintegration of much of the Afghan army, Soviet soldiers were required to be directly involved in patrols and offensives in the provinces as well as in guarding the cities. By 1983, the Soviet forces in Afghanistan consisted of an army, 105,000 strong, together with air force units which included many squadrons of fighter planes and over 400 helicopter gunships. These were supplemented by Soviet military advisers.

A number of the major population centres, including Kandahar, Herat and Ghazni, fell periodically under the control of the resistance forces. These were able to engage in strikes against Soviet positions, drawing on the support of residents, despite punitive bombardments. Herat and Kandahar were subjected to repeated bombing raids. Raids on Herat in the spring of 1983 destroyed a large area of the city and led to around 3,000 civilian casualties.

The road system was one of the principal targets of the insurgents so that, by cutting sections of road for periods of time or engaging in ambushes of armoured patrol vehicles, they could disrupt communications, weaken the supply and logistics operations of military forces and undermine the process of trade and provisioning between cities.

The Soviet Union invested heavily in the creation of a logistics infrastructure to support its operations, such as to indicate that it planned to remain in the country for some time and, possibly, establish a permanent military presence. These included all-weather airport runways and major improvements in transport facilities across the river Oxus, to facilitate cross-border travel.

While providing military assistance, the Soviet Union also sought to strengthen the Afghan state. Soviet advisers were placed into government ministries in very large numbers to help them build their capacity, but, as noted above, they were constrained by the continuing departure of civil servants. They also faced a long-standing system of patronage, accompanied by corruption, and a reluctance to take responsibility which required every minor decision to be referred to the minister. Anthony Hyman thus commented:

> Corruption is pervasive in the Afghan civil service, from top to bottom of the hierarchy, an accepted lifestyle which has been repeatedly challenged but never suppressed by reforming governments. The reasons for the prevalence of corruption are generally understood to be two interrelated factors: a survival into the present day of traditional patterns of behaviour, in which gifts for favours received are considered entirely natural; and as a direct result of fixing official salaries at levels far below bare subsistence for many state employees. Yet the criterion of need is certainly not what has determined exactions in bribes and private payments – the most outrageous offenders have often been the best-paid senior officials, who had full opportunity to exploit their seniority.[21]

Anthony Hyman also commented:

> Another aspect of corruption is nepotism, the patronage of relations by induction and promotion of family or friends in state service, at the expense of capable civil servants lacking patrons. Although a meritocracy did emerge, with many Afghans of humble birth occupying posts of high responsibility by the 1960s, nepotism has kept down the morale as well as the general standard of efficiency in the administration.[22]

The ability of the civil service to operate was also affected by a reduction in the customs revenues on which the government largely relied for its tax base, with resistance forces controlling many of the borders. The government administration therefore relied increasingly on Soviet financial support for its survival.

Because of the continuing exodus of civil servants, whether because of the climate of fear or the low morale, Soviet advisers found themselves in a position in which the administrative capacity that they needed to run the country was simply not there. The situation would have been worse if the writ of the government had extended beyond the urban areas. Ministries were able to function with only one quarter of their pre-1980 staff because the Afghan Government actually controlled such a small part of the country. It would also have been worse if, through its efforts and the efforts of others, the provision of education had not considerably improved over the previous few decades. There was, therefore, a potential core of educated people able to run a government.

The Soviet Government exercised particular control of key departments such as defense, the interior, communications and the intelligence service, as well as the party apparatus and the central committee of the PDPA.

By the time of the PDPA coup, Afghanistan had already established strong trade links with the Comecon States, in spite of Daoud's policy of seeking a diversification of both trade and aid partners. With the cessation of most aid from Western governments, and from those within the Islamic world, in 1980 the Afghan Government became absolutely dependent on the Soviet Union for aid and credits. The bulk of the non-military assistance from the Soviet Union (worth around $300 million in 1982) came in the form of commodity assistance to provide wheat, sugar, rice and textiles, among other products. By 1981, the Soviet Union provided about 65 per cent of Afghanistan's imports.[23] By 1983, over 70 per cent of Afghanistan's trade was with Comecon states, compared to 39.5 per cent in 1978. Most of this was in the form of barter agreements. In 1982, the USSR provided 84 per cent of machinery and transport equipment imports, 65 per cent of cotton fabric and 96 per cent of refined petroleum products.

Trade between Afghanistan and its northern neighbour was greatly facilitated by the opening, in June 1982, of the 'Friendship Bridge' across the Amu Darya, between Termez and Hairaton. This provided the first rail and road bridge between the two countries and thus created a terminus for the Soviet railway system on the Afghan side of the border. The Afghan port of Hairaton was provided with new facilities to enable it to better serve as a trade and communications centre. The Afghan economy thus became increasingly integrated into that of the Central Asian Republics of the USSR. The process of supplying Soviet forces was simultaneously strengthened.

Due, in part, to attacks by resistance forces, the little industrial production that existed in April 1978 had virtually ceased to exist by 1981. Thus, ginned cotton production decreased by 73 per cent between 1978 and 1982, cotton textile output by 50 per cent, sugar production by 97 per cent and the production of vegetable oil by 73 per cent.[24]

The principal exception to this decline was the Soviet-run natural gas industry at Shiberghan, whose operations were heavily protected. Industries such as fertilizer and cement, which exported heavily to the Soviet Union, benefited from substantial Soviet aid to keep their production at a reasonable level. Further, bakeries were able to use Soviet wheat imports to maintain their output.

Only as it became clear that the resistance could not be overcome by military means alone did some policy makers, both military and civilian, within the Soviet Government advocate a greater level of engagement with the population, aimed to encourage a detachment from the resistance forces. However, opinions were always divided as to the balance to be aimed at between the use of force and a more conciliatory approach.

Thus, from the summer of 1981, the PDPA Government was actively seeking to engage with tribal leaders, as an adjunct to military operations, to offer them tribal or regional autonomy. It was hoped, thereby, to create zones which would distance themselves from the resistance.

The policy of engagement took a further step forward with the replacement of Babrak Karmal by Muhammed Najibullah, as president, in 1986. The latter, in his determination to establish links with tribal and religious leaders across the country, demonstrated his willingness to abandon the previous focus on the creation of a socialist state. There was therefore a greater emphasis on the centrality of Islam and traditional values. The government also neutralized some sectors of the opposition, through local pacts and by payments of 'allowances' to tribal leaders. This approach had some success, particularly after the withdrawal of Soviet troops from Afghanistan in February 1989. A key contributory factor was the growing popular disillusionment with the Mujahidin, which was over their failure to agree on a power-sharing formula that might have permitted them to form an alternative government at that time. However, there were also indications that those who did cooperate with his government did so in order to prevent military offensives being undertaken against them rather than out of any sense of commitment to the regime.

Najibullah's efforts were nonetheless undermined by the reputation which he had earned as a result of his role as the previous head of the intelligence service, KHAD. He was more successful in the north of the country than in the south, with the provinces bordering Pakistan being particularly resistant to his Government.

The policy of engagement was further undermined by continued Soviet support for the intelligence service and the police. Soviet assistance was provided, from the outset, to support a rapid expansion in the police force. An initial goal was to bring numbers up to 60,000 by the middle of 1983. The 6- or 18-month training courses that were used in 1980 were replaced by three-month courses in 1982. The intelligence service, KHAD, was given particularly generous funding, to enable it to place a network of agents in all State offices and also carry out intelligence functions across the country, under Soviet supervision, in order to identify possible opposition elements. Training courses were provided by the KGB and by East German intelligence experts.

Large numbers of arrests continued to be made each month. In consequence, the educated class still felt at risk and the departure of the intelligentsia, which had been increasingly in evidence during the previous period, continued, with many taking refuge in Europe or North America. This feeling of vulnerability did not cease with the more conciliatory approach of President Najibullah. Those who were seen as a threat to the State continued to be targeted by the intelligence services.

The education sector suffered considerably from the conflict, with schools damaged or destroyed in bombing raids on rural areas. There were also attacks on government schools by resistance forces, who objected to the content of the curriculum. Many schools were burned down or forcibly closed. A serious shortage of qualified teachers was in evidence, with large numbers leaving the country. This shortage was even apparent in the urban areas. With the PDPA drawing heavily on former teachers for its membership, a part of the teaching profession had been diverted into administrative functions.

Kabul University inevitably suffered from the purges of the PDPA government of 1978–9, as did the professionals who would send their children to university. Student confidence was also affected by the risk of being forcibly recruited to the army from the university campus. The number of students registering for higher education fell from 20,000 in 1978 to 4,000 in 1981.

Within the University, the previous focus on English, German and French was replaced by Russian language studies, with Soviet citizens undertaking the tuition rather than the teachers from US, West German and French universities who had previously spent periods of time in Kabul under cultural cooperation agreements.

Further, thousands of Afghan students embarked on higher education courses in the Soviet Union or the Comecon States each year.

Soviet advisers became heavily involved in the propaganda process, through support to television, radio and the printed press. A fundamental reorganization of the Afghan media was one among a number of strategies aimed to attract activists for the PDPA. In focusing on the urban population, the Soviet Union sought to target schools, students and youth in general, together with factory workers, soldiers and state employees. In addition, young children were organized in cadres of Pioneers, on the Soviet model. The Soviet Union thus saw the PDPA as their primary vehicle for consolidating and extending their influence and power in Afghanistan over the long term.

Agreements were thus drawn up between the Afghan Government and the Soviet Union and East Germany to improve the professional skills of Afghan journalists. In March 1983, East Germany set up a course in 'progressive radio journalism', for which it donated printing presses and communications equipment. In addition, the Czechoslovak Socialist Union of Youth facilitated the publication of Darafsh-e-Jawanan (Youth Flag), the weekly outlet of the Democratic Youth Organisation, in order to help in the recruitment and education of youth cadres. Anthony Hyman comments that 'the effects of a more sophisticated approach to state propaganda were already apparent in 1982'.[25] However, these messages had to compete with the BBC World Service Persian and Pashto broadcasts, which were widely listened to and enjoyed considerable credibility.

Funding from the Soviet Union may also have made it possible to recruit and pay the thousands of members of militia forces, who volunteered to serve in local areas across the country from 1981 onwards. Many of these were from urban or semi-urban groups. The principal functions of the militia were to guard state property and communication lines and also check on the movement of resistance groups through their areas. In addition, special border militia were set up along the border with Pakistan in the provinces of Kunar, Paktya and Nangarhar from the spring of 1982. All civil servants and other state employees were expected to serve in Civil Defence Units, to guard their offices or factories at night.

The initial emphasis on the use of overwhelming force led to a rapid acceleration in the exodus of the population to Pakistan or Iran. The population was also influenced, in their decision to leave Afghanistan, by the fact that their homeland was perceived to have been occupied by a non-Islamic power. This justified a migration, on religious grounds. By the end of 1979, 400,000 Afghans had fled to Pakistan and 200,000 to Iran. A year later, the combined total in both countries had reached 1.9 million. By the end of 1983, Pakistan was already hosting 3 million refugees. Iran had a population of 2.3 million Afghans by 1986. When the refugee population peaked in 1990, Pakistan contained 3.3 million Afghan refugees and Iran 2.9 million.

The Soviet military intervention had the effect of strengthening the resistance. In both Pakistan and Iran, but particularly in Pakistan, the refugee populations served as a foundation for insurgency movements into Afghanistan. This cross-border insurgency was also, as noted above, able to draw support from the population that had been able to remain in Afghanistan. In a situation where the efforts of the Government and the Soviet forces to win over elements of the population were of very limited success, the Soviet army thus became bogged down in a guerilla war which it always struggled to address.

By 1985, the Soviet leader, Mikhail Gorbachev, was already considering an eventual withdrawal of Soviet forces from Afghanistan in the context of efforts to radically reform the Soviet machinery of government. He was concerned that the bureaucratic inertia created by the Brezhnev years had brought the economy to a state of crisis which needed drastic solutions. In seeking to free up the command economy, he recognized that the Afghan venture was one which could not be afforded, either economically or politically. It also constrained his efforts to build up his relationship with the USA, in the hope of attracting investment into the Soviet economy. However, it is also likely that increasing public discontent over the war, and the casualties that it was creating, was influencing the opinion of the Soviet Government. Those who fought in the Afghan war were returning disillusioned and angry. This would have fed into the concerns felt by President Gorbachev. It is therefore likely that internal factors within the Soviet Union were of greater significance than the strength of Afghan resistance in influencing the Soviet decision to withdraw. However, the failure of Soviet troops to make any real progress, in spite of an all-out effort to try to defeat the resistance in 1986, would have also weighed heavily in the balance.

Finally, the Soviet Union opted to withdraw militarily from Afghanistan in February 1989, under the provisions of the Geneva Accords of April 1988. It left behind a PDPA government, which managed to stay in power until after the Soviet Union itself collapsed in 1991.

Conclusions

The Soviet intervention differed from those of the British in that the PDPA regime of 1978–9, although sympathetic to Moscow, had emerged independently, albeit with a degree of support from the Soviet Union. However, the survival of the regime was seriously threatened as a consequence of its own actions. The Soviet Union was therefore intervening to support its own protégé.

Whereas the British justified their interventions in the light of their assumed right to pursue their imperial ambitions, the Soviet Union presented theirs as an act of self-defence against the actions of 'imperialists'. However, it was perceived by the wider international community as a naked act of aggression. This perception was very much enhanced by the fact that the Soviet Union sent in a very substantial force and, at the same time, installed a new President by force, as the British had done in 1839. It is significant that the Soviet Union sought to justify the intervention after the event, whereas the USA took steps to secure international support before it went in. Thus, although the Soviet Union took steps, through various consultative mechanisms, to establish internal legitimacy for the Afghan government, this was subsequent to Babrak Karmal's assumption of the presidency.

While the British may, on the basis of their colonial arrogance, have hoped to impart some of their values onto the Afghan population, they did not actively set out to do so. The Soviet Union, in contrast, was seeking, through the PDPA, to impose its own societal vision. However, it is arguable that they would have preferred to achieve this through the cautious approach to reform adopted by President Daoud. It would have been apparent to the Soviet Union, from early on in the rule of the PDPA Government, that the impatience demonstrated by the PDPA leadership to bring about a complete transformation of Afghan society, by imposing value systems which were at variance with those prevailing not only in the rural areas but also in the cities, was proving to be counterproductive. It would also have been clear that the purges of fellow socialists and of intellectuals, liberals and professionals, was weakening the support base of the government and alienating the very class who might have been sympathetic to a gradual process of reform. It is also clear that the Soviet Union took definite steps to encourage the PDPA to slow down their reform programme and also to demonstrate allegiance to Islam. It was, therefore, the PDPA which had assumed the right to impose socialist values, rather than the Soviet Union.

Yet, at the same time, the Soviet Government was willing to fund and support an intelligence service which was guilty of major human rights abuses, in order to maintain the regime and so protect its own strategic interests. Further, its forces were, themselves, directly party to abuses. In one incident, 1,170 men and youths were shot dead in the village of Kerala, in the eastern province of Kunar after an act of defiance. Twenty Soviet advisers in Afghan uniforms were in command of the force that perpetrated this massacre.[26] As a result, the regime was associated with a foreign ideology and was seen to have acted with great brutality and insensitivity in order to promote this ideology.

It was also the case that the representatives of the Soviet Union in Afghanistan demonstrated the same colonial arrogance as the British had done before them. The Soviet Ambassador behaved as an effective Viceroy and the arrogance of Soviet advisers, both in the armed forces and within the government administration, was reported to have a highly negative impact on the morale of the Afghans who worked with them.

The overt attack on Afghan societal values was presented, by the resistance forces, as an attack on Islamic values. This was also seen as an attack on the honour of women. The initiatives introduced by the PDPA to impose literacy on women and girls inevitably raised questions as to the potential role of women outside the home. This provoked defensive reactions from men, concerned to protect the honour of women within their families and to also ensure that the traditional roles of women within the domestic sphere continued to be performed. It also generated fears that the important role of women, as the primary vehicles for passing traditional and Islamic values from one generation to another, would be undermined if they were exposed to external and, particularly, non-Islamic values. This enabled the exiled radical Islamic parties to claim leadership of the resistance and also to declare a jihad.

There was, perhaps, not the same absolute disregard for the interests and wishes of the population as had been evident during the British interventions. There was, at least, a recognition that the population needed to be persuaded of the benefits of socialism and that it was not enough to offer material incentives to that end. The centrality of Islam to Afghan society was therefore recognised at an early stage. However, the brutality of the PDPA government and the use of military might against the population by Soviet and Afghan forces did not lend itself to the level of acceptance that the Soviet Union had an interest in engaging. It was not until the late 1980s that such an acceptance began to be apparent, in response to a shift in approach by President Najibullah. The population would, therefore, have felt violated and humiliated by the intervention, as it had done during the British interventions, and there was the same need to assert personal dignity through a reliance on Islam.

The radicalism of the resistance forces would have created the conditions for another manifestation of the British interventions, a tendency to objectify and depersonalize the resistance forces. Thus, while the Soviet Government, on one level, recognized the need to engage with the population to listen, learn, understand and show respect, it was capable, through the actions of its forces, of resorting to extreme violence, brutality and cruelty. This included operations which deprived the population of its livelihood and also denied the resistance fighters the means to find shelter and food. In response, the population were led to also objectify the Soviet forces, to the point where any form of violence was justified. A cycle of violence thus ensued in which each side resorted to ever greater brutality and cruelty. Further, the brutality of the Soviet forces increasingly mobilized the population against them so that those organizing acts of violence were able to retreat into the population and draw support. There was, therefore, a radicalization process in which hard-liners came to positions of leadership. This radicalization process increasingly permeated the population so that a critical mass of opposition was built up to the point where the Soviet Union no longer had the resources, or the political climate, to maintain its position.

The Soviet Union also justified itself on the basis that, by seeking to impart socialist values, it was replacing societal values, which it regarded in a negative light, with ones which would be of benefit to the population.

This was key to the maintenance of morale within the Soviet army although this morale was quickly sapped. Further, there was the hope that, by sending Afghans for further training in the Soviet Union and Comecon States, a new generation of socialists could be created.

Soviet assistance to Afghanistan over the ten years from 1979 to 1989 was largely geared to the protection of Soviet interests. Thus, the major part of its investments was in the supply of Soviet troops and military hardware, together with the provision of training and equipment to the Afghan army. The intelligence services also received considerable support, as did the media. The provision of higher education opportunities in the Soviet Union and Comecon States was a further priority, with obvious potential benefits in terms of expanding the proportion of the population who were committed to socialist ideals.

The Soviet Union also placed a large number of advisers into the government administration in order to build up its capacity and bring its systems into line with those in Soviet Union. In addition, it advocated a centralised planning model, based on five-year plans and State control of key elements of the infrastructure. However, the injection of advisers proved to be of limited effectiveness in the face of a long-established practice of patronage and corruption, combined with a continuous haemorrhaging of government staff through departures into exile and the purges of the intelligence service. The efforts of the Soviet Union to build up and reform the police force also came up against the endemic corruption which had characterized the force for decades.

Conversely, there was little investment in the creation of sustainable livelihoods for the population, although an important safety net was provided through the supply of food and other essentials to the urban population at subsidized prices. The obvious exception was the financial underpinning that the Soviet Union made to the army, the civil service and the PDPA itself. This ensured the employment of 250,000 people. However, this was not sufficient to avoid serious levels of hardship for much of the population. With most of the rural areas under the control of the resistance, there was virtually no support for the agriculture sector, on which most of the population depended.

Investment in industry was mostly limited to enterprises which were producing for export to the Soviet Union, namely natural gas, fertilizer and cement. These were primarily in the provinces to the north of the Hindu Kush range, which the Soviet Union had, historically, seen as within its sphere of influence. This was both because these represented a continuation of the Central Asian plains, leading up to a defensible boundary of the Hindu Kush, and because the population, as Uzbeks, Tajiks and Turkmen, were ethnically linked to the populations of Central Asia.

The combination of resources provided by the Soviet Union to support military operations and help sustain the infrastructure of the state, including its intelligence and propaganda functions, were sufficient to keep the Soviet-backed Government in being for so long as Soviet support was provided, even after Soviet troops had withdrawn. However, once the Soviet Union itself ceased to exist in 1991, the PDPA Government lacked the wherewithal to sustain itself.

The aid provided by the Soviet Union from 1979 was therefore largely allocated to the financial underpinning of an Afghan government which had already alienated the population through its purges and its resort to force, brutality and culturally insensitive behaviour in seeking to impose its reforms. Contained within this underpinning was support to the Afghan army and intelligence services. Further, the Soviet Union included, in what it regarded as its official assistance to Afghanistan, the supply of Soviet troops and weaponry. This aid was therefore acceptable to the Government but not to the population.

In spite of the provision of resources on a massive scale, the Soviet Union failed to create the conditions for a stable government in Afghanistan to emerge or to establish a permanent military presence. Its failure was largely due to the absolute conviction held by the PDPA government that, in order to address injustices within the society and give expression to its utopian vision of a socialist state, it needed to move quickly and, if necessary, resort to force. There was, therefore, no attempt to implement a gradual process of reform and to build on what existed. Further, rather than, for example, establishing a literacy programme, presented in the context of traditional and Islamic values, for the rural areas, the government made it clear, through its propaganda, that it was seeking to impose an ideology that was quite at variance with those values. The fact that it was a secular ideology was significant although any attempt to impose, for example, the Christianity of the Russian Orthodox Church would have been equally opposed.

Further, the PDPA Government manifested not only a total disregard, and absence of respect, for existing societal values but also a determination to eradicate them. It further demonstrated, in its early efforts to implement its reform programme at the local level, a resort to brutality which rapidly alienated the population. The ignorance of the young party cadres sent to the countryside to bring the reforms into being also led to actions which were grossly insensitive. They thus failed to take into account, for example, the absolute importance of upholding the honour of women or the respect with which elders were held within the society. There was also no attempt to research the nature of existing inter-relationships between landowners, tenants, sharecroppers and landless labourers before setting in motion a land reform programme.

The ability of the Soviet Union to win public support, through its investment in the propaganda process, was, therefore, seriously undermined by the fact that it was associated with the PDPA regime.

It was, therefore, the case that the Soviet Union, which showed every indication that it would have preferred a gradual process of reform within Afghanistan, found itself in a situation in which it was having to pick up the pieces from the over-zealous approach of the PDPA Government.

The attempt to build a socialist state was further undermined by the distress and outrage caused by the large number of deaths in custody of those arrested and detained as political prisoners by the PDPA regime, prior to the Soviet intervention. The regime therefore made enemies of that element of society which might have been sympathetic to its ideals, if introduced without coercion and an associated reign of terror.

It could be argued that the Soviet Union could have done more to rein in the Afghan Government at an early stage, but it is clear that it was already advocating a strategy of conciliation before it actually embarked on its military intervention. By the time it did intervene, for reasons which were largely linked to its own strategic interests, the conditions were no longer conducive for any programme of socialist reform, even one that was gradual and had regard to existing values.

As the level of violence committed by Soviet forces grew, in response to the growing strength of the resistance, so the anger felt by the population towards the government was also directed against the external invader. The rallying cry of the Islamic jihad was a powerful element in giving identity to the resistance and in further strengthening it. The fact that a high proportion of the population had opted for exile, and had therefore uprooted themselves, created an environment in which resistance forces could engage in guerilla warfare and retreat across the border where they could not be pursued. This was a war which the Soviet Union had no chance of winning, in spite of its efforts, through the PDPA Government, to take a conciliatory approach in its dealings with the population.

Thus, although the Soviet Union had invested significantly in the Afghan economy during the 25 years leading up to its military intervention, this was of no weight in comparison with the actions of the PDPA in seeking to impose socialist values on the population. Further, the insensitivity demonstrated, and the brutality used, seriously alienated the population. The subsequent violence committed by Soviet forces on the population accentuated this sense of alienation.

The fact that it also led to a large-scale exodus from both rural and urban areas placed much of the population in very different political environments, those of the refugee camps of Pakistan and the cities of Iran. They were therefore removed from any influence that the PDPA government or the Soviet Union might exert through the media or through engagement with tribal or other leaders.

In addition, the PDPA government lost its potential capacity to build a support base within the urban population through its purges of intellectuals, liberals and professionals. The absolute intolerance shown to anyone who did not share their particular vision therefore had a major impact. The Soviet Union may have hoped to establish a permanent military presence in Afghanistan, but it failed.

A dominant theme during the period in which Soviet troops were based permanently in Afghanistan was, therefore, the balance between military offensives, aimed to defeat the insurgency, and efforts to encourage the population to distance themselves from the insurgents by engaging with them and demonstrating respect for traditional and Islamic values. It was clear, by the time of the Soviet intervention, that there was no longer any possibility of persuading the population of the benefits of socialism. It had been too discredited by the brutality of the PDPA and by its clear association with a foreign power. Further, the physical presence of that foreign power, engaging in military offensives against villages, was deemed to be an affront, a humiliation. Thus, far from encouraging the population to accept socialist values, the Soviet intervention had brought about a staunch defence of traditional and Islamic values such as to lead to a new radicalism. The existence of the radical Islamic parties within the Mujahidin provided a potential vehicle for the expression of radical values, but there nonetheless remained a broad spectrum of opinion, which was sympathetic to those values, amongst those engaged in the resistance.

5

THE BUILD-UP TO THE
US-LED INTERVENTION

US, Saudi and Pakistani support to the resistance

The exodus of refugees

The targeting of the intelligentsia by the PDPA led professionals to leave the country in their thousands from the summer of 1978 onwards. This was when it became clear that anyone who was remotely liberal, or independent in their thinking, was at risk and that those who were arrested very often didn't survive the torture and appalling prison conditions that they faced. The country thus lost doctors, engineers, university teachers and civil servants, either to exile or to the ranks of the disappeared. By January 1979, camps for 30,000 of these refugees had been set up in Pakistan. Daily bombing raids by the Afghan military on rural areas, combined with brutal treatment on the ground, led tens of thousands more to flee to Pakistan, this time from villages.

For those who sought exile in Pakistan, refugee camps were set up the length of the Afghan border. Here, refugees were provided with tents, from which they built their own mud housing, together with access to water supply, sanitation, health care, education, vocational training and income-generation opportunities.

Much of the aid to the camps in Pakistan was provided by the UN system, together with international and Afghan NGOs. Among the UN agencies, UNHCR worked with the Pakistan Government to set up the camps, provide tents and oversee camp administration, together with the supply of food, water, health, education and other services. UNHCR also supplied other essentials, such as plastic sheeting and cooking utensils. The World Food Programme delivered food to the camps, mostly wheat and pulses. UNICEF oversaw education provision, working with NGOs.

Thus, for example, the Swedish Committee for Afghanistan supported schools, DACAAR organized the supply of water, the Ockenden Venture set up income-generation projects and the Austrian Relief Committee provided vocational training.

Some of the international NGOs operating in the camps originated as solidarity committees set up in various European countries, including the UK, Sweden and Austria. These were established as a direct response to the Soviet intervention, either out of sympathy for the Afghan population or as a means of raising the profile of the intervention within the context of Cold War tensions. An initial focus on awareness raising activities thus gave rise to decisions to also provide tangible support to the Afghan population.

Other NGOs were established medical relief charities such as Medecins Sans Frontieres, Medecins Du Monde, Handicap Internationale and Action Contre La Faim. A global link with refugees was another factor. The Danish Refugee Council thus joined forces with other Danish organizations to form the Danish Committee for Aid to Afghan Refugees (DACAAR). The British NGO, The Ockenden Venture, built on its experience with Vietnamese refugees to lend support to Afghans in Pakistan.

A number of NGOs also came in from Saudi Arabia and the Gulf. These sought to give expression to Islamic concepts of charity through programmes for orphans and widows. Support was also given for education programmes, through madrasahs (quranic schools) and other institutions.

The dozen or so Afghan NGOs operating in the camps were primarily medical in nature and were, in many cases, the initiatives of Afghan doctors who wished to provide treatment to the war wounded coming across the border as well as meet the ongoing medical needs of those already in the camps.

The NGOs operating in the camps were unable to avoid the fact that they were operating in a highly politicized environment. The Mujahidin parties set up recruiting offices in the camps, with particular parties dominant in particular camps. Some of the Mujahidin parties also set up their own primary and secondary schools, and even universities, in the refugee camps in the hope of bringing up a new generation of adherents. Fighters would go into Afghanistan from the camps and would return to them after their operations.

The highly politicized character of the camps inevitably influenced the distribution of aid, particularly when the camps were first set up. Anthony Hyman comments as follows:

> The system under which the Pakistan Government dispensed its 'Islamic charity' to Afghan refugees was, from the first, calculated (whether consciously or not is another matter) to increase the power of the exile parties, since relief aid in cash and in kind was channelled through the parties. This indirect system certainly removed much of the strain from Pakistani officials as the refugee problem rapidly grew from 1978, but it increased rivalries between exile parties and actually provided the justification for mere factions to register as parties. The Afghan fundamentalists, already well established in Peshawar, were naturally at an advantage in extending their influence over both Afghan refugees and resistance groups across the borders.[27]

Thus, while the NGOs saw themselves as providing services of a humanitarian nature, and would not differentiate between members of one Mujahidin party or another in so doing, they were inevitably supporting an insurgency operation at the same time as they were providing for civilians who had fled a situation of armed conflict. However, this situation was not unique to the Afghan conflict. There have been many examples, historically, in which refugee camps have become bases for cross-border insurgency operations.

The Mujahidin parties were not only able to draw on refugee camps for recruits but they were also able to generate resources from individuals, organisations and governments within the wider Islamic world on the basis of pan-Islamic solidarity. They thus presented themselves as engaged in a popular resistance struggle, with Islam as the rallying point, against a secular power. In so doing, they built on a collective need to assert a shared value system, namely that of Islam, in the face of a denial of those values by the colonizer. At the same time, they sought to counter any feelings of humiliation, thus suffered as a result of the perceived disregard and disrespect for Islamic values, as individuals and as the global Islamic community. A pan-Islamic movement thus became an anti-imperialist movement.

Fundraisers for the Mujahidin parties were able to fundraise in private Arab circles and also from Afghan labourers working in Saudi Arabia or the Gulf. However, the resistance movement also relied heavily on existing stocks of weaponry and on being able to replenish these easily in the arms workshops of Darra Adam Khel, to the south-west of Peshawar, in Pakistan's tribal territories. Levies were also imposed on the population in 'liberated areas' to help pay for the war. In addition, the resistance would secure supplementary weaponry through its attacks on Afghan and Soviet military transports and posts.

Further support was provided from within Pakistan through largely tacit assistance. Thus, the Pakistan Government did not obstruct the efforts of the Mujahidin parties to organize politically, fundraise or publicize their cause, provided that due discretion was observed.

Hazara leaders, representing the major part of the minority Shi'a population of Afghanistan, set up small offices in Quetta, and in Iranian cities, from August 1979, in order to raise funds and publicise their cause. However, the provision of aid to the Hazara parties by Iran has always been secondary to wider strategic considerations.

The resistance movement also benefited from substantial resources provided by the USA, Pakistan and Saudi Arabia. Initially, the USA was slow to give this. The US government did not want, in the immediate aftermath of the Soviet military intervention, to be seen to be providing arms to the resistance because of the significant implications that this would have for its already tense relations with the Soviet Union. It also did not wish to commit US forces to a situation in which they would be directly confronting those of the Soviet Union. It was, in any event, preferable to place Afghan resistance fighters in the firing line rather than US soldiers. The willingness of Pakistan to be used as a vehicle for US arms supplies, initially provided covertly, to be delivered to the Mujahidin was, therefore, of great benefit.

Pakistan was willing to play this intermediary role because it was consistent with its own strategic objectives. It had always been conscious of its weakness relative to India and aimed, as its primary goal, to strengthen its position by creating an Islamic bloc encompassing Pakistan, Afghanistan and the Central Asian republics of the USSR, so as to achieve what is referred to as 'strategic depth'. To this end, it worked to support Islamist movements in both Afghanistan and Central Asia in the hope of building an alliance between these and a growing body of adherents to Islamist ideologies within Pakistan, notably within the army.

Pakistan was also open to any support that could be provided to strengthen its own armed forces. This was partly in response to violations of Pakistan's airspace – over 200 during 1980 alone – by warplanes and helicopters from Afghanistan. The Government of General Zia was concerned that any one of these border incidents could escalate into hostilities which would then be used to justify a punitive intervention by Soviet or Afghan forces. It was well aware that the weaponry available to its own forces was far inferior to that of the Soviet Union and that it would therefore come off badly from any confrontation. The General was also mindful of his own internal unpopularity, manifested in the imposition of martial law, and of the international opprobrium that had been attached to him as a consequence of his hanging of the previous Prime Minister, Zulfikar Ali Bhutto, in 1979. It was, therefore, very much in his interests to secure strong backing from the USA.

However, he rejected an initial offer of $400 million, half in economic assistance and half as arms sales credit, from the US Government as being insufficient to justify the strong reactions that any increase in Pakistan's military capacity would provoke in Moscow or New Delhi. Only when the government of Ronald Reagan offered a much larger aid package, in the spring of 1981, did Pakistan agree to a deal. In addition to the direct aid that it received, Pakistan was also rumoured to have diverted, into its own arsenal, an element of the military resources provided by the USA for the Mujahidin.

The USA initially used Egypt as a cover for its arms supplies, providing arms to the Egyptian Government to replace arms delivered to the Mujahidin from Egypt's own arsenal of Soviet-supplied weaponry. In acting as the conduit for these arms supplies, Pakistan was able to increase its credibility with Saudi Arabia and the Gulf States and, thereby, strengthen its relationship with them.

Hisb-e-Islami, under the leadership of Gulbuddin Hekmatyar,

was one of seven Mujahidin parties, out of many more, to which the Pakistan Government agreed to give resources, drawing on the funding provided by the USA and Saudi Arabia. There were doctrinal differences between Hisb-e-Islami and another major party known as Jamiat-e-Islami. Although both parties had been formed in Kabul University circles in the 1960s and 1970s and both espoused radical Islam, Jamiat-e-Islami sought to build an Islamic state on existing societal structures while Hisb-e-Islami took the view that existing structures should be replaced by a new cell-based structure. In addition, Jamiat-e-Islami was largely made up of Tajiks, the ethnic group which lives in the northeast of the country, while Hisb-e-Islami was predominantly Pushtun. Jamiat-e-Islami therefore saw Hisb-e-Islami as potentially aiming to re-establish the Pushtun dominance of government which had characterized the previous three centuries. Jamiat-e-Islami, in contrast, was actively seeking to achieve a greater representation of the non-Pushtun population in the governance process. A third radical party was Ittihad-i-Islami, led by Abdul Rasoul Sayyaf. This party had strong links with Saudi Arabia and espoused Wahhabism, with its emphasis on dress and behavioural codes. Sayyaf felt a greater affinity to Jamiat-e-Islami than he did to Hisb-e-Islami.

The remaining four of the seven Mujahidin parties registered with the Pakistan Government were broadly defined as conservative, being more anchored in traditional values. However, three of them supported the creation of an Islamic state, albeit with a less intellectual approach than that of the radical parties. These were another faction of Hisb-e-Islami, led by Yunus Khalis, Harakat-e-Islami, led by Nabi Mohammadi and the Afghan National Liberation Front, led by Sibghatullah Mujadidi. The Taliban were to draw many of their supporters from Khalis' Hisb-e-Islami and from Harakat-e-Islami. The fourth party was NIFA, led by Pir Gailani. This supported the return of the former King, Zahir Shah.

The role of Pakistan in supporting the resistance led to continuing criticism in both the Afghan and Soviet media. The view was taken that, if Pakistan and Iran could be persuaded or intimidated into exercising greater control of cross-border movements of insurgents, the resistance would be weakened. This very much echoes the post-2001 situation.

The increased injection of US military resources into the Mujahidin from 1986 onwards, which included the much-publicised delivery of Stinger missiles, is widely reputed to have turned the tide of the war in the Mujahidin's favour. However, it is much more likely that internal factors within the Soviet Union were dominant in the decision-making of the Kremlin.

Further arms were provided to the Mujahidin by China, Saudi Arabia and Egypt. Training was, in addition, said to have been provided to the Mujahidin forces by Chinese, Pakistani, American, British, West German and Israeli agents and military instructors.[28]

Saudi Arabia also agreed to match US funding for the Mujahidin, dollar for dollar. Much of this was directed at Hisb-e-Islami of Gulbudin Hekmatyar and Ittihad-i-Islami of Abdul Rasoul Sayyaf, as the most radical of the parties and the most akin to Saudi Wahhabism.

The strength of the resistance forces was enhanced by the arrival of volunteers from other parts of the Islamic world. Saudi Arabia, in particular, actively organized the recruitment of volunteers to fight alongside the Mujahidin and provided resources to support their training. Among a number of Peshawar-based recruitment offices was one, known as Al-Qaida, in which Osama bin Laden had a facilitating role. Hisb-e-Islami and Ittihad-i-Islami were also commissioned to provide much of the training for the Saudi volunteers.

Saudi Arabia also took the opportunity to promote Wahhabism within Pakistan, building on a close affinity between it and the Deobandi vision which had long been established in the Indian subcontinent. A manifestation of this was a mushrooming of Islamic madrasahs, or Quranic schools, in Pakistan, including the refugee camps.

The aid provided by various funding sources within Saudi Arabia, for an expansion of madrasahs in Pakistan, supported the ambition of the Pakistan President, Zia Al-Haq, to increase the number of soldiers within the Pakistan army who were committed to a radical Islamic perspective. Both Saudi Arabia and Pakistan were, at this time, financing and supporting the development of Islamist centres and educational facilities in the Ferghana Valley of Uzbekistan.

However, although the Saudi Government was willing to be a partner of the USA in supporting the Mujahidin, it was resistant to requests from the US Government that the latter might establish bases on Saudi soil for the use of rapid deployment forces. Other Gulf States were also resistant.

Substantial funding was made available by the USA to NGOs, from 1986 onwards. However, it was only a small number of, primarily, US NGOs which received the major part of this funding. These included the University of Nebraska at Omaha, which played a major role in supporting the education sector and in drawing up a curriculum. These and other NGOs later linked with the Afghan Interim Government in Peshawar to ensure that their policy was consistent with the policy of what was seen as the government-in-waiting.

Although this funding was largely used for humanitarian purposes, the emphasis on education, in particular, was clearly geared to influencing values within the population. Further, while NGOs welcomed the additional funding, it was linked to a politically driven goal of supporting the resistance to undermine the Soviet military presence. The aid community thus became, to a degree, politically tainted by its association with the US government even though a majority of European NGOs were securing funding from both public and private donors who were independent of the USA.

Aid to refugees in Iran

In Iran, most refugees were expected to survive in the urban areas of the country without specifically earmarked assistance, while being permitted to work in certain designated menial occupations. They were also entitled to receive the subsidies on basic essentials that the Iranian population enjoyed, together with access to state health care and education. This was of a greater quality than that provided in the refugee camps in Pakistan. Additional support was provided by local Komitehs and private organizations.

In addition, Iran set up some camps along the border. These camps were largely resourced by the Iranian Government, together with the Iranian Red Crescent Society. UNHCR played a very minor role in the provision of services to the camps, due, in part, to the unwillingness of donor governments to fund humanitarian operations in Iran. The Iranian Government was also very resistant to any large Western presence and wished to avoid the large expatriate community that was a characteristic of the refugee situation in Pakistan.

Iran provided support, in some cases including arms supplies on a small scale, to specific organizations, through which the Hazara population of Afghanistan engaged in resistance operations against the PDPA Government and the Soviet forces. Among these was Sazman-i-Nasr, which drew inspiration from the Ayatollah Khomeini and thus pursued the model of Iran's Islamic revolution. Also supported was Harakat-e-Islami. Both parties maintained offices in Iran. However, Iran's war with Iraq took precedence over any considerations of how it might influence outcomes in Afghanistan.

Later, Iran sought to bring the various Shi'a Hazara parties together under one umbrella. Various structures came and went before they coalesced, under the name of Hisb-e-Wahdat, in 1989. As well as seeking to influence the population ideologically, it was hoped that Hisb-e-Wahdat would be able to strengthen the position of the Shi'a population, in political and economic terms, and so address the extremely low status which it had suffered historically. However, Iran was reported to have provided greater levels of funding for some of the Peshawar-based Mujahidin parties, particularly Hisb-e-Islami.

At the same time, Iran supported a cross-border insurgency movement into western Afghanistan, using the refugee camps in its eastern provinces of Khorasan and Sistan-Baluchistan as a base for these. This was supplemented by propaganda against the Soviet military presence.

Aid to Afghan refugees in India, Europe and North America

In addition to the support provided by Pakistan and Iran to Afghan refugees, India permitted at least 20,000 to seek exile within its borders. These were primarily from the intelligentsia and the professional class and arrived by air from Kabul. Among these were Sikhs and Hindus who had settled in Afghanistan, from the Indian subcontinent, to engage in commerce.

Of the European and North American States, it was only Germany which provided visas and allowances to Afghans on any scale. Others, in spite of their expressions of sympathy and solidarity for the Mujahidin, were reluctant to permit the entry of Afghan refugees in more than very small numbers.

Aid to populations in Mujahidin-held areas

Those who lived in the rural areas had to survive without government support. This was inevitably difficult when Soviet forces were engaging in bombing offensives or search operations. Many of those who remained in Afghanistan therefore suffered serious privations as it became increasingly unsafe to cultivate their land. The food shortages that followed the destruction of crops and livestock brought about a rapid growth in malnutrition, which affected women and children in particular. These shortages were compounded by a decline in the number of able-bodied villagers to work the land as young men joined the resistance or were killed or injured. There was a major increase in the incidence of diseases such as pneumonia and TB, as villagers were compelled, by bombing raids, to take refuge in mountain caves and suffered the effects of exposure to damp and cold conditions. Serious psychological conditions, due to the stress from aid raids, were also observed.

The population suffered, in addition, a loss of basic services. Estimates by the Afghan Government, in February 1983, concluded that over half of the country's schools and hospitals (1,814 schools and 31 hospitals), 111 basic health centres, 75 per cent of communication lines, 800 heavy transport vehicles, 906 peasant cooperatives and many other development projects had been damaged or destroyed. This was exclusively attributed to the operations of resistance forces and made no mention of the impact of bombing raids by Soviet or Afghan forces.

The medical services that were needed, to care for the war wounded, were, in consequence, no longer available in many areas. The large number of civilians who suffered injuries as a result of the heavy bombardment of villages, or from booby-trap bombs or anti-personnel mines, were therefore seriously at risk.

Some limited medical assistance was provided by Medecins Sans Frontieres and Aide Medicale Internationale which, between 1980 and 1983, sent over 300 doctors and nurses on short missions into Afghanistan to care for the sick and wounded. In addition, the Afghan Doctors Society established five major and 21 small clinics in Afghanistan, to which it dispatched hundreds of young Afghan men and women who had been trained as paramedics. Another important actor was the de-mining NGO, The HALO Trust, which offered medical care alongside its de-mining work in northern Afghanistan.

Additional assistance, in the form of wheat or cash, was provided to populations in Mujahidin-controlled areas by humanitarian agencies operating cross-border from Peshawar and Quetta in Pakistan. These would normally link with one or other of the Mujahidin parties who would, typically, collect the wheat or cash at the border and transport it by donkey to vulnerable families in their areas of control. The agencies would exercise a degree of supervision by sending staff into Afghanistan periodically to monitor how the aid had been spent.

While this form of delivery carried a significant degree of risk in terms of the aid reaching, in full, those for whom it was intended, it was felt that, through monitoring visits, it was ensured that families living on the margins were given support which they would not otherwise have received.

It is also the case that there were legitimate concerns for the welfare of people still living in Afghanistan and caught up in the ongoing conflict. It would have been extremely difficult for NGOs to establish normal aid operations while Soviet forces were carrying out bombing raids or searching villages and, it could be argued, they did their best in the circumstances.

By giving aid through particular Mujahidin parties, the NGOs involved were inevitably aligning themselves both with the Mujahidin side and with some Mujahidin parties over others. At the time, this partiality was felt to be justified because of the outrage felt, over the Soviet intervention, by those NGOs that emerged out of solidarity committees. It should, however, be stressed that not all NGOs operated cross-border in this way and those that did tie their colours to the Mujahidin mast, at this stage, took steps to operate on the basis of neutrality and impartiality once the Soviet forces withdrew.

By the time that the Soviet forces withdrew, the Afghan economy had been severely damaged. Agricultural production was at half its pre-war level, partly because of destruction but largely because of neglect, with so much of the population living in exile. The irrigation systems and flood protection structures, on which much of agriculture depended, had fallen into disrepair. Livestock numbers were also seriously depleted. The major highway system, which had been constructed to a high standard by the USA and Russia during the 1960s, had lost its tarmac surface and was heavily potholed.

The electricity generating facilities which supplied the cities were only operating at part capacity, if at all. Water supply and sanitation were also badly affected. The little industrial production that existed before the intervention had reduced to a small fraction of its previous level.

US support for a Mujahidin government-in-waiting

As the 15 February 1989 deadline for Soviet withdrawal approached, the international community was convinced that the Soviet-backed Government would not survive the departure of Soviet troops. This was in spite of the failure of mediation efforts by the envoy, Diego Cordoves, appointed by the UN Secretary General in 1983. These had involved regular meetings with representatives of the resistance, Pakistan, Iran, the Soviet Union and the USA, in the hope of identifying possible elements to form the basis of a negotiated settlement. The Geneva Accords of April 1988 built on these efforts.

In the continued hope that the fragmented Mujahidin parties would cohere around a single political platform, Pakistan and the US Government sought to facilitate the creation of a government-in-waiting through what was referred to as the Afghan Interim Government. Thus, under the gaze of the world's media, the various Mujahidin parties were brought together in Peshawar in February 1989 to agree on a power-sharing arrangement. By the end of the three days of deliberations, it was clear that agreement was not in sight and that doctrinal, ethnic and personal power-related issues were presenting insuperable obstacles.

The greatest fissure was between Jamiat-e-Islami, led by Ahmed Shah Masoud, and Hisb-e-Islami, led by Gulbuddin Hekmatyar. Jamiat-e-Islami resented the fact that their fighters had borne the brunt of the Soviet military offensives while receiving only a small fraction of the resources provided by the USA and Pakistan. They also resented the fact that Hekmatyar had been particularly favoured by the USA, and by Pakistan's Inter-Services Intelligence, and was being seen as a future leader of Afghanistan and, thereby, a key element in Pakistan's goal of creating an Islamic bloc encompassing Pakistan, Afghanistan and the Central Asian Republics as a counterweight to India.

In spite of this fragmentation, the USA and Pakistan persisted in their efforts to build the seven parties into an alliance which could take over the Afghan Government in the event of the fall of the Soviet-backed Government. They also supported and financed the bureaucracy of the Afghan Interim Government, with its separate ministries, in Peshawar.

The differences that had undermined efforts to create a government-in-waiting also weakened the capacity of the Mujahidin to bring about the anticipated fall of the Soviet-backed Government of Muhammed Najibullah, which retained control of the urban areas of Afghanistan. A Mujahidin offensive against the Afghan army near Jalalabad in March 1989 failed miserably, and the Mujahidin were not able to capture ground until they took Khost in April 1991. However, they were in a position to act as an irritant to the government by rocketing Kabul on almost a daily basis.

The ability of the Soviet-backed Government to withstand Mujahidin offensives was greatly helped by the fact that it could draw on additional support from what was known as the Jozjani militia, headed by the Uzbek leader (from Jozjan in northern Afghanistan), Rashid Dostam. This militia had a reputation for particular ferocity.

The disunity of the Mujahidin led to a growing fragmentation of power within the rural areas of Afghanistan. This fragmentation was used by President Najibullah to weaken the Mujahidin resistance by striking deals with local power holders. Although Soviet forces were no longer present, the ongoing fighting between the Soviet-backed Government and the Mujahidin created an insecure environment. Further, the divisions between the Mujahidin were leading to localized conflict within the rural areas. The aid community was therefore heavily constrained in accessing populations at risk even though NGOs had arrived in Peshawar, in force, in the expectation that they would be needed to support a return of the refugees.

An initial rush to spend money was a characteristic of this early stage as agencies slowly adjusted to the fact that the Soviet-backed government had not fallen and that refugees had not returned. A consequent haste to establish programmes in areas of Afghanistan close to Peshawar was replaced by greater realism as agencies discovered, through experience, that the security situation in the country was more fragile than they had anticipated. However, the greater availability of funding did mean that the refugee camps benefited from an enhanced quality of services.

Because of their close association with the Mujahidin, NGOs were not, with only a couple of exceptions, willing to operate programmes in the urban areas controlled by the Soviet-backed Government or work cross-line from the cities into the rural areas. Quite apart from any considerations of affinity to the Mujahidin cause, NGO staff would have been put at risk from the Mujahidin parties, given the climate of fear that existed, if they were known to be working in Government-controlled areas. In any event, with many of the NGO staff, at that time, connected to one or other of the Mujahidin parties, such a move would have been strongly opposed within the organizations.

However, from 1989 onwards, NGOs felt the need to move from their solidarity committee roots to establish themselves as neutral, impartial organizations working on the basis of professional standards. An image of neutrality and impartiality was also important if they were to be able to deliver aid to all areas of Afghanistan, regardless of the links that particular Mujahidin parties had with particular geographical areas. In transiting areas controlled by certain power holders, in order to reach those controlled by others, it was important not to be associated with one Mujahidin party over another. This was not always easy to achieve, as particular NGOs were already widely known as having links with particular Mujahidin parties, but it was an aspiration that NGOs gradually worked to achieve. With the same objective, they also brought in staff who were independent of the Mujahidin as existing staff left. Many of these were technocrats. This helped enhance their professional image as they built a reputation for their engineering, medical or other skills.

The departure of Soviet troops, combined with the poor image of the Mujahidin at this stage, will have helped maintain morale amongst what was left of the Afghan national army. In fact, the conciliatory approach taken by President Najibullah since 1986 had, by 1989, created broad-based support for his government within the urban areas. The climate of fear and purges of the early PDPA years had been replaced by a more benign environment, with President Najibullah frequently referred to, by the population of the cities, as an ox, by virtue of the relative stability that he provided.

It was in Peshawar that such a climate of fear emerged. This arose from the threat that intellectuals were seen to pose to the Mujahidin parties' efforts to impose their societal vision on the refugee population. A spate of assassinations of liberals such as Professor Sayyid Majruh, who ran the Afghan Information Centre, compelled Afghans in senior positions within the aid community to seriously constrain their movements. The intense atmosphere of paranoia was accentuated by the distribution of what were called 'night letters', threatening all those who were seen to be undermining Islamic values. Hisb-e-Islami, which had a strong presence in Pakistan, was rumoured to be behind these threats but there were many organizations in existence with similar perspectives. The ruthlessness and doctrinal intolerance which characterized the early PDPA regime were therefore also to be found on the Mujahidin side.

Conclusions

In looking at the lessons that can be learned from the provision of aid to refugees and to the populations of Mujahidin-held areas during this period, we can certainly conclude that it was highly politicized. The military support provided by the USA to the Mujahidin was clearly aimed to weaken the Soviet Union. The additional assistance provided to the Afghan Interim Government would have been based on the hope that a friendly government could have been created in Afghanistan, which would have accepted a strong US influence, if not a US military presence. The support to the UN system and NGOs was a secondary by-product of this strategy, to ensure that the refugee population, on which the cross-border insurgency relied, had adequate food and provisions. The UN and NGOs had no choice but to accept the unfortunate reality that their operations were not politically neutral and, for some NGOs, the decision to be partial was one that they were willing to make.

It is also the case that, at this stage, the UN and NGOs were bit-part players on a global stage. The power that they enjoyed was relatively small in terms of influencing outcomes. Thus, in spite of being part of a major operation to support three million refugees in Pakistan, they were caught up in a complex web of power games, including those created by the presence of Mujahidin parties in the refugee camps, over which they had no control.

In considering power dynamics over this period, the dominant factor was the ability of the Soviet-backed Government to stay in power, until the collapse of the Soviet Union deprived it of the resources on which its survival had depended.

The failure of the Mujahidin parties to unite, and the consequent fragmentation process in the rural areas, created a situation of political fluidity within Afghanistan. In Pakistan, the strong power base of the more radical of the Islamic parties had a major influence on the political environment, with a targeting of liberals and intellectuals being a serious consequence.

Yet it is not clear that the other players succeeded in the objectives that the delivery of military and other assistance was intended to achieve.

Whether the USA was successful in weakening the Soviet Union, through its support to the Mujahidin, is debatable. The resistance was already strong within Afghanistan before the USA lent it support. However, it never ceased to be fragmented and US support, if anything, increased that fragmentation by strengthening Hisb-e-Islami at the possible expense of other groups. This, in turn, helped fuel the subsequent civil war of 1992–6. Hisb-e-Islami would not appear to have had sufficient impact, in confronting Soviet forces, to justify the level of resources provided to it. Other Mujahidin groups are viewed as having been far more effective with much fewer resources. The role of Stinger missles in turning the course of the war continues to be controversial and it is likely, as has been noted above, that internal factors within the Soviet Union, with their roots going back decades, were far more influential.

However, while neither the Soviet Union nor the USA could be regarded as having achieved their objectives, the unintended consequences of their interventions, combined with those of Pakistan and Saudi Arabia, have had enormous implications.

Thus, the funding and other support provided by Saudi Arabia for an expansion of madrasahs in Pakistan created the conditions for a radicalization of the political environment, and it has had considerable implications for power dynamics within both Pakistan and Afghanistan. This programme of expansion helped facilitate the ambition of President Zia al-Haq to strengthen adherence to radical Islam within the Pakistan army and so support insurgency operations against India in Kashmir. It also, in conjunction with the operations of radical Islamic parties such as Jamiat-al-Ulema al-Islami, created an environment in which the Taliban movement emerged. The power of this movement has been further strengthened by a network of radical Islamic organizations, often referred to as Al-Qaida, which arose out of the many volunteers from other parts of the Islamic world who fought in the Afghan jihad.

A related question is whether the efforts of the UN and NGOs to deliver humanitarian assistance, either in the refugee camps or in Afghanistan, were undermined by the various power dynamics around them. In the refugee camps, it is likely that the efforts of the UN and NGOs to deliver food and other assistance would have been, to a degree, influenced by power dynamics within the camps, including possible influences linked to the Mujahidin parties. The Pakistan Government, including the intelligence service, may also have played a role, either positive or negative, arising out of their contacts with these parties. However, such dynamics do not appear to have been sufficiently serious to lead to significant inequalities of access to assistance. The delivery of food assistance is always problematic, in any event.

It could certainly be argued that the ability of the aid community to access populations at risk in Afghanistan was seriously constrained by Soviet military operations. Aid personnel would therefore have been vulnerable to offensives against villages where these populations lived and to attacks, largely from the air, while they were travelling to these villages. However, aid agencies had no previous history of working in Afghanistan and would not have sought to deliver assistance if it had not been for the Soviet intervention.

Pakistan steps into the power vacuum

The break-up of the Soviet Union towards the end of 1991 meant that the PDPA Government in Kabul was no longer in receipt of the subsidies on which its existence depended. It was, therefore, only a matter of time before it ceased to be sustainable. The end came in April 1992, after the Uzbek militia leader, Rashid Dostam, and Ahmed Shah Masoud negotiated with key elements in the PDPA Government for a peaceful transfer of power to a Mujahidin government. Again, the USA and Pakistan sought to bring their own protégés, notably Hekmatyar, into the act but without a successful negotiated outcome. In the end, the struggle for power between the non-Pushtuns, represented by Masoud and Dostam, and the Pakistan and US-backed Pushtuns was settled through a resort to arms.

It was largely Pakistan that sought to influence outcomes in Afghanistan after 1991. The attention of the USA was diverted elsewhere once the Soviet Union had ceased to exist. The departure of the big players, the Soviet Union and the USA, created a power vacuum into which Pakistan neatly stepped, in pursuit of its goal of strategic depth.

Pakistan immediately called a meeting in Jalalabad of the Mujahidin parties with a view to influencing the composition of the future Mujahidin government. However, this meeting failed to reach agreement and, within a day of Masoud's forces entering Kabul, the forces of the Hisb-e-Islami leader, Gulbuddin Hekmatyar, started to rocket Kabul from their base at Charasyab, to the south of Kabul.

Heavy fighting continued across the capital, with the city reduced to virtual anarchy, and travel was highly restricted by the numerous checkpoints held by the various groups. It became particularly intense in August 1992, resulting in a large-scale exodus of professionals to the northern city of Mazar-i-Sharif.

In the west of Kabul, Hisb-e-Wahdat took the opportunity to establish a foothold from which to assert its right to be a key player in any negotiations for a future government. It thus hoped to redress the historical marginalisation of the Hazara population within both the political and economic domains. Fighting soon broke out between this group and Ittihad-i-Islami and this continued over the rest of the year. In response, Masoud's forces went on the offensive in support of Ittihad-i-Islami, in February 1993, and perpetrated what became known as the Afshar massacre, in bombarding an entire Shi'a neighbourhood. Thereafter, Hisb-e-Wahdat's position was much weakened.

Hekmatyar continued to rocket Kabul and, in January 1994, he was joined by Dostam, who was aggrieved that Masoud had not honoured their previous power sharing agreement. From 1 January, for about ten days, rockets literally poured onto Kabul from Charasyab in the south and Dostam's positions in the northeast of the capital, leading people to flee in panic in their hundreds of thousands. About 30,000 people reached Pakistan but it proved necessary to set up new camps for displaced people near Jalalabad. These came to accommodate over 200,000 people. By this stage, much of southern Kabul was reduced to rubble, but the fighting continued over the rest of the year, with the population suffering considerable privations.

While the Mujahidin were fighting for control in Kabul and Kandahar, Herat and the north-west of Afghanistan enjoyed relative stability under the former resistance fighter, Ismail Khan. Rashid Dostam operated his own fiefdom from Mazar-i-Sharif, albeit engaged in ongoing conflict with Ismail Khan for control of eastern Badghis. Jamiat-e-Islami, under Ahmed Shah Masoud and President Rabbani, controlled the northeast while Hisb-e-Wahdat controlled the central Hazarajat. In the east of the country, the Mujahidin commander, Haji Qadir, held sway over Nangarhar and parts of the adjoining provinces while another major commander, Hazrat Ali, maintained a tight hold on Laghman, to the north of Nangarhar.

Pakistan, which had, hitherto, been continuing to place its hopes in Hekmatyar, began to look elsewhere for ways of achieving its goal of an Islamic bloc encompassing Pakistan, Afghanistan and the newly independent Central Asian Republics. Over the summer of 1994, it took active steps to build influence in these Republics. To this end, Pakistan's Interior Minister, Nasrullah Babar, undertook a journey across Afghanistan to see whether it was possible to travel by land across Afghanistan to Central Asia and thus establish a trade route.

His journey, undertaken in October 1994, was successful but his convoy was attacked to the south of Kandahar. A group of religious students came to the rescue, having recently formed the group in response to behaviour, amongst the commanders battling for power in Kandahar, which they found unacceptable. The students had studied at Quranic schools or madrasahs in Pakistan, whence came the name Taliban (students). Pakistan saw an opportunity to strengthen this group.

The Taliban were able to quickly build popular support because of disaffection over the failure of the Mujahidin to provide a secure government. They thus took Kandahar in November 1994 and, thereafter, much of the southern provinces over the ensuing months. By February 1995, they were at the outskirts of Kabul and captured Charasyab from Hekmatyar. They were also able to briefly take western Kabul before being pushed back by Masoud's forces. In the process, they captured the leader of Hisb-e-Wahdat, Abdul Ali Mazari, who died in mysterious circumstances in their custody.

Herat was the next target, which they took in September 1995. This was achieved without a fight. They then moved northeast into Badghis but failed to make any headway. A year passed before a further attempt was made on Kabul, in September 1996, but only after Jalalabad had first been taken, earlier that month. The move on Kabul involved some fighting but Masoud opted to withdraw rather than subject the capital to a long battle.

Immediately on taking power in Kandahar, the Taliban sought to impose their vision on the population. This vision of radical Islam drew on a combination of traditional practice in Afghanistan, the Deobandi school of thought and Wahhabism, with a strong emphasis on dress and behavioural codes.

However, the Taliban were not particularly draconian, at this stage, in requiring the population to comply with their behavioural and dress provisions. For the population of the rural areas, these did not differ markedly from the prevailing norms and the Taliban, in their determination to complete their conquest of Afghanistan, did not want to divert their energies by bothering with how people dressed and behaved at the village level. In fact, their presence was very light during the first year and the Pushtun tribes were largely left to get on with their lives so long as they acquiesced to Taliban rule. This the tribes were willing to do for so long as they continued to value the improved security that the Taliban had brought, and for so long as the Taliban did not interfere in their lives or seek to forcibly recruit new fighters from their populations.

The Taliban were somewhat harsher when they took Herat in that they placed an absolute ban on women working and girls being educated. In Kandahar, this had not been a major issue as very few women worked and female education was generally regarded as a low priority in the highly conservative society of the city. However, Herat had, historically, been the major cultural centre of Afghanistan. Thus, even though it was also conservative, it had supported education for girls on a significant scale and employed a large number of female teachers. These suddenly found themselves unable to work and so education for boys was curtailed as well as for girls.

The end of rocketing by Hekmatyar's forces made it possible for Kabul to enjoy a period of security and stability for over a year, in spite of military engagements between the Taliban and Masoud's forces on the edge of the city. In consequence, efforts were made to re-establish the governance process and strengthen the bureaucracy. However, a Taliban blockade of the capital over the winter of 1995–6 brought about considerable shortages.

In Central Asia, a civil war in Tajikistan led to an exodus of refugees to northern Afghanistan, while the Fergana Valley, which sits astride Kyrgyzstan, Uzbekistan and Tajikistan, saw the emergence of a growing Islamist movement, supported by Saudi Arabia.

The USA and Europe were, at this stage, little involved in affairs to do with Afghanistan. Although the arrival of the Taliban in 1994 caused some concerns, it did not lead these governments to give priority to the country. They simply maintained what they called a watching brief while opting not to accord diplomatic recognition to the Mujahidin government.

This period saw many population movements. Initial optimism, following the fall of the Soviet-backed government, led to a large-scale return of over 100,000 refugees from Pakistan over the summer of 1992. The rate of return then slowed as the optimism turned into disillusionment in response to the heavy fighting in Kabul. During the following years, the numbers returning were relatively small and were offset by the exodus of January 1994. However, 1993 saw another large return from Iran after it had signed a repatriation agreement with UNHCR and Afghanistan and had strongly encouraged certain groups of refugees to return, stimulated by the bulldozing of most of the refugee camps along the border.

The large-scale return of refugees from Pakistan and Iran was offset by a common tendency of returning refugees to establish some family members in their villages or neighbourhoods of origin and then return to their countries of exile to seek work. Further, some family members had gone back to their villages during the 1988–92 period to undertake some initial rebuilding work to homes and irrigation systems before bringing the rest of the family back. Many of those who returned in 1992–3 were living close to the Pakistan or Iran borders. There was, therefore, a situation in which a single family would have members on both sides of the border and there would be a continuing process of moving back and forth to seek work, undertake repair work, and so on.

The European Commission became a major donor over this period and also became supportive of innovative ways of working. Primary among these was a willingness to support long-term rural development programmes, working in partnership with beneficiary communities, in spite of the absence of an effective government.

A key development was the departure of US funding, on any scale, from 1993 onwards as Afghanistan was removed from the list of priority countries for US foreign policy. The view was, therefore, taken that, having achieved the weakening of the Soviet regime that they sought, there was no further need to inject resources into the country. The fact that Afghanistan was severely damaged was not seen as a sufficient justification. Strategic interests therefore prevailed.

The US Government now regards this as a major error on their part in that, by taking their eye off the Afghan ball and by failing to support a reconstruction process and, thereby, improve living standards, they created an environment in which the Taliban could build popular support. However, a much greater level of reconstruction assistance would have been needed than was being provided at that time if the US was to make a significant difference to the reconstruction process. Further, the success of the Taliban in building public support was largely due to the failure of the Mujahidin parties to form a stable government. It is not clear that the US Government would have been able to persuade the various parties to cohere around agreed objectives, even if it had given greater priority to Afghanistan after 1991. However, it might have been more difficult for elements within Pakistan to lend active support to the Taliban conquests if the Pakistan Government had felt under greater scrutiny from the USA.

Notwithstanding the decline in the volume of external assistance for Afghanistan, the relative improvement in security brought about in areas such as Herat and the northeast, as well as in the southern provinces after the emergence of the Taliban, made it possible for the UN and NGOs to access populations and so operate programmes with a reasonable degree of efficiency and effectiveness. As a consequence, major rural development programmes were established, benefiting from the three-year funding cycles of the European Commission and others, and from the experience gained in exploring community development approaches. The brief period of stability in Kabul, from the spring of 1995 to the summer of 1996, was also a relatively positive period from the point of view of the delivery of assistance.

In addition, in spite of the involvement of Pakistan in orchestrating outcomes in Afghanistan, the UN and NGOs were operating in a less politicized environment, in that they were no longer associated with a superpower. It was therefore possible for them to establish greater neutrality and impartiality in the face of the fragmented political environment.

The Taliban colonization process: 1996–2001

The Taliban capture of Kabul in September 1996 created a very different political environment from that which existed before. Hopes that the Taliban would moderate through the experience of running a government soon disappeared as it became apparent that they were to deal harshly with the population of Kabul. Further, the decision of the Taliban to capture the Shomali Valley, in the immediate aftermath of their seizure of Kabul, led to several years of conflict which destroyed an important area of agricultural land and also left Kabul as an economic backwater. As a result, Kabul became a dead economy, with the population heavily dependent on food aid from the UN.

The Taliban also dealt punitively with the non-Pushtun minorities as they sought to complete their conquest of the country. Their initial effort to take Mazar-e Sharif in May 1997 resulted in a massacre of Taliban soldiers, and they were quick to take revenge when they finally captured the city in August 1998, massacring several thousand people, mostly Hazaras. When they quickly moved south from Mazar to take control of the Hazarajat, more Hazaras were killed. However, agreement was finally reached with one of the Hisb-e-Wahdat leaders for him to run the area as a semi-independent fiefdom, under their overall control.

The Taliban then moved on the northeast, but it took them until September 2000 to take the town of Taloqan and they were still embarked on their conquest of this final corner when the USA intervened in Afghanistan in October 2001.

The Taliban were only accorded diplomatic recognition by Pakistan, Saudi Arabia and the United Arab Emirates (UAE). Iran was extremely wary, because of the very evident antipathy of the Taliban, and their international supporters, to Shi'as, and this wariness increased after several Iranian diplomats were killed in Mazar-e Sharif in August 1998.

The USA, at this stage, made tentative overtures to the Taliban, from 1996 onwards, in connection with potential interest in a pipeline route through Afghanistan to transport gas from Turkmenistan to Pakistan. A US company, UNOCAL, competed with an Argentinean company by the name of Bridas to secure contracts with the Taliban.

However, even this minor level of communication came to an abrupt halt after the USA launched air strikes on Afghanistan in August 1998, in response to terrorist attacks on the US embassies in Nairobi and Dar es Salaam. The US Government immediately called on the Taliban to hand over Osama bin Laden, who had taken sanctuary in Afghanistan after being expelled from the Sudan. The Taliban instead took him under their wing in Kandahar and, thereafter, a growing process of communication between him and the Taliban leadership led to a radicalization of the movement. This manifested itself in various ways. These included an obvious sympathy with pan-Islamic issues, such as Palestine, in contrast to a previous disinterest in the wider Islamic world. It also manifested itself in the destruction of the Buddhas of Bamyan in March 2000. A further outcome was the growing development of training camps in Afghanistan, aimed, primarily, to impart military skills to foreign fighters helping the Taliban in their process of conquest, but with the side-effect of resourcing a potential process of terrorist activity elsewhere.

The USA also distanced itself from the pipeline project, following the air strikes and consequent high profile lobbying from women's organizations in the USA against any deals with the Taliban. The financial viability of the project had also become less certain, with alternative pipeline routes within Central Asia being more actively promoted.

Although the Taliban established a government which progressively controlled a large area of the country, their goals were very limited. Like Abdur-Rahman at the end of the nineteenth century, their primary objective was to achieve a conquest of the country and to ensure security within the conquered territories. Of equal importance was the creation of an Islamic state based on Shari'a Law, requiring the population to behave and dress appropriately to accord with their highly conservative creed. Unlike the radical Islamic movements in Egypt and Iran, they did not see the alleviation of poverty or ill health as part of their goal.

While there continued to be a willingness to permit the aid community to provide health care to women, subject to certain conditions, there was no shift in their previous refusal to allow the UN or NGOs to employ Afghan women. The Taliban also maintained their stance that women and girls should not be educated beyond the normal instruction in Islam. The delivery of assistance therefore became much more problematic after the Taliban takeover of Kabul in 1996, in that a government now existed but it was one which accorded very low priority to the provision of basic services to the population.

After 1996, it also became virtually impossible to deliver aid in front-line areas such as the Shomali Valley or in regions which the Taliban were seeking to conquer. Further, the exodus of over 200,000 people from the Shomali Valley to Kabul in 1997 necessitated a significant humanitarian response. The World Food Programme was already operating a large bakeries programme in the capital, through which consumers could purchase bread at subsidized prices, and this had to be expanded to provide for the new influx. Further, the population was inevitably affected by the effective collapse of the Kabul economy. This increasingly suffered from the loss of an important source of food, with the Shomali Valley no longer producing on any scale, and it also progressively ceased to function as a trading post, as traders were forced to find other routes following the closure of the Shomali Valley. Its potential function as the seat of the government administration was very much weakened by the failure of the civil service to function in any meaningful way, with limited exceptions, after the years of the Mujahidin Government. A further exodus of senior civil servants after the arrival of the Taliban had accelerated this. By 2001, the bakeries programme was feeding a very high proportion of the population and NGOs were doing their best to provide medical care and supplementary feeding to people at risk. Begging was increasingly in evidence, particularly by women. Children, in large numbers, were compelled by economic circumstances to use their ingenuity to seek out income-earning opportunities. Some of these were supported by projects operated by NGOs for street children as well as by orphanages.

In spite of these efforts, the Taliban saw the work that the UN and NGOs were doing in the country as of very limited value. At the same time, they were deeply suspicious of foreign agencies, and of Afghans working for them, lest they subtly imbue the Afghan population with western or liberal values. The Taliban were clearly concerned that Afghan traditional and Islamic values would be progressively undermined by the prevailing global value systems. These were seen to be heavily influenced by US values and were felt to represent a serious threat to Islam and Afghan cultural mores. It was therefore regarded as important to build a cocoon around Afghanistan to protect it from these external influences. However, international aid workers were, in the eyes of the Taliban, potential vehicles for bringing these external values into Afghanistan. Further, the largely educated professional Afghans employed by NGOs were seen as liberal and, potentially, secular and un-Islamic. It was therefore feared that these might actively seek to resist the efforts of the Taliban to implant their societal vision within the country

The Taliban continued to tolerate the aid community, to some degree, possibly in recognition that there might be some value in having them provide health and agricultural support services, in particular, to the population. But there was a high degree of ambivalence in their position, which always led them to question whether what they saw as the limited benefits that NGOs might bring would be offset by the negative influence that they might have on the population.

There was particular unease about the involvement of NGOs in the provision of education. Education had been a sensitive political issue since the efforts of Amir Amanullah in 1929, to introduce limited education for girls, had provoked a backlash from tribal and religious leaders, which had led to his overthrow. The expansion of education from the 1950s onwards was seen by the Taliban as having been responsible for the emergence of the PDPA and the consequent coup of April 1978, which had, in turn, led to the Soviet military intervention of December 1979. It was also seen as responsible for the creation of the Mujahidin parties and the doctrinal differences which had, amongst other factors, contributed to the inter-factional fighting in Kabul of 1992–6. The Taliban were aware of the efforts of individual Mujahidin parties, and other political movements, to build a supporter base through the establishment of schools and, even, universities. Education was not seen, therefore, as value neutral. Any education provision by international NGOs was thus regarded as, potentially, a vehicle for Western governments to introduce their own norms into Afghan society, or for Afghan intellectuals employed by NGOs to undermine traditional or Islamic values. For the Taliban, the relatively simple education provided by the madrasahs was all that was needed to ensure that the population were aware of their Islamic heritage.

This made it necessary for the UN and NGOs to negotiate with the Taliban in relation to all programmes. The ease with which this could be carried out varied from one area to another, and from one period to another, and was heavily dependent on the approach of individual Taliban Governors, with some being more flexible and pragmatic than others. However, these local representatives were frequently rotated meaning that, for example, education programmes for girls which were tolerated by one Governor might be banned by his successor.

It was particularly difficult for expatriate women to negotiate with the Taliban and the latter would often refuse to speak to them if they attended a meeting, even if they were the sole representatives of their agencies and there was important business to discuss.

At times, the power that tribal leaders or other representatives of beneficiary communities wielded made it possible for them to challenge local Taliban representatives and insist, for example, that girls schools be allowed or that restrictions on NGO activities be lifted. To a degree, therefore, the Taliban were dependent on tribal structures for their support base and could be persuaded by pressure from tribal elders.

The Taliban were particularly suspicious of NGOs which were overtly Christian, lest they seek to actively evangelize. These organizations came under considerable scrutiny and some were finally forced to leave the country.

NGOs were also seen as decadent in their behaviour by virtue of the more liberal approach of their expatriate staff to communication between women and men. There was a consequent fear that they would have a corrupting influence on the Afghans that they came in contact with. Aid personnel had to be especially circumspect. Expatriate men therefore took care to ensure that they were not alone with Afghan women. Both women and men, within the expatriate community, dressed modestly so as not to cause offence. Social gatherings were normally small scale and low key. However, there were the inevitable lapses into inappropriate behaviour which provoked strong responses from the Taliban.

In their concern to contain what they saw as the contaminating influence of aid workers on the population, the Taliban insisted, in July 1998, that all NGOs with bases in Kabul move into a polytechnic building on the edge of Kabul. However, NGOs were resistant to being in one, publicly known, location. They were aware of historical incidents in which crowds had suddenly been fired up in response to a perceived action which was deemed to be offensive. Among these was the attack on all the Shelter Now International premises at Nasirbagh camp, near Peshawar, in 1990. There was a consequent fear that they would become a symbolic target of a mass attack if they were in one building. There was, therefore, a preference to remain in separate offices scattered around the city where they could try to keep a low profile. However, the Taliban stood their ground and a majority of NGOs left the city. Subsequent negotiations made it possible for NGOs to return to Kabul to occupy individual premises, but the radicalization of the political climate in the aftermath of the US air strikes of August 1998 made many reluctant to do so. Thus, while some did return, the numbers were never as great as they were prior to July 1998.

There were also growing threats to Afghans employed by international agencies arising from their perceived association with Western and, therefore, secular values. These pressures intensified with the radicalization of the political environment and often included death threats from the more hard-line of the Taliban. Over time, political pressures combined with work and family pressures to lead one individual after another to decide to seek asylum in the West. It was often those in senior positions within agencies that were targeted, because they tended to be the better educated and more liberal. As this process accelerated during the 1999–2001 period, international NGOs lost large numbers of their managerial staff and often faced serious programming difficulties. However, actual assassinations were very few at this stage and westerners were not actively targeted, in contrast to the situation that has existed since 2003.

However, international NGO staff did find the atmosphere increasingly hostile from 2000 onwards. This was accentuated by the arrival of a growing number of volunteers from other parts of the Islamic world, many of whom had more hard-line attitudes towards westerners and liberals.

Donors began to play a much greater role in the determination of policy after 1998, in response to growing sensitivity over the provision of aid to Afghanistan under Taliban control. The British Government placed a ban on any programmes which helped build the capacity of the Afghan Government, in however small a way. It also withdrew funding from NGOs whose expatriate staff worked in or visited Afghanistan. At the same time, both the UK and the USA introduced a ruling that its nationals could not serve with the UN in Afghanistan.

In considering power dynamics over this period, we could argue that the Taliban wielded considerable power, with Pakistan providing significant logistical and other support to facilitate the process of conquest. The climate of fear that they generated constrained the behaviour of the population and led to an exodus of intellectuals and professionals, whether employed by the aid community or the government service. This weakened the capacity of aid organizations to deliver services. But, in spite of the restrictions imposed by the Taliban, the aid community retained much of the power that it had held, during the 1992–6 period, to determine policies and priorities in relation to the provision of agricultural support, health care, water supply, sanitation, water supply and, to a much lesser degree, education. The lack of interest from the Taliban meant that there was very little by way of a policy framework or national planning process through which the aid community should operate. The UN agencies and NGOs therefore continued with the framework which had been established prior to 1996, while modifying it to the new political environment.

At the same time, the USA was increasingly concerned that the Taliban were providing a training ground for potential terrorists and that they were also providing sanctuary for Osama bin Laden. The arrival of growing numbers of volunteers from other parts of the Islamic world, following the US air strikes on Afghanistan, led the USA to view the situation in Afghanistan in highly negative terms. There was also interest in the establishment of a permanent military presence in Afghanistan in pursuit of US strategic interests with regard to Iran, China, Pakistan and Central Asia. The stage was, therefore, set for a US-led intervention in Afghanistan if a sufficient justification could be found. The attacks on the World Trade Centre provided such a justification.

6

THE US-LED MILITARY
INTERVENTION

Legitimacy

The US-led military intervention of 7 October 2001 was, to a significant degree, an outcome of the terrorist attack on the World Trade Centre of 11 September 2001. The US Government was under pressure to be seen to be doing something, in response to what was seen as a major assault on the US homeland, and was able to build on the fact that Osama bin Laden had, through the US air strikes of August 1998, already been presented, in the public eye, as a serious threat to the West. There was ample evidence that, following the air strikes, Afghanistan had become increasingly used as a base for the training, in military and other skills, of Islamic radicals from across the world. It was therefore easy to provide, to the US public, an argument that the attack on the World Trade Centre was organized from within Afghanistan and that Osama bin Laden was the mastermind. The evidence for this argument remains difficult to establish, but the political consensus on this question was sufficient to justify a warning to the Taliban that, unless they handed over Osama bin Laden, there would be serious consequences. The USA also presented its intervention as a moral crusade in that it sought to overthrow a regime whose values it expressly criticized and to establish, in its place, a democratically-elected government.

The US Government was able to secure the support of the UN Security Council through Resolutions 1368 and 1373.

Resolution 1368 of 12 September 2001 provided that:

The Security Council

Reaffirming the principles and purposes of the Charter of the United Nations,

Determined to combat, by all means, threats to international peace and security caused by terrorist acts,

Recognizing the inherent right of individual or collective self-defence in accordance with the Charter,

1. *Unequivocally condemns*, in the strongest terms, the horrifying terrorist attacks which took place on 11 September 2001 in New York, Washington DC and Pennsylvania and regards such acts, like any act of international terrorism, as a threat to international peace and security;

2. Expresses its deepest sympathy and condolences to the victims and their families and to the people and Government of the United States of America;

3. Calls on all States to work together urgently to bring to justice the perpetrators, organizers and sponsors of these terrorist attacks and stresses that those responsible for aiding, supporting or harbouring the perpetrators, organizers and sponsors of these acts will be held accountable;

4. Calls also on the international community to redouble their efforts to prevent or suppress terrorist acts, including by increased cooperation and full implementation of the relevant international anti-terrorism conventions and Security Council resolutions, in particular resolution 1269 (1999) of 19 October 1999;

5. Expresses its readiness to take all necessary steps to respond to the terrorist attacks of 11 September 2001 and to combat all forms of terrorism in accordance with its responsibilities under the Charter of the United Nations;

6. Decides to remain seized of the matter.

The Security Council Resolution 1269, referred to in Resolution 1368, 'stresses the vital role of the United Nations in strengthening international cooperation in combating terrorism and emphasizes the importance of enhanced coordination among states, international and regional organizations'. It then 'calls upon all States to take, inter alia, in the context of such cooperation and coordination, appropriate steps to... deny those who plan, finance or commit terrorist acts safe havens by ensuring their apprehension and prosecution or extradition'.

UN Security Council Resolution 1373 of 28 September 2001 recognizes 'the need for States to complement international cooperation by taking additional measures to prevent and suppress, in their territories through all lawful means, the financing and preparation of any acts of terrorism'. It also reaffirms:

> ...the principle established by the General Assembly in its declaration of October 1970 (resolution 2625 (XXV) and reiterated by the Security Council, in its resolution 1189 (1998) of 13 August 1998, namely that every State has the duty to refrain from organizing, instigating, assisting or participating in terrorist acts in another State or acquiescing in organized activities within its territory directed towards the commission of such acts.

It further states that all States shall 'deny safe haven to those who finance, plan, support or commit terrorist acts' and 'ensure that any person who participates in the financing, planning, preparation or perpetration of terrorist acts is brought to justice'. Finally, the Security Council 'expresses its determination to take all necessary steps in order to ensure the full implementation of this resolution, in accordance with its responsibilities under the Charter'.

The United Nations Charter states: 'All members shall refrain, in their international relations, from the threat or use of force against the territorial integrity or political independence of any state' (Chapter 1, Article 2.4). It further states: 'Nothing in the present Charter shall impair the inherent right of individual or collective self-defence if an armed attack occurs against a member of the United Nations, until the Security Council has taken measures necessary to maintain international peace and security' (Chapter VII, Article 51).

The US Government therefore drew on the UN Charter as its primary justification, stating that it was acting in self-defence in response to an armed attack initiated from outside its borders. This was extended, using UN resolutions relating to terrorist activity, to present the case for self-defence against terrorist attacks committed by an external aggressor. It was also extended to assert that it was acceptable to overthrow another government if that government failed to comply with its responsibilities to clamp down on terrorism committed within its borders against another state. In addition, it was able to exercise significant leverage within the UN, by virtue of its economic, military and political supremacy on the global stage, to ensure that it secured the necessary mandate. It is noteworthy that the British parliament, for example, supported the UN mandate with little debate.

Jenny Warren[29] comments:

> The phrase 'an armed attack' has generally been understood, within the United Nations remit to maintain peace between nations, to mean an armed attack by another state. Following the terrorist attack in America, however, the United States and its NATO allies, including Britain, interpreted Article 51 as sanctioning the use of force against a state that harbours a terrorist group, one that was directed from abroad, that was of 'global reach'.

She also states:

> The United States and its NATO allies used the argument of self-defence against terrorism for the first time as justification for their military intervention in Afghanistan. Now, the US Defense Secretary has claimed self-defence as the legal basis for all the United States' military interventions throughout the world... In this way, the plea of self-defense, where no clear aggression by another state has occurred, can become the justification for hegemonic military intervention by powerful states – the same plea

that was made by the Soviet Union as justification for its invasion of Afghanistan in 1979 – and creates the legal basis for a dangerous anarchy in international relations in the new multipolar world of powerful states.

In seeking to secure international sanction for its military intervention, the USA was able to go so far as to use another nation state to effectively declare war and, what is more, to use an Islamic nation. Thus, CNN reported, on 17 September 2001 that 'the Pakistan Government, led by President Gen. Pervez Musharraf, will ask the Taliban, Afghanistan's rulers, to hand over suspected terrorist, Osama bin Laden, in three days or face massive military action led by the United States'. On 7 October 2001, less than a month after the attack on the World Trade Centre, the US launched air strikes on Afghanistan.

Strategy

However, the decision to engage militarily in Afghanistan had additional benefits for the US Government, other than the perceived need to remove the potential for Afghanistan to provide a training ground for radical Islamic activists. It also provided an opportunity to take forward a strategy drawn up by neo-conservative elements within the US administration through what is termed 'The Project for the New American Century'.

The website for 'The Project for the New American Century' states that it is 'a non-profit educational organization dedicated to a few fundamental propositions: that American leadership is good both for America and the world; and that such leadership requires military strength, diplomatic energy and commitment to moral principle'. The Project's Founding Principles state:

As the 20th century draws to a close, the United States stands as the world's most preeminent power. Having led the West to victory in the Cold War, America faces an opportunity and a challenge. Does the United States have the vision to build upon the achievement of past decades? Does the United States have the resolve to shape a new century favourable to America's principles and interests?

[What we require is] a military that is strong and ready to meet both present and future challenges: a foreign policy that boldly and purposefully promotes American principles abroad; and national leadership that accepts the United States' global responsibilities.

Of course, the United States must be prudent in how its exercises its power. But we cannot safely avoid the responsibilities of global leadership or the costs that are associated with this exercise. America has a vital role in maintaining peace and security in Europe, Asia and the Middle East. If we shirk our responsibilities, we invite challenges to our fundamental interests. The history of the 20th century should have taught us that it is important to shape circumstances before crises emerge and to meet threats before they become dire. The history of the past century should have taught us to embrace the cause of American leadership.

The thinking of the Project for the New American Century is clearly set out in Rebuilding America's Defenses: Strategy, Forces and Resources for a New Century.

This states:

At present, the United States faces no global rival. America's grand strategy should aim to preserve and extend this advantageous position as far into the future as possible. There are, however, potentially powerful states dissatisfied with the current situation and eager to change it, if they can, in directions that endanger the relatively peaceful, prosperous and free conditions the world enjoys today. Up to now, they have been deterred from doing so by the capability and global presence of American military power. But, as that power declines, relatively and absolutely, the happy conditions that follow from it will be inevitably undermined.[30]

and:

> Without a well-conceived defense policy and an appropriate
> increase in defense spending, the United States has been
> letting its ability to take advantage of the remarkable
> opportunity at hand slip away.[31]

and:

> In broad terms, we saw the project as building upon
> the defense strategy outlined by the Cheney Defense
> Department in the waning days of the Bush administration.
> The Defense Policy Guidance drafted in the early
> months of 1992 provided a blueprint for maintaining US
> preeminence, precluding the rise of a great power rival,
> and shaping the international security order in line with
> American principles and interests.[32]

The neo-conservatives thus made it clear that they wished to
prevent any possible rivals on the global stage from challenging the
pre-eminent position that the USA enjoyed. In addition, they set out
to increase US military spending so as to provide the Government
with the resources to maintain that pre-eminence:

> The surplus expected in federal revenues over the next
> decade, however, removes any need to hold defense
> spending to some preconceived low level... the willingness
> to devote adequate resources to maintaining America's
> military strength can make the world safer and America's
> strategic interests more secure now and in the future.[33]

Further, they anticipated that, in order to maintain their military
superiority, they would need to engage in a number of major
offensives at the same time and also establish an ongoing military
presence in regions of strategic importance.

The report thus establishes four core missions for US military
forces:

- Defend the American homeland;
- Fight and decisively win multiple, simultaneous major theater wars;
- Perform the 'constabulary' duties associated with shaping the security environment in critical regions;
- Transform US forces to exploit the "revolution in military affairs".

It goes on to say: 'To carry out these core missions, we need to provide sufficient force and budgetary allocations'. Among the measures identified to achieve this, it comments that the United States must:

> ...reposition US forces to respond to 21st century strategic realities by shifting permanently-based forces to South-East Europe and South-East Asia and by changing naval deployment patterns to reflect growing US strategic concerns in East Asia.

It further proposes to: '...increase defense spending gradually to a minimum level of 3.5 to 3.8 per cent of gross domestic product, adding $15 billion to $20 billion in total defence spending annually.' [34]

It is clear from the document that China was seen as a major potential threat, necessitating the establishment of permanently-based forces in South East Asia. Further, with China sharing a border with Afghanistan and with several of the Central Asian Republics, the creation of an ongoing military presence in Afghanistan was evidently of value as a means of helping to contain that threat.

The following paragraph in the report is also of considerable relevance:

> America's global leadership and its role as the guarantor of the current great-power peace relies upon the safety of the American homeland; the preservation of a favourable balance of power in Europe, the Middle East and surrounding energy-producing region, and East Asia; and the general stability of the international system of nation states relative to terrorists, organized crime and other 'non-state actors'.[35]

The Central Asian Republics are clearly part of the 'surrounding energy-producing region' mentioned. In addition, Afghanistan has its own gas and oil reserves which have, hitherto, largely been untapped. Further, Afghanistan is of significance in considering 'the general stability of the international system of nation states relative to terrorists, organized crime and other "non-state actors"'. It is not only seen as a potential haven for the orchestration of international terrorism but also as the major producer of opium poppy, with mafia-style organized criminal networks central to the production and trafficking processes. Afghanistan also shares a border with Pakistan which contains important 'non-state actors', in the form of radical Islamic organizations potentially disposed to support and resource international terrorism. A further strategic interest of the USA was to address the risk that Pakistan might be taken over by a radical Islamic government, with its finger on the nuclear trigger. A presence in Afghanistan enabled the USA to establish a close relationship with President Musharraf and to support him against threats to his regime. The case for creating a permanent military presence in Afghanistan was therefore strong.

Afghanistan also offered a springboard from which US forces could deploy within the surrounding region to areas where it would be difficult to secure the authority of governments to establish US bases. This included Pakistan, Iran and most of the Central Asian Republics. It would also provide a centrally located resource from which simultaneous wars could be engaged in or against two or more of Afghanistan's neighbours, with Pakistan, Iran and China all seen as potential threats.

The report thus states: 'The United States must retain sufficient forces able to rapidly deploy and win multiple simultaneous large-scale wars and also to be able to respond to unanticipated contingencies in regions where it does not maintain forward-based forces.'[36] Further, all three of these States were seen as potential nuclear powers: The report comments that:

> ...US nuclear force planning and related arms control policies must take account of a larger set of variables than in the past, including the growing number of small nuclear arsenals – from North Korea to Pakistan – perhaps soon

Iran and Iraq – and a modernized and expanded Chinese nuclear force.[37]

In order to challenge these potential powers, the report stresses that 'American troops, in particular, must be regarded as part of an overwhelmingly powerful force'.[38]

The case for establishing a strong military presence in Afghanistan is also made in the following paragraph:

> Over the long term, Iran may well prove as large a threat to US interests in the Gulf as Iraq has. And even should US–Iranian relations improve, retaining forward bases in the region would still be an essential element in US security strategy, given the longstanding American interests in the region.[39]

It is important to note, in this context, that the need to support international military operations in Afghanistan was used to justify approaches to Uzbekistan and Kyrgyzstan to establish bases in those countries, from which logistics support could be provided to US-led coalition operations in Afghanistan. However, Uzbekistan, having agreed to the deployment of US forces in Uzbekistan in 2001, withdrew from the arrangement in July 2005, after US criticisms of its human rights record. The Kyrgyz Government, having also permitted the USA to establish a base in 2001, set more demanding terms in October 2005. The latter response was, in part, influenced by pressure from China and Russia, which were deeply concerned about an increased US military presence so close to their borders. The two major powers had already come together with the Central Asian Republics in June 2001 to form what was known as the Shanghai Cooperation Organisation, in which Iran, India, Pakistan and Mongolia have Observer Status. This has given Iran a degree of protection from the USA.

To maximize the potential presence of US forces in strategically important areas, the report proposes the creation of a network of what were termed as 'forward operating bases' across the globe. These would be designed to hold relatively few permanent soldiers but have the infrastructure onto which a larger force could quickly be put into place if US interests were actively threatened, or if they needed to be strengthened in pursuit of a particular strategic goal.

The report thus states:

> As a supplement to forces stationed abroad under long-term basing arrangements, the United States should seek to establish a network of 'deployment bases' or 'forward operating bases' to increase the reach of current and future forces. Not only will such an approach improve the ability to project force to outlying regions. It will help circumvent the political, practical and financial constraints on expanding the network of American bases overseas. These deployment or forward operating bases can range from relatively modest agreements with other nations as well as modest improvements to existing facilities and bases. Prepositioned materiel would speed the initial deployment and improve the sustainability of US forces when deployed for training, joint training with the host nation, or operations in time of crisis.[40]

To summarise, therefore, the USA had major strategic and commercial interests in Central and South Asia which could be usefully protected or strengthened through the establishment of a permanent military presence in Afghanistan. Its preoccupation with Iran as part of the Axis of Evil drove it to find ways of putting the squeeze on that country. The encirclement of Iran, to the extent possible, by US bases, was an apparent part of that strategy.

It is of interest, in this regard, that the USA took the opportunity of temporary instability in Herat to take control of Shindand Airbase, in western Afghanistan, in September 2004. This was in spite of the fact that it already had substantial bases in Bagram and Kandahar, as well as many smaller bases in Afghanistan, from which offensives could, potentially, be organized against Iran. The USA also had a network of bases in the Arabian Gulf and had, in addition, established a military presence in Iraq. It had thus almost completed the circle around Iran. However, as at the beginning of 2008, Iran's northern borders were free of US bases in that it had not established a military foothold in the Caucasus or Turkmenistan.

The actual US-led military intervention of 7 October 2001 was also consistent with the doctrine drawn up by The Project for the New American Century, in that it set out to demonstrate overwhelming US power. The global population was therefore presented with powerful images, on their TV screens, of precision strikes, from the air, on targets of apparent strategic importance. The fact that these included ancient planes which had been rusting on the tarmac of Kabul airport for many years was not publicized, although the media did cover two attacks on warehouses belonging to the International Committee for the Red Cross as an indication that some bombs were going astray.

The USA was mindful of the highly negative image created by the Soviet forces physically invading Afghanistan, with Soviet troops flying in to take control of key locations and overthrow the Government, while a much larger force crossed the border from the north. It therefore expressly set out to minimize the number of US soldiers who were actually present in Afghanistan. To this end, the USA looked to Mujahidin and militia groups to follow up, on the ground, what US bombing raids had achieved from the air. US planes would then support the offensives of these groups by strafing Taliban forces engaged in battle or by bombing targets identified by the Mujahidin or militia groups. These, as it subsequently turned out, were often the homes or bases of individuals or groups against which there were scores to settle. The USA was therefore being used to alter power dynamics on the ground.

In the south of the country, the USA struck deals with various Mujahidin commanders, such as Hazrat Ali in Laghman and Gul Aga Sherzai in Kandahar, to help them defeat the Taliban. However, the Taliban were able to retreat to Pakistan when their positions proved to be difficult to defend and the indications are that they opted not to defend these to the last, deciding, instead, to withdraw in order to regroup.

In northern Afghanistan, the USA relied heavily on the forces of Jamiat-e-Islami and Rashid Dostam. These were greatly helped by the fact that the Taliban forces in the north were not able to easily escape, nor were they able to secure new supplies. They therefore made easy targets for US bombing raids. This meant that the remaining Taliban forces in the north were quickly destroyed as effective military units. Of those who were not killed, some managed to escape by air when Pakistan was allowed to organize a rescue mission for their nationals. Others found themselves imprisoned by Jamiat-e-Islami or, primarily, Dostam's forces and many met a terrible death from suffocation in metal containers. US and other international Special Forces participated in the interrogation of those captured and many were taken off to Guantanamo Bay for further questioning.

The Taliban chose to withdraw from Kabul rather than fight to the death, and it was Jamiat-e-Islami forces which walked into the capital to take control of it. This created a de facto reality in which Jamiat-e-Islami militia continued to maintain a presence in the city.

It also created a situation in which Jamiat-e-Islami was in a strong position to bid for key ministerial posts at the Bonn Conference of December 2001, which brought together international donors to plan for the creation of an interim government. The three key posts of Defence, Foreign Affairs and Interior went to members of Jamiat-e-Islami. This caused resentment amongst the Pushtun, Uzbek and Hazara populations.

The Bonn Conference set in motion what was termed the Bonn Process. This stipulated that a traditional assembly of representatives from across the country, known as a Loya Jirga, would be convened in June 2002 to elect a transitional government. It also stipulated that a draft constitution would be drawn up, to be ratified through a Constitutional Loya Jirga, and that presidential and parliamentary elections would be held.

The Loya Jirga of June 2002 brought together those who wielded power through the gun in the various localities of Afghanistan, and it was accompanied by significant levels of intimidation. Women delegates found it particularly difficult to influence the debate and many of those who were outspoken found themselves subject to subsequent intimidation, including death threats.

Intimidation also accompanied the Constitutional Loya Jirga of December 2003, the presidential election of October 2004 and the parliamentary elections of September 2005. The agreed constitution was a carefully crafted document which gave due regard for the centrality of Islam within the population, while also ensuring that basic human rights enshrined in international conventions were included. There was, therefore, provision that men and women were equal before the law. It provided, in addition, that women would have a quarter of the parliamentary seats earmarked for them. The parliamentary elections even resulted in some female candidates winning seats in their own right rather than because of the positive discrimination afforded to them through the constitution. However, the conservative political climate which continued to prevail meant that women had to continue to fight to have their voice heard, and the position of women within the home remained extremely restricted.

The Bonn Process also failed to address the fact that, following the US-led military intervention, power largely reverted to those who had held power at the local level before the arrival of the Taliban. Some of these had their power reinforced through deals which the US-led coalition forces struck in order to have local militia engaged in counter-terrorism operations instead of US soldiers. There was, therefore, little incentive for these power holders to cooperate with the government in Kabul.

The government also had very limited resources to offer to the population to wean them away from dependence on local power holders. The international community was slow to deliver reconstruction assistance on any scale, due, in part, to a reluctance to disburse funds to a government structure which had almost no capacity to function.

In addition, the Government lacked an effective army, police force or judiciary which could provide protection to the population from local armed power holders. A climate of impunity therefore prevailed in which the rule of the gun presided over the rule of law.

President Karzai found himself having to continually strike deals with local power holders in order to maintain his position, and he was not able to play a strong hand in this regard while his government remained so limited in its capacity to deliver.

His position was also undermined by the fact that he was widely perceived as having an over-close association with the US Government. This image was very much reinforced by the role that the first US Ambassador to Afghanistan, Zalmay Khalilzad, assumed in operating as a virtual viceroy. This was particularly evident at the Loya Jirga of June 2002, when Mr Khalilzad appeared to play an instrumental role in the process.

Mr Karzai's image was not helped by the fact that many of

the actions of the US-led coalition forces seriously alienated the population. In the course of their counter-terrorism operations, troops engaged in behaviour which was regarded as insulting to prevailing mores, including bursting into homes, searching women and failing to demonstrate respect to tribal elders. They also caused many civilian casualties through air raids conducted when troops on the ground identified possible Taliban locations or came under attack. They have only apologized or provided compensation for these actions on a very few occasions. Further, they were reported to have caused accidents through aggressive driving.

Clearly evident also was a tendency, by US-led coalition forces, to objectify the population so that all Afghans were apparently regarded as suspects when international forces were conducting house searches. There were many reports of US forces failing to engage effectively with the population, with the result that US soldiers were said to feel considerable fear of their adversaries. This has manifested itself in episodes in which US troops, in particular, have simply 'lost it' and fired indiscriminately into crowds, in the wake of terrorist attacks or traffic accidents in which they felt in an exposed position.

There was, in consequence, no real effort to listen, learn and understand. International forces therefore failed to take sufficiently into account the importance of Islam and of pan-Islamic sentiments. As with the British interventions of the nineteenth century, cultural arrogance, combined with insensitive behaviour, led to perceived affronts to traditional and Islamic sensibilities and alienated the population. However, the brutality associated with searches and with air raids, with their consequent civilian casualties, was an important component in the alienation.

This pattern was less in evidence amongst the troops of some of the other countries contributing to international forces in Afghanistan. A greater emphasis on engagement with the population in the training that soldiers receive in countries such as the UK, Canada or The Netherlands served to reduce the propensity to objectify the population and, thereby, the intensity of the fear that is felt in relation to the population.

The population was also aggrieved by what were perceived as attacks on Islam, with many influenced by Taliban accusations that there existed a Christian crusade by the USA against the Islamic

World. Feelings of antipathy were heightened by the US-led intervention in Iraq of March 2003 and evident US support for the Israeli intervention in Lebanon of July 2006.

The reputation of the US government was further tarnished within Afghanistan, as well as internationally, by its decision to create its own network of detention facilities, both within Afghanistan and globally, at Guantanamo Bay, Bagram, Kandahar and elsewhere. The use of these facilities, to question and hold suspects, received widespread publicity, and there were also many Afghans who had direct experience of family members who had been seized, interrogated and indefinitely detained.

Thus, while the Government of Hamid Karzai has been found, by the US Department of State, to be responsible for, among other human rights abuses, cases of arbitrary arrests, extra-judicial killings, torture and poor prison conditions[41], it is the USA which has come in for the greatest criticism on account of its treatment of prisoners in Guantanamo Bay and at the various detention centres in Afghanistan. In the case of the US-led intervention, it was US forces that were most directly involved in the interrogation of suspects, whereas with the Soviet intervention it was the Afghan Government.

According to Human Rights Watch:

> The US military continues to operate in Afghanistan without any legal framework, such as a Status of Forces Agreement with the Afghan Government, and to detain hundreds of Afghans without any legal process. US forces, at a minimum, are obligated to treat detainees in accordance with the fundamental guarantees provided by international humanitarian law.[42]

Those who have been arrested by the USA are not the intellectuals who were actively targeted by the PDPA, the Mujahidin and the Taliban. Rather, it is the rural population which has found itself at risk of arrest, torture and imprisonment during the post-2001 period, on account of its suspected sympathy for the Taliban, Al-Qaida, Hisb-e-Islami or other radical elements. As with the Soviet intervention, there has been a tendency to be over-suspicious, meaning that people have been taken in for questioning with initial evidence that they represent a threat to the Government that is, at best, tenuous.

Preident Karzai was acutely aware of public sensitivity with regard to the excesses of international forces and expressly set out to be vocal in his criticism of them. It was also Karzai's Government which took upon itself the task of engaging with the population, at large, and with the insurgents. It was not, therefore, left to the international community to play this highly complex role.

Public antipathy helped fuel the Taliban insurgency. The insurgency clearly increased in intensity following the intervention in Iraq, manifested in a growing number of terrorist attacks on targets associated, by the Taliban, with a US-led state-building process. These included government ministers, government officials, members of the national army and police, aid workers and private-sector construction workers engaged on major US-funded projects such as the main highway system. A further strengthening of the insurgency was evident from the spring of 2006, when the ability of the Taliban to regroup and build up their resource base over the previous four years enabled the movement to present a serious challenge to international military forces.

However, the need to be seen to be going after Osama bin Laden meant that strategies were adopted which were not necessarily consistent with the aim of preventing the establishment of a Taliban presence in Afghanistan. In particular, counter-terrorism operations involved significant levels of brutality and insensitivity, which ran counter to the need to build support within the population so as to prevent the Taliban doing likewise.

While the US-led coalition forces were engaged in counter-insurgency operations against the Taliban in the southern provinces, a UN-mandated stabilization force, known as the International Security Assistance Force (ISAF), was established in Kabul from December 2001. This was empowered to protect members of the government and government buildings but not to provide protection for the individual citizen. In spite of the presence of ISAF, two government ministers were assassinated in the capital during the first year of the Bonn Process.

ISAF was initially commanded by a succession of countries, which individually contributed troops on a six-month rotation. Turkey was thus followed by the UK which was, in turn, followed by Germany, in combination with The Netherlands. During the last of these rotations, logistics support was provided by NATO. By this stage, it was proving difficult to secure commitments from other countries to take on the leadership role. The USA and other NATO member states therefore saw NATO as a suitable structure for this purpose. In August 2003, NATO took up overall command of ISAF, with a view to ultimately taking responsibility for the operations of all international forces in Afghanistan.

As noted above, the USA was concerned to maximize its military presence in Afghanistan, in pursuit of its own strategic interests, but wished to lend this greater legitimacy by having other countries on board. When the opportunity presented itself to have international forces in Afghanistan commanded by NATO, the USA was strongly supportive.

The role of ISAF was expanded in October 2003, when Germany was asked to take responsibility for security in the northern province of Kunduz. Over the following year, it was further expanded to other parts of the north: Mazar-e Sharif (under UK control), Badakshan (Germany) and Baghlan (Netherlands). The Mazar-e Sharif area was one in which Dostam's militia, Jamiat-e-Islami and Hisb-e-Wahdat frequently resorted to armed clashes between themselves and, in which, therefore, there was potential for an external force to intervene to prevent the escalation of conflict and also mediate. In the summer of 2005, new ISAF operations were set up in the north-west: in Herat (Italy), Badghis (Spain), Ghor (Lithuania) and Farah (USA). There was a further expansion to the southern provinces of Helmand (UK), Kandahar (Canada), Uruzgan (Netherlands), Zabul (USA), Daikundi and Nimroz in July 2006. The remaining eastern and south-eastern provinces were transferred to ISAF command in October 2006, mainly under US leadership. In addition, the US military continued to operate its own programme, aimed at capturing high value targets such as Osama bin Laden and Aiman al-Zawahiri.

The ISAF operation was structured through Provincial Reconstruction Teams, which were theoretically modelled on the Provincial Reconstruction Teams (PRTs) set up by the US-led coalition forces in the southern provinces. However, the latter were essentially civilian-orientated military operations aimed to win the 'hearts and minds' of the population through small aid projects and so gain intelligence in pursuit of counter-insurgency operations. The ISAF PRTs had a stabilization mandate and so included, for example, police training and mentoring, the uncovering of weapons caches, support to disarmament programmes, and negotiations with local power holders geared to a reduction in inter-factional tensions. The reconstruction projects established by ISAF PRTs were often supportive of security sector reform by, for example, providing resources for court houses or police posts, as opposed to the construction of schools or digging of wells typical of the US PRTs. International forces also had a major role in providing training for the Afghan National Army.

However, in taking on the southern provinces in July 2006, ISAF faced immediate problems in endeavouring to stabilize an area in which the counter-insurgency operations of the US-led coalition forces had already seriously alienated the population. Its strategy of winning over the population through a softer touch than the USA had adopted was met with suspicion. Its efforts were also undermined by a campaign of intimidation by the Taliban, which involved threatening households that any cooperation with foreign forces would result in death and reinforcing this by killing so-called spies. At the same time, ISAF forces found themselves the targets of determined, well-organised, attacks by Taliban forces and were compelled to operate a de facto counter-insurgency operation rather than the stabilization one that had been intended. The situation was further aggravated by the fact that they were operating in an area, in Helmand, which had, for decades, been a major centre of the opium trade.

ISAF forces were, therefore, dealt with as though they were US forces. No differentiation was made for the fact that many were Europeans. In fact, British forces were viewed as legitimate targets because of the British military interventions in Afghanistan of the nineteenth century and because of their major role in the US-led intervention in Iraq. They were thus seen as yet another target associated with the US-led state-building process.

This polarization process, between those who were working to implement the Bonn Process and those who were seeking to undermine it, left the population in a situation of profound ambivalence. On the one hand, there was growing disenchantment with the government in Kabul. It was seen as corrupt and as having failed to bring security or the necessary level of reconstruction to ensure that livelihoods were met. There was also considerable anger, as noted above, over the behaviour of US-led coalition forces and over global affronts to Islam. There was therefore a degree of sympathy for the Taliban, reinforced by their use of intimidation and fear, because they offered a return to the good security that they had provided when they were in government. They were also seen as defenders of Islam. On the other hand, the people were mindful of the considerable restrictions that the Taliban had previously imposed and of the climate of fear they had created. Thus, while there was considerable fear of what a return of the Taliban would bring about, there was little or no hope that the international community could necessarily produce anything better.

However, the international military had concluded, by the end of 2006, that they would not be able to defeat the insurgency by military means alone. The willingness of the population to lend active or passive support to the Taliban was therefore seen as the determining factor in the success of the counter-insurgency operation.

A key determinant for the population was an expectation that international forces would, sooner or later, find the going too difficult in Afghanistan and seek a face-saving mechanism for withdrawal. It was anticipated, in this regard, that the Afghan National Army would not be able to provide an effective defence against a sustained Taliban offensive and that the Taliban would be able to take the southern provinces without too much difficulty.

There was also fear that the various militias operating in the north and centre of the country, and broadly acting on behalf of the Uzbek, Tajik and Hazara populations, would have been too weakened by the disarmament process, which the Afghan Government had been engaged in since 2001, to defend their territories against a Taliban advance.

In addition, it was anticipated that Afghanistan's neighbours would jockey for position to maximize their respective influence in Afghanistan. The Afghan and US Governments had already accused Pakistan of permitting the Taliban insurgency to be supported within its borders and of not doing enough to counter this support. It may certainly have been the case that elements within Pakistan were providing arms and other resources as well as recruits, as had occurred while the Taliban were in power. By this stage, Jamiat-al-Ulema al-Islami had joined forces with other radical Islamic parties to contest the election of October 2002 in North-West Frontier Province (NWFP) and Baluchistan. The coalition, known as the MMA, achieved overall control in NWFP and significant influence in Baluchistan. It is possible that some of the radical Islamist parties which were thus engaged in the political processes in NWFP and Baluchistan were sympathetic to the Taliban and were providing it with support. On the other hand, there were indications, by the end of 2007, that Jamiat-e-Islami had become estranged from the Taliban because it was seen as insufficiently radical. Whether the Pakistan Government had a role in the provision of direct support to the Taliban is open to question. However, it is possible that Pakistan's intelligence service, ISI, was in some way linked, if only in so far as the operations of the Taliban were consistent with its strategy of seeking to create strategic depth.

There was therefore an expectation that, if international forces were to withdraw, Pakistan would seek to fill the vacuum. It was also anticipated that India, China, Russia and Iran would almost certainly seek to counter any increase in Pakistan's influence. The emergence of the Shanghai Cooperation Organisation in 2001 was significant, in this regard, in representing a rearranging of the regional chess board.

US strategy was, therefore, based on the creation of a democratic government to lend legitimacy to its nominee, Hamid Karzai, for the post of President and so underpin its wider regional strategies. However, the actions of the US military, including its use of detention facilities, more than offset any goodwill that might have been generated by the democratic process. The process itself was also seen as flawed in bringing to parliament those who wielded power through the gun. Further, in spite of the apparent legitimacy accorded to its intervention by the UN, the perception in the public mind in Afghanistan was that the USA had intervened in pursuit of its own interests and could not be relied upon to provide long-term support to their country.

7

THE RELATIONSHIP
BETWEEN US STRATEGY
AND THE AID PROCESS

In an ideal world, the principal donors would have sat around the table at Bonn and Tokyo and reflected on how to make Afghanistan a better place without, at the same time, being influenced by their own agendas. This would have necessitated the full involvement of the principal Afghan actors, including the Taliban, and would have had regard to agreed perceptions on levels of need relating to issues such as livelihoods, health care, education and agricultural support, as well as the importance of building up the infrastructure of the state, its army, police force and judiciary.

To a degree, there was such a process. The key donors were present at the Bonn Conference of December 2001 and a wider group of donors met at the Tokyo Conference in January 2002. The United Nations Development Programme (UNDP), the World Bank and the Asian Development Bank played a key role in drawing up an interim programme. They estimated the cost of delivering this programme as at a level of $14.6 billion over ten years. In the event, $4.8 billion was pledged for a five-year period.[43] Much emphasis was placed by UNDP on the fact that donor attention was likely to be short-lived and that it was necessary to get as much done as possible within the initial two to three years. This created an urgency to the situation which may have inhibited a process of reflection.

However, the image of the international community working effectively together in support of Afghanistan hid a very different reality. The USA was very much the dominant player and Afghans were scarcely represented in the major decision-making processes that followed the Bonn Conference.

It was thus reported, in the early part of 2002, that the US State Department was convening weekly teleconferences, involving the heads of the World Bank, UNDP, USAID, the UK Government's Department for International Development (DFID), the Special Representative of the UN Secretary General and the Deputy Special Representative of the UN Secretary General for Pillar 2 (assistance programmes).[44] To an extent, therefore, the DFID was given greater access to the centre of power than the other donors, but it was still very marginal as a player. The Afghan Government was not even represented.

Further, the US Ambassador was, in many respects, acting as the de facto President. At the same time, the US Embassy was operating as one of a number of parallel governments, along with the UN, the wider donor community and the very much weaker NGO network. However, it wielded much greater power than the actual government or the other parallel governments.

The US was therefore in the driving seat from the beginning and was not always mindful of the need for other international donors to be aware of what it was doing. There was, therefore, a two-tiered donor environment in which the US, as the largest donor, was formulating development plans and seeking to orchestrate outcomes without necessarily consulting the Afghan Government or the wider group of donors.

The situation was not helped by the fact that the US Government was much less transparent in its decision-making process than other governments. With the exception of USAID, information regarding how much had been allocated, for what purpose and over what period was not always easily available on US Government websites.

The US Government was therefore concerned to establish, in Afghanistan, a compliant government which would enable it to pursue its strategic interests with a minimum of restraint. A major part of the resources allocated were geared to the creation of a long-term military presence through the establishment of a network of bases. To a considerable degree, therefore, the USA did not have an interest in involving the Afghan Government or the wider international community in its plans. Yet it needed to persuade them to lend it their support. This was largely done with reference to the threat that international radical Islamic organisations posed to global security and the risk that Afghanistan could again become a base for international terrorism. For the major donor governments, this was an argument that they were prepared to accept. They were therefore willing to provide troops for both stabilization and counter-insurgency operations. It is important to note, in this regard, that the US government, in securing buy-in from other Western states and Japan for its military intervention, was also achieving international backing for its state-building enterprise.

A further major priority of the US Government was to ensure that the newly created Afghan Government would establish a regulatory framework through which private sector investment could be maximized. The National Development Framework, issued in the spring of 2002, and the Interim Afghanistan National Development Strategy, published in January 2006, have both presented a model of the Afghan Government minimising its own involvement in the economy and contracting out, or issuing invitations to tender, to the private sector.

In so doing, the USA may have had regard to the potential opportunities available in relation to Afghanistan's oil, gas and mineral reserves and the possibility of a pipeline being constructed to transport gas from Turkmenistan, across Afghanistan, to Pakistan.

However, the priority given to the provision of development assistance geared to the livelihood, health care, education and other needs of the population was relatively low. Thus, the per capita allocation for reconstruction assistance to Afghanistan was very significantly less than the average for Bosnia, Kosovo, Rwanda or East Timor. It would not appear, therefore, that the US Government gave significant priority to persuading the Afghan public of the benefits of its intervention.

At the same time, the US Government made considerable efforts to persuade the US public of the need for its continuing involvement in Afghanistan. The US intervention had been prompted by the terrorist attack on the World Trade Centre of 11 September 2001 and the US government needed to demonstrate that it was going after the potential orchestrator of the attacks in the form of Osama bin Laden. The US obsession with 'the bad guys' gave them no choice but to search for the individuals thought to be responsible.

The decisions of the US Government as to how to use its resources were, therefore, significantly influenced by its perceptions as to how best to convince the US public that the intervention in Afghanistan had been a success. Thus, alongside the relatively low profile actions which were aimed to secure the long-term interests of the USA were others which may, to a degree, be regarded as geared to public relations objectives.

The creation of a democratic process had enormous public relations significance in that it was clearly linked to the often-expressed ambition of the US Government to export democracy to countries where it was lacking. Thus, while the process was clearly flawed, it enabled the US Government to claim that it had brought democracy and, by association, 'freedom' to Afghanistan.

The donor community, across the board, was also persuaded that this was an effective use of funds during the initial period. This was even though, in the light of the insurgency, there might have been a case for reconstruction assistance to be provided at a high level at that stage and for the electoral process to be deferred.

Certainly, the level of financial and human resources provided for the Loya Jirga, the Constitutional Loya Jirga and the presidential and parliamentary elections was considerable. If comparable resources had been provided for education, health care, agricultural support and the creation of additional sources of livelihood, the outcome, in terms of improvements to those services, would have been significant.

Substantial US aid funding was also provided in support of its counter-terrorism operations. This included sizeable subsidies to particular power holders and the use of aid projects for 'hearts and minds' operations, to facilitate both force protection and the gathering of intelligence.

It was also seen to be important to address the high levels of opium and heroin production in Afghanistan. This was clearly necessary, given the risk that Afghanistan could develop into a narco-mafia state. However, the international community has been singularly unsuccessful in its efforts, in the face of vested interests within the Government and regional police forces. Initiatives to eradicate opium have been largely cosmetic, with corruption undermining their effectiveness, but they have seriously alienated the population. This is particularly serious in areas where the international military are seeking to persuade the population to detach themselves from the insurgents. In fact, the Taliban have been able to capitalize on public anger and also provide a degree of protection for opium farmers.

It could certainly be argued that the considerable resources allocated for counter-narcotics programmes could have been more effectively used in building up the agriculture sector over a period, so as to create sustainable alternative livelihoods. However, this has always been a sensitive political issue in donor countries where heroin consumption is a serious problem and there is inevitably considerable pressure on politicians to be seen to be doing something.

The USA has also, as noted above, allocated significant resources to the Afghan National Army and Afghan National Police, with the aim of devolving the task of defending Afghanistan against external aggression to indigenous forces. The US Government has also been mindful of the need to minimize US casualties. The creation of a national army thus enabled the US military to look to others to fight the same cause, as did the payment of subsidies to various Mujahidin commanders and militia leaders.

The willingness of other European and North American countries to provide military personnel and resources, with the theoretical objective of stabilizing the country but with the de facto outcome of supporting the ongoing counter-insurgency operation, served the same purpose. It also created the image that the international military presence was not simply geared to US interests but had the backing of the international community.

Political considerations complemented human rights ones in giving the issue of women's rights a high profile. It was, therefore, helpful, in justifying the military intervention in Afghanistan, to make graphic references to the restrictions imposed by the Taliban on women and to present the international community as saviours creating an environment in which women could recover their lost freedoms. The provision of support to the Ministry of Women's Affairs was one element in this approach, along with many smaller initiatives by the USA and other international actors.

Support also came from the international community for the creation of the Afghan Independent Human Rights Commission, to further create the impression that it was serious about the rights of women and other human rights. At the same time, the Office of the UN High Commissioner for Human Rights was persuaded that it was no longer necessary to retain the role of the UN Human Rights Rapporteur for Afghanistan after his report had spoken critically of abuses by the US military in Afghanistan.

However, the high priority given by the international community to the maintenance of the Karzai Government in being meant that the government had to take serious account of religious and other conservative opinion. Thus, while it was clearly important for the serious human rights violations suffered by women in Afghanistan to be addressed, support for women's rights became secondary to US interest in the survival of the regime. In spite of this, there was a pronounced tendency in the international media, at least during the initial period, to present actual and potential progress on the situation of women in over-optimistic terms for propaganda purposes.

In fact, the international media presented overall progress in Afghanistan in over-glowing terms over the first year. But this was before the US-led intervention in Iraq prompted the campaign of terrorist activity in Afghanistan, which dented the image that all was well. Public statements by politicians in Western capitals made constant reference to the number of children in school and the number of refugees who had returned as key indicators of success. This was in spite of ample evidence that the number returning again to Pakistan and Iran was substantial. In fact, the Afghan refugee population in Pakistan in 2005, at 3 million, was no less than it had been in 1992 or 2002.

The decision to accord a high profile to the return of refugees from Pakistan and Iran linked with the wish of many European governments to justify a return of their Afghan refugee populations to Afghanistan. It was, therefore, very much in their interests to present the military intervention in Afghanistan and the subsequent State-building exercise as a success. In the UK, for example, the Home Office Reasons for Refusal would consistently describe the conditions in Afghanistan as very substantially better than they were. Thus, while the international community allocated relatively little funding to strengthen the capacity, through improvements in the agriculture sector, of returning refugees to survive on the land, it gave considerable weight, in its public relations work, to the apparently sustainable return of refugees from Pakistan and Iran.

Western governments also ignored the fact that the Afghan economy could not sustain its population and that it relied heavily on the ability of households across the country to send one or more sons to work as migrant labourers in Pakistan or Iran. Western donors did not seek to establish whether those returning to the villages of Afghanistan were managing to secure sufficient incomes, from agriculture and other sources, to feed their families. The questions were not asked of key agencies such as UNHCR and information provided to donors was quantitative, based, for example, on the number of houses improved with UNHCR assistance, rather than analytical in nature.

It was therefore left to research bodies such as the Afghanistan Research and Evaluation Unit to conclude that households had to diversify in order to survive and that labour migration was a major survival strategy. Western donors also failed to respond to reports by UNHCR which indicated that Afghans in Pakistan and Iran were subjected to considerable pressures, including forcible deportations on a large scale in the case of Iran. UNHCR could not, therefore, rely on the support of the international community in its efforts to persuade Pakistan and Iran to conform to the protection mechanisms laid down in the 1951 Convention on Refugees.

A further priority of the US Government, with support from other international actors, was to create a 'free' and effective media in Afghanistan. There was a very evident view, in this regard, that the intervening power had the right to impose its values on the population, particularly with regard to the situation of women. However, this was modified by other perspectives within the wider international community which were more anchored in the realities of Afghan society. US support to the media was also aimed at the creation of a political environment and a set of values which would be conducive to its strategic objectives. In this, it was reasonably successful in that Tolo TV, owned by an Afghan entrepreneur, became a popular entertainment channel. However, the effectiveness of the newly-created Afghan media in influencing public attitudes and values was offset by easy access to alternative media sources such as the BBC, Al-Jazeera or internet sites and by informal networking which disseminated information about, for example, the behaviour of US forces in Afghanistan. Public access to information was also greatly enhanced through major investment by the international private sector in telecommunications, including both mobile phones and internet access.

The mushrooming of media outlets provoked a strong reaction from conservative elements. The Mujahidin parties, which continued to play a prominent role within the government of President Karzai, expressed vociferous concerns over the influence of Western attitudes, and they used the power they had in the parliament to actively challenge the media on some of the content of its programming. Objections were raised, in particular, to the way in which women were portrayed in the media. There was additional concern at the easy availability of pornography sites on the internet.

The assistance given to the Afghan media, to inculcate a more liberal set of values, was thus seen as part of a package of measures which created echoes of the Soviet intervention. As Chris Johnson has noted:

> History – not only in the experience of working with the Taliban but also in earlier attempts by the communist government to push through rapid change – suggests that social change in Afghanistan cannot be pressed from outside.[45]

The efforts of the USA to promote its values were also undermined by the growing power of the Taliban in the south of the country. This power inevitably influenced the overall political environment as President Karzai took steps to give greater weight to religious and conservative opinion in his efforts to erode the Taliban support base. Women therefore felt intimidated into continuing to dress and behave in a conservative manner even though they were now able to access employment and girls were able to attend school.

The international personnel living in Kabul took account of this environment in conditioning their own behaviour, although there were inevitably situations in which individuals behaved insensitively. There was the ever-present risk of a backlash against the superficial liberalism that the expatriate population represented. Further,

Western dress codes were deemed to be morally unacceptable, and the failure by some Western women to adopt a more conservative form of dress, akin to the looser clothing worn by women in Afghanistan, helped fuel stereotypes of the West as 'decadent'.

The riots in Kabul that resulted from a traffic accident in May 2006, in which US forces fired on the crowd, demonstrated very vividly how a single incident could spark a mass reaction. Thus, while the international community was taking a more subtle approach to the process of seeking to influence attitudes and values than did the PDPA or the Taliban, its very presence was seen, by many, as an affront to traditional and Islamic sensibilities. The fact that the international community was also associated with a US-led state-building process and, thereby, with the intervention in Iraq, Guantanamo Bay and the behaviour of international forces served to compound this.

The USA and other donors also needed to take account of the fact that any investment that they made in education would be seen, by the Taliban, as aimed to inculcate Western values into the population. However, the level of investment, while significant, could have been very much greater if serious priority had been given to the need to overcome the impact of over twenty years without effective education provision, and to also address the skills shortages brought about by the continuing exodus of professionals over that period. Yet the international community made frequent use, for public relations purposes, of statistics demonstrating the increased number of children in school and, in particular, of the increase in the number of girls in school. It talked much less about the quality of that education.

It should be noted, in considering the vulnerability of schools and teachers to attack, that the Taliban are very much aware of the efforts of the former Soviet-backed Government to use education in order to build up support for their movement. They are also aware of similar efforts by some of the Mujahidin parties, who ran schools and even universities in the camps. They therefore consider any initiative to expand education in the present context as a product of the ambitions of the USA to promote its value systems. The Afghan Government is seen as a passive vehicle, in this regard, as are NGOs involved in the delivery of education.

The new Afghan Government was thus presented to the US public in an entirely positive light, even though it contained many individuals whose human rights record was not significantly better than that of the Taliban. In fact, donors were very reluctant, after 2001, to address existing or previous human rights abuse, taking the view that these were secondary to the need to create security and build up the infrastructure of the state. This gave a clear message to the various power holders in Afghanistan that they had impunity.

The USA was also presented as a force for good in that, having 'liberated' Afghanistan from the Taliban, it was now working to build up the infrastructure of the Afghan State and combat terrorism, in order to 'make the world a safer place'.

It is noteworthy that the donor community placed no conditions on the deployment of its nationals to Afghanistan after the US-led intervention. This was in strong contrast to the restrictions imposed on US and UK personnel during the Taliban period by their respective governments. It is also noteworthy that it was acceptable to direct resources to build the capacity of the Afghan Government after October 2001, yet it was quite unacceptable to the US and UK Governments to do so while the Taliban were in power. These policy positions, taken during the Taliban period, may therefore be seen as examples of assistance to the population being potentially reduced on political grounds, rather than on the basis of need.

The view that the situation which existed after the Bonn Agreement was entirely positive also influenced the security rating that existed for expatriate personnel. Thus, the number of UN expatriate staff who were authorized to be based in Kabul increased from 15 people in 2000, when the Taliban were in power, to 450 in October 2002.[46] This was in spite of the fact that the security situation in the capital was, in many respects, worse in 2002 than it had been in 2000. It was certainly more complex and less predictable. Further, expatriates were more at risk of being actively targeted, by the Taliban, after 2002 than they were during the period of Taliban rule.

The position that the post-Bonn Government was a success coloured the conditions under which aid was given and even the assessment of risk to expatriate personnel, and yet this position was clearly taken for political purposes. There was therefore a wish fulfilment. Donors chose to believe, or, at least, to indicate that they believed, that they had created a functioning democratic government which had committed itself to adhere to international norms and human rights standards. Anything which did not conform to this myth was carefully omitted in statements by donor governments.

The US government thus placed considerable emphasis on the image that it was creating with the US public, but it gave scant attention to how its actions were perceived within the Islamic world. Thus, in establishing detention facilities at Guantanamo Bay and within Afghanistan in order to demonstrate to the US public that it was taking punitive action against those who were seen to represent a threat to US and international security, it further angered and alienated Muslim opinion. The USA therefore made the cardinal mistake of ignoring the potential for mass movements to develop on the back of shared grievances. It thus failed to take account of the fact that, if those who had emerged into leadership positions within Al-Qaida, or other radical organizations, were located and arrested, others would come to take their place if there was a sufficient sense of collective anger.

It is far from clear that the organization known as Al-Qaida, which recruited volunteers from Saudi Arabia to fight alongside the Mujahidin against the Soviet forces in Afghanistan, was the all-powerful organization that it was presented as being. The indications are that it was part of a loose network of organizations committed to the use of violence against the USA, albeit an inspirational one.

However, the USA did have good reason to be concerned at the existence in Afghanistan, during the latter part of the Taliban period, of a network of training camps in which volunteers from other parts of the Islamic world received training in military skills. Their motivations were various. Many sought to undermine the regimes of the countries in which they originated, viewing them as too closely aligned with the USA or insufficiently Islamic. Others expressly set out to commit terrorist attacks against US targets. Yet others were willing to support the Taliban in their efforts to create a state based on Shari'a Law.

Behind this willingness to volunteer were identifiable issues of major concern. There was thus widespread anger over US support for a particularly oppressive approach by the Israeli Government towards the Palestinian territories, manifested in the construction of a dividing wall and in the use of significant levels of violence against Palestinian populations in both Gaza and the West Bank. The fact that gruesome images of this violence were daily broadcast on Al-Jazeera television further intensified the feelings of outrage. Although President Clinton had worked hard to address the Palestinian issue, with some degree of success, he was only able to go so far because of the strength of the pro-Israel lobby in the USA amongst both Jewish and fundamentalist Christian populations. The abiding impression, therefore, was that the USA was solidly behind Israel.

Public opinion was also negatively influenced by the US military presence in Saudi Arabia following the Gulf War of 1991, which was deemed to be an affront to the holy places in Mecca and Medina. The US air strikes on Afghanistan of August 1998 had further radicalized opinion, as had the offensives of Moscow against Chechnya.

A failure to give sufficient weight to the sense of shared grievance led the USA, with UK backing, to compound the sense of grievance many times over with a series of actions which generated such a degree of anger that violence against perceived US and other Western targets became inevitable. Primary among these actions was the US-led intervention in Iraq of March 2003. This was felt as a massive humiliation across the Islamic world.

The US-led intervention in Iraq thus had the effect of galvanizing opinion across the global Islamic community, with the result that Afghanistan became identified as part of a wider cause, aimed to secure the removal of international forces from both Iraq and Afghanistan and a cessation of US support for Israel. This enabled the Taliban to secure donations from Muslims across the globe and to also draw on the technology used in terrorist attacks in Iraq. This meant that, alongside the resources provided by the USA and other donors for the priorities that they identified in Afghanistan, there were other, substantial, resources provided to strengthen the insurgency.

The disclosure of the behaviour of US military personnel at Abu Ghraib prison in Iraq and at various detention facilities in Afghanistan also had a major impact. The detention of what were almost exclusively Muslim suspects at the prison at Guantanamo Bay, and the widespread publication of reports on conditions there, further fuelled perceptions that the West was engaged in a crusade against the Islamic world.

The accessibility of Muslim populations across the world, through satellite television, to visual images of violence against fellow Muslims certainly played a role in creating a shared sense of grievance. Also important was the increasing ease with which information could be downloaded through the internet. Anti-Islamic statements issued by public figures in the West were immediately available through multiple websites to interested individuals throughout the Islamic world. Thus, when President Bush spoke of 'Islamic fascists', this provoked a strong and instantaneous reaction. Cartoons in a Danish newspaper that portrayed the prophet, Mohammed, in a very perjorative light led to demonstrations across Afghanistan in which many died.

The sense of shared grievance was felt across the generations, amongst farmers and labourers as well as amongst intellectuals. It was, in addition, felt amongst Muslim populations within the West, as manifested in the terrorist attacks on the London tube and bus systems of July 2005.

The US Government could have clearly sought to influence public opinion in the USA in favour of a policy of engagement with the Islamic world, aimed to address the major grievances. Instead, it pandered to the prejudices of some of its own constituencies which included, as a dominant element, fundamentalist Christians with a very myopic view of the world outside the USA. It therefore created a political environment in which the US media was encouraged to produce negative stereotypes of Muslims and to also instil fear through frequent references to the potential for terrorist activity to directly impact on the population. This climate of fear created a sufficient level of consent for the US Government to use its income from taxation to significantly increase its defence budget. It also enabled it to impose greater controls on personal freedoms, through the Patriot Act, in pursuit of counter-terrorism objectives.

It is important to consider, in relation to the evident expansion of the Taliban movement from the spring of 2003 onwards, whether, had the USA not intervened militarily in Iraq, the Taliban would have placed the same focus on the use of terrorist attacks as they did. The Taliban were certainly beginning to regroup during 2002 but needed to build a support base. They were able to do this to a degree, both in the southern provinces of Afghanistan and within Pakistan, using the rallying call that Afghanistan had been invaded by the USA. However, the international presence in Afghanistan was not a major cause within the wider Islamic world, at that stage. It was, therefore, difficult for the Taliban to generate resources from that wider world.

It could, reasonably, be argued that the role of Islam as a galvanizing force has been even greater during the post 2001 period. Thus, while the Soviet intervention created the conditions for a radicalization process, the US-led intervention in Iraq justified a global jihad against the US military presence in Afghanistan.

Thus, in seeking to provide resources to the Afghan population, the international community was facing a situation in which the Taliban were also resourced to provide some of the functions of the state, notably security, law and order.

The combination of the resistance movement and the campaign of terrorism also made it increasingly difficult to deliver reconstruction assistance. Thus, the aid programmes delivered by the UN and NGOs were progressively withdrawn from more and more areas or were reduced in scale. Further, the reconstruction assistance that was delivered to insecure areas could not be easily overseen, and so quality control inevitably suffered. This affected public perceptions of the value of the aid provided.

A central flaw in the counter-insurgency approach of the international military was the assumption that the support of the population could be won through relatively small amounts of reconstruction assistance. This led to an expectation that, if areas could be temporarily 'liberated', NGOs could come in to provide reconstruction assistance, which would then encourage the population to withhold support for any renewed intervention by the insurgents. The view taken by a majority of NGOs, that it was not safe for them to operate in areas which had recently been retaken by international military forces, tended to be dismissed as a failure on their part, rather than a reasonable and considered response to the situation.

This assumption, by the international military, that reconstruction assistance is the key to consolidating military gains also downplayed the negative influences, such as the impact of civilian deaths, affronts to sensibilities and the brutality and humiliation involved in forced searches of homes. The population was assumed to be easily 'bought', to be primarily influenced by material gain rather than personal honour and dignity.

Further, the efforts of international forces to compensate for civilian deaths, caused as an outcome of their military operations, through offers of schools or clinics were seen as insulting. On the few occasions that direct compensation was given to the families of those killed, this was often on such a small scale as to be derisory. For example, when US forces fired indiscriminately at civilians after a terrorist incident in Nangarhar in March 2007, the compensation offered was only $2,000 for each of the eight people killed.

Aid therefore tends to be unacceptable when it is accompanied by force, brutality or by behaviour which is disrespectful, insulting to the dignity of the individual or culturally insensitive. The assumption consistently made by the international military, that the desire for material benefit will prevail over all other considerations, is thus deeply flawed.

What the international community has failed to do is to provide aid on a sufficient scale to seriously impact on people's daily lives, and in areas which clearly benefit the population. Thus, while there has been investment in rural development, health care and education, in particular, the level of funding has left considerable gaps in provision. It does not, therefore, take much, by way of negative influences, for the population to feel that the benefits of aid are of little consequence.

Further, there was media-induced optimism, in the early stages, that reconstruction assistance would be delivered on a sufficient scale to make a real difference. Disillusionment soon followed when this failed to happen. It also led to anger over the existence of elites, within the government and amongst the plethora of international advisers, which were living in obvious affluence.

The provision of aid needs to be placed in the context of economic realities. In a situation where the majority of the population is having to survive on the land, the level of investment in agriculture needs to be sufficiently large to make a difference. Alternatively, additional income-earning opportunities have to be made available through the creation of manufacturing or service-sector outlets. If aid is delivered on a relatively small scale, it may not make a sufficient difference to people's lives for it to be seen as significant, even in the areas where it is delivered. Further, it may not benefit the whole of the population in the areas concerned. In addition, there will be many areas where aid has not been provided at all. This may lead to perception that, overall, nothing much has been done.

There is always the risk that the aid giver will overestimate the degree of difference that a project will make to people's lives, relative to the many other factors which condition their daily struggles to survive. Further, there is a tendency to assume that the rural population can live through agriculture alone whereas the reality, in Afghanistan, is that a high proportion of households have relied, for many decades, on being able to send one or more sons to Pakistan or Iran, or to one of the urban centres of Afghanistan, to look for work. The provision of support to the agriculture sector may therefore reduce the need to opt for labour migration as an economic strategy but, from the experience of the author, it is unlikely to be sufficient to totally remove that need.

It is arguable that reconstruction assistance delivered in the immediate aftermath of the Bonn Agreement might have delivered enough to make the population feel that progress was being made and so avoided the later disenchantment with government that developed, and also the public sympathy for the Taliban. However, this would have required a willingness to take risks with security while the country was theoretically in a stabilization process. It would also have required an organizational capacity amongst the donor governments which was not readily available. On the other hand, the failure of the international community to show sufficient tangible progress during that initial period, in spite of the sense of urgency impressed upon them at the Tokyo Conference, has undermined confidence in the Afghan Government amongst the Afghan population.

However, in considering how to allocate resources, the USA had to set the serious economic situation against the fact that the interim government of Hamid Karzai lacked popular legitimacy. There was, therefore, a perceived need to provide it with this legitimacy through an electoral process. Yet that Government continued to be closely associated with the USA and it is arguable that its failure to provide security and reconstruction assistance at a sufficient level has undermined any credibility accorded to it through the electoral process. The international community would appear, during the initial stage at least, to have failed to take account of the historical cynicism of the Afghan population towards their governments. The creation of a veneer of democracy was therefore of marginal significance to the population by comparison with concerns relating to the failure of the Afghan Government to improve security, ensure adequate livelihoods and address corruption.

Further, a parliament was created to ensure the accountability of the civil service to the population before that civil service had developed the capacity to deliver services on any scale.

There was also the related issue of whether the US practice of directing a high proportion of its aid through US contractors made for the best use of resources. In one example, USAID awarded a $218.6 million contract, in March 2007, to the US company BearingPoint Inc. The principle objectives were said to be:

- to strengthen the performance of ministries, businesses, non-governmental organizations, universities and local governments;
- to establish permanent, sustainable capacity in the public, private and higher education sectors;
- to build the skills of key personnel in the Afghan public and private sectors, through scholarships.

This links to a pattern through which US aid is largely geared to US commercial and foreign policy interests. Thus Earthscan Publications, in the Reality of Aid 2000, reported, in their US section, that '71.6% of its bilateral aid commitments were tied to the purchase of goods and services from the US'.

Corpwatch published a document in October 2006, under the title 'Afghanistan Inc.', to assess the role of US private sector contractors operating in Afghanistan. The report notes that another US company, Louis Berger, received $665 million in contracts from the US Government up to September 2006 to build roads, dams, schools and other infrastructure, including 81 clinics, in Afghanistan. It used subcontractors for this work.

A further US company, Chemonics International Inc., worked

through a US Government initiative, known as Rebuilding Agricultural Markets Program (RAMP). Two US companies, Dyncorps and USPI, have played a major role in the provision of security for reconstruction projects.

There were many other examples of US companies working on reconstruction projects or helping sustain the US military operations in Afghanistan. The primary concern of the Afghan Government, in relation to the presence of these companies was that they represented poor value for money. The former Afghan Foreign Minister, Abdullah Abdullah, thus commented on 18 May 2007, in an interview with Canada's CanWest News Service, that 'international contracts tend to be subcontracted several times, with each person taking a piece of the pie. The result is that only about $30,000 of an international donation of $100,000 will end up being applied to the actual project.'

There was, thus, a high level of cynicism amongst the Afghan public about the relative benefits of aid, provided by the US Government, to Afghans as opposed to US companies. This inevitably coloured perceptions of the international presence, overall, so that, when the international military stated that reconstruction assistance was a vital component of their counter-insurgency strategy, the population inevitably reflected negatively on much of the assistance that had been delivered to date. This negative perception was compounded by the fact that, due to insecurity and other factors, it was not possible for donors, such as the USA, or their contractors to exercise sufficient supervision of funded projects. This often resulted in poor quality outputs, which further fuelled public cynicism.

Equally important was the need for those who did engage in Afghanistan to be better controlled so that the resources allocated were transparent. Regrettably, in many immediate post-conflict situations, there are inevitably some who take advantage of the chaos. The safeguards are not normally in place to prevent this, or to stop international companies, for example, securing over-advantageous rights to mineral or other resources in the heat of the immediate post-conflict situation. Such situations also tend to attract individuals who are willing to take considerable risks in return for high rewards.

Given that the USA was the major donor, although roughly on a par with the European Commission and European donors combined, could it have used its resources more effectively? Further, if more resources had been used on reconstruction during the initial year instead of on the creation of military bases and the pursuit of radical Islamic networks, how would that money have best been spent? Would it have reduced the risk of terrorist activity or the likelihood of a Taliban-orchestrated insurgency emerging?

In considering these questions, we may reasonably take the view that it was unlikely that the US would have wished to postpone the creation of a network of military bases in Afghanistan when this was one of its primary objectives, as part of their strategy of establishing a network of forward operating bases around the world. Its concerns with regard to Iran, Russia and China made this a more urgent priority than the more nebulous task of reconstructing Afghanistan. The USA also attached high priority to the creation of a democratic process, which required a very substantial allocation of both financial and human resources over a four-year period.

However, the reconstruction of Afghanistan was clearly a much lower priority than that of the Balkans, East Timor or Rwanda, judging by the relative allocation of resources to the country. It is not clear why this was. Was it because the infrastructure was so depleted that the absorption capacity was very limited? Was it based on a fear that too much money injected too quickly into an unstable environment could have a major destabilizing effect? Or was it that donors did not wish to fund salaries for government servants at a level which the government could not afford long term? As it was, it is clear that the sudden availability of much larger resources did place strains on the existing NGO infrastructure. There was also the inevitable risk that an injection of resources into the government, before it was ready to absorb it, would have further fuelled corruption. However, after the initial drought-related funding, the NGO network, on which much of the population continued to depend for the provision of basic services, faced considerable problems securing the funding that it needed to maintain services at their existing level. There was, therefore, scope to do more if additional resources were made available.

If, therefore, aid had been provided on a sufficient scale in the areas that made a significant impact to people's lives (namely in agriculture, health care, education, water supply and sanitation), it might have positively influenced those parts of the population which were, for example, not directly affected by the negative actions of the international military. If these populations had experienced the Afghan Government and the international community as bringing obvious tangible benefits, it might have made them less inclined to support the Taliban. However, they would have still been affected by perceptions that the West was behaving badly towards the Islamic World and by reports of negative actions of the international military elsewhere in Afghanistan. They would also have been affected by the intimidation and climate of fear created by the Taliban.

However, it would have been extremely difficult for those who had been victims of house searches by the international military or of who had lost relatives in air raids by the international military, to be positively influenced by the provision of aid.

To conclude, the USA was not successful, through the use of aid, in achieving its strategic objectives in that it failed to persuade the Afghan population to acquiesce in the significant international presence and to accept, as legitimate, the government of President Karzai. At the same time, its military presence seriously undermined the ability of the aid community, including the UN, the International Committee of the Red Cross and NGOs, to continue providing basic services to the population. As a result, the population was, in many areas, denied access to services which had been available prior to 2001.

To seek to deliver aid as a means of winning hearts and minds is therefore ineffective. The provision of aid should, more appropriately, be the outcome of a sense of responsibility to address poverty and disadvantage. It should, therefore, be an end in itself rather than a means to another end.

8

THE SPECIFIC IMPACT OF DEVELOPMENT AND HUMANITARIAN ASSISTANCE

In considering this question, it may be first useful to reflect on the nature of the Afghan economy as it was at the beginning of 2002.

The progress that had been made by the population, with support from the UN and NGOs, in restoring the agricultural base from 1989 to 1999 was seriously undermined by the 1999–2001 drought. NGOs were already working to get food aid to affected communities before the onset of winter when the US military intervention commenced. Programmes had to be put on hold for several weeks as a result of the intervention, provoking fears that the targeted villages would not be reached in time. Fortunately, the snow was late in arriving and the World Food Programme, supported by NGOs, performed an impressive logistical exercise to deliver the food before it was too late.

However, families were still struggling to survive in the face of mounting debt. A high proportion had lost livestock. Many had been forced to sell their land. Migration of young men to Pakistan or Iran was a common survival strategy. The situation was compounded by the fact that the Taliban had placed a ban on opium cultivation in 2000. This meant that an important source of seasonal labour, for the opium harvest, was not available.

At the beginning of 2002, an estimated three million Afghans were living in Pakistan and 1,482,000 in Iran. A proportion of these had originally left Afghanistan in response to the Soviet military intervention and were living in refugee camps or in one of the urban areas of Pakistan or Iran. Those who had fled to Iran as refugees were, for the most part, resident in the cities. However, both Pakistan and Iran experienced a continuing influx and exodus of Afghans as they sought to work in one or other country for temporary periods.

Both Pakistan and Iran were actively promoting a return of their Afghan populations to Afghanistan from the beginning of 2002. This was being facilitated through tripartite agreements signed with the Afghan Government and the UN High Commission for Refugees (UNHCR) to assist returning refugees, through a Voluntary Repatriation Programme, with sacks of wheat, cash grants and items such as plastic sheeting.

Apart from agriculture, migration and small scale trading, there were few other sources of income. The manufacturing base was virtually non-existent. The carpet trade was largely being organized through the refugee camps in Pakistan. The only extraction of mineral resources was in the lapis lazuli mines in the northeast. Gas production in the north had all but ceased.

The potential for growth was impeded by the poor state of the roads. The Taliban had tarmacked part of the Kabul–Kandahar highway and also part of the highway from Torghundi, on the Turkmen border, to Kandahar. Otherwise, the two highways were reduced to the concrete slabs on which the original roads had been built. Elsewhere, roads were largely earth or gravel and heavily potholed. In wet conditions, they often became impassable due to mud. Many high altitude areas could not be accessed by vehicle and the roads that existed faced a constant risk of landslides.

Potential manufacturing growth was also constrained by the very limited supply of electricity. In Kabul, this was dependent on the Sarobi Power Station, to the east, which required significant refurbishment. As a result, electricity supply was extremely erratic and only available on a very small scale.

The telephone system was also barely functioning. It was necessary to go to the central Post Office to make an international call. Communication between residents was not possible. International agencies depended on satellite phones.

The Kabul economy was also suffering from the fact that the Shomali Valley, to the north, had been a conflict zone since 1996 and was virtually dead. Not only did this remove a major agricultural area from production but it also meant that Kabul was no longer on the trade route from Central Asia to Pakistan. Mazar-e Sharif, in northern Afghanistan, was also affected. Instead, trade was passing through Herat and Kandahar, which were doing relatively well, economically. As a result, much of the population of Kabul had been living on food aid for the previous five years. Begging was commonplace.

However, the good security that the Taliban were providing in the areas under their control had made it possible for the UN and NGOs to deliver education, health care, agricultural support and drinking water sources across the country. Although the funds available for this purpose were much less than after the Bonn Agreement, they could be used more cost-effectively because agencies were able to build up long-term relationships with communities. This meant that they were able to enter into partnership arrangements under which communities would also contribute resources and, more importantly, participate fully in the planning process. Agencies also had to spend much less on security. The aid community had thus provided an important safety net for vulnerable communities and also ensured that basic services were provided to the population throughout the country at a certain level. There was therefore a consistency which proved not to be achievable after Bonn.

At the same time, the capacity of the Afghan Government to deliver services to the population in the immediate aftermath of the Bonn Agreement was extremely constrained. The civil service had barely functioned since the fall of the Soviet-backed government, even though thousands of government staff remained theoretically on the payroll and were, in many cases, turning up for work each day. The situation had been aggravated by significant pressures placed on civil servants by the Taliban, arising from a perception that they were liberal, and possibly secular, in outlook. As a result, large numbers of government workers had left their jobs and, in very many cases, the country. Some ministries, such as the Ministry of Public Health, retained sufficient capacity for the UN and NGOs to engage with them for policy making and implementation purposes. The intelligence services also functioned reasonably well although they were closely linked to Jamiat-e-Islami. However, many ministries were effectively empty shells in which the Minister and a few advisers would determine policy but had no real capacity to implement it.

The Ministries were also, following the Bonn Agreement, effectively fiefdoms of their ministers, in which patronage determined appointments rather than merit. This inevitably reinforced a tendency towards corruption which had been endemic since the pre-1979 period. A legacy of an over-bureaucratic system, in which even the most minor decisions were passed up to the minister, paralysed the decision-making process. The very low salaries of government staff also meant that they needed to do other work in addition to their government service. This inevitably led staff to keep their reserves of energy for their other jobs. As a result, the work ethic was not as much in evidence as it would ideally have been even though many staff were committed to their jobs.

The low salaries also offered an inducement for civil servants to demand additional payments from the public for bureaucratic services provided. While not all civil servants were in a position to benefit from such opportunities, the culture of corruption thus created proved difficult to shift when efforts were made to reform the government service.

In addition, many ministries had introduced cumbersome regulations with which the population had to comply. This meant that aid organizations and private sector operators were having to spend unreasonable lengths of time on bureaucratic matters, which both undermined productivity and served as a major disincentive for private sector investment in the economy.

The Government also had no money. There was no functioning tax collection system and the revenue from customs duties at the various border crossings was mostly being retained by local power holders. The government was, therefore, heavily dependent on international donors to provide it with the resources to both pay its staff and deliver services.

An early priority of the international community was to establish mechanisms through which the Afghan Government could build its capacity to manage donor funds. With the cooperation of the then Finance Minister, Ashraf Ghani, measures were taken to invest in an expansion of the human resource capacity of the Ministry of Finance. Experts were brought in from donor governments, from the World Bank and from large Western accountancy firms. Systems were introduced to track payments by donors and to allocate funds through a budgetary process.

The World Bank played a major role in supporting the Ministry of Finance to set up systems which complied with international regulations. This gave it considerable influence in mainstreaming the Afghan economy within the international financial system.

Following the example of other post-conflict situations, the World Bank, with support from donors, introduced several trust funds through which donor funding could be channelled to the Government for specific purposes. Primary among these was the Afghanistan Reconstruction Trust Fund (ARTF), a multilateral arrangement operated by the World Bank, with a management committee including the Asian Development Bank, the Islamic Development Bank, UNDP, the World Bank and the Afghan Ministry of Finance. The Government was required to account for the use of these funds through an audit process. The ARTF was used to fund the Government's salary bill, among other items of expenditure. This included the salaries of thousands of teachers across the country, channelled through the Ministry of Education.

Among the other beneficiaries of this trust fund system was the Ministry of Reconstruction and Rural Development, which introduced a nation-wide rural development programme known as the National Solidarity Programme. This provided grants to village communities to implement projects prioritized by village councils set up for the purpose. Facilitation of the consultation process was carried out by NGOs, while village councils implemented the work themselves or would contract out to private sector operators or other NGOs. The Ministry of Public Health was a further beneficiary, to enable it to administer a network of primary health care services across the country, contracted out to NGOs and private sector organizations, through the Basic Package of Health Care.

The budget process through which the National Solidarity Programme and the Basic Package of Health Care operated was the National Development Framework (NDF). This document stipulated that the Government would determine policy for the various areas of responsibility that it took on, but it would look to the private sector and NGOs to implement programmes in key sectors such as health care, education and rural development. It is not clear whether this approach was adopted because it was consistent with US policy, and the philosophy of the World Bank, that the role of government should be kept to the minimum, or whether it was based on a recognition that NGOs were already operating in the country and therefore had the capacity which the Government lacked. However, there was a strong focus in the NDF on strengthening the role of the private sector, both Afghan and international, and on creating a regulatory framework for the private sector to operate.

The NDF focused on what were seen as the key priority areas. These included support for the reintegration of returning refugees, an expansion in education and vocational training, and the creation of mechanisms through which livelihoods could be enhanced and safety nets provided for those who were unable to secure a sufficient income. Among the safety net programmes, the National Emergency Employment Programme sought to provide employment through public works. Linked to the creation of livelihoods was the development of Afghanistan's natural resources, including oil, gas, copper, coal, iron ore, salt, quarry materials, marble, industrial minerals and precious stones. In recognition of the fact that many returning refugees would gravitate to Kabul and other cities, urban development was seen as a further area in need of attention. The reconstruction of the main highway system, particularly the national ring road, as well as the many secondary roads which linked villages to provincial and district centres, was also identified as a high priority. In addition, the Government aimed to ensure an adequate supply of electricity, water and sanitation to the population and, at the same time, build up telecommunication links across the country. The creation of a rule of law, through a process of security sector reform aimed to strengthen the army, police force and the judiciary and remove weapons from the various militia, was also seen as of high importance. Public administration reform, to build up the capacity of the civil service and establish systems and processes which would make it accountable and uncorruptible, was a further aspiration.

The Interim Authority, and the Transitional Administration which followed it, produced three budgets based on the NDF. In March 2002 expenditures were budgeted at $460 million, with an additional $23 million to clear wage arrears accumulated prior to the Interim Authority's tenure. The budget was primarily allocated to the wages and salaries of government employees and other expenses. Some $83 million was to be financed by domestic revenue and $400 million by external sources. The subsequent budget, published in March 2003, included two main elements: an ordinary budget of $550 million and a national development budget of $1,700 million. The Government committed itself to raise $200 million towards the ordinary budget, while international donors agreed to fund almost 90 per cent of the national development budget.

This same focus also underpinned a document, known as 'Securing Afghanistan's Future', which was presented to international donors at a conference held in Berlin, Germany, in March 2004. This document stated that 'Afghanistan is aiming for a small yet effective government whose role will, as far as possible, be limited to ensuring the security and safety of citizens, creating an enabling but properly regulated environment for the private sector and ensuring that all citizens have access to basic services'. Thus, in the same manner as the NDF, there remained a strong emphasis on the role of the government as being to provide a regulatory framework for a robust private sector. The report made it clear that there would be no State-owned enterprises, but did envisage some investment by the state to lay the foundations for future private-sector activity.

The programme anticipated annual growth of 9 per cent in the legal economy, based on agriculture, mining, industry (including construction, transport, telecommunications and manufacturing) and services. It recognized that this growth rate would still leave a vulnerable population of around 4 million, who would need support through social welfare initiatives. Meanwhile, a stated aim of the Afghan Government was to raise the per capita annual income from less than $200 to $500.

The document further envisaged that the Government would seek to finance the wage portion of its recurrent expenditure in five years and the entire recurrent budget in nine years. Some $13,500 million of the $27,500 million nine-year budget was allocated to improvements to the physical infrastructure, while $2,700 million was assigned to education, $2,600 million to security measures, $2,300 million to livelihoods and social protection, $1,400 million to health care, and $400 million to culture, media and sport. Of the $27,500 million, $7,200 million was needed to fund the Government's recurrent expenditure. The balance would be designated to specific projects, including major capital ones. Primary among these was to be the reconstruction of the major highway system.

The report noted that, apart from agriculture, the economy depended very heavily on small-scale enterprises, primarily at the household level. It identified potential for expansion through the development of hydropower and the exploitation of gas reserves in northern Afghanistan, which were estimated at 120 billion cubic metres. Private investment opportunities were also to be sought further to develop telecommunications and to explore and extract new oil reserves, together with substantial mineral reserves, including coal, iron ore, salt, copper, quarry materials, marble, industrial minerals and gemstones. The report nonetheless noted that 'investor perception of the difficulties of doing business in Afghanistan constrains funding from international markets for exploration and development'. The opening of several international banks in Afghanistan from 2003 onwards was considered significant in facilitating both international trade and inward investment.

In identifying the constraints to economic progress, the report stated that 'until key concerns around the security situation and the extent to which rule of law is followed are addressed, the level of private investment will be limited'. The document stressed that the low level of general education, the shortage of specific professional skills and poor health indicators were undermining the capacity of the country to achieve significant growth in the short term. It added that 'investments in human and social capital will not be productive if citizens do not enjoy basic protections and guarantees' and emphasized that 'an integrated strategy must address core structural issues of human rights, human security and the rule of law'. Concern was expressed about the 'increasingly heavy demands. . . being placed on national resources and capacities, not least by large numbers of returnees and ex-combatants seeking to reintegrate, and by the rapid growth of urban centres'. In this context, 'pressures by asylum countries to accelerate the rate of return' were said to exacerbate the 'significant pressure on already fragile national resources'. It also commented that there 'are currently strong and concentrated interests in Afghanistan who are angling for a weak central government which will allow them to undertake narcotic production and illegal natural resource exploitation'.

In focusing on capacity considerations, the document presented a key dilemma that confronts the Government as a result of, for example, its heavy dependence on NGOs to provide education and health services: the need for an ongoing international presence constrains the Government in its quest to build up its institutional base because it is unable to offer terms and conditions of employment that are competitive with those provided by international organizations and the diplomatic sector.

This became a particular issue after the US-led military intervention because neither the Mujahidin nor the Taliban Governments were in a position to give priority to an expansion of the civil service. The aid sector was also not resourced to provide employment on a sufficient scale to compete with any serious attempt to build up the government service. However, the Bonn Agreement brought, in its wake, a huge influx of international personnel to open embassies, security companies and Kabul-based headquarters of companies, eager to exploit the opportunities that typically arise in high profile post-conflict reconstruction situations. The UN needed extra staff to enable it to take on new programmes such as the Disarmament, Demobilisation and Reintegration Programme and the organization of the huge electoral process. The number of NGOs also increased as new agencies came in to respond to the well-publicised drought, and the availability of additional, albeit temporary, funding made it possible for NGOs to significantly expand their programmes. In addition, the World Bank and the Asian Development Bank set up Kabul offices.

Many of the additional international personnel needed translators, interpreters, drivers and office staff. Long-established NGOs found themselves losing their Afghan managers to less demanding but better paid jobs with other international bodies. Afghan NGOs, in turn, lost their staff to international NGOs as well as to a wider group of organizations.

Efforts to achieve a standardization of wage levels were of no effect. The level of competition for the relatively small number of educated Afghans left in the country, a high proportion of which had been working in the NGO sector, was simply too intense. Further, the Government was not in a good position to generate sufficient revenues, even in the medium to long term, to pay its civil servants a salary on which a family could survive. With much of the economy in what has been termed the 'informal sector', from which it was difficult to generate tax revenues, and with a high proportion of the population living at a marginal level of survival, the Government was dependent on a combination of customs revenues, business tax on a few companies and income tax on, for the most part, international personnel. The income thus generated was not sufficient to wean the Government away from its considerable dependence on income from international donors and, therefore, it was not able to build a sustainable resource base that could support more competitive salary levels.

In order to attract a limited number of qualified or skilled Afghan staff, the Government had to resort to incentive programmes, including the payment of relatively high wages to key personnel. A few were even paid salaries at international levels, supported by earmarked funding by UNDP and donor governments.

For this and other reasons set out below, the Government was a long way from establishing an effective civil service able to implement its development programme when, in January 2006, it launched the Interim Afghanistan National Development Strategy. The key priority areas identified in this five-year development plan were security, governance and the rule of law, human rights, sustainable economic and social development, and counter-narcotics.

The document reaffirmed the underlying principle of the NDF – namely that the Afghan state would seek to create an environment in which the private sector can flourish, and that it would also seek to minimize its own role as a service delivery entity by contracting out to private sector organizations and NGOs.

The agricultural economy was seen as the principle vehicle for economic growth although this growth was expected to be relatively slow. To maximize agricultural productivity, the strategy included mechanisms to improve access to markets, provide sources of power, and support the creation of cold storage facilities. The government planned to take initiatives to strengthen non-farm economic opportunities within the rural areas, in the hope of reducing migration to the major cities. It also set out to increase the availability of credit to rural communities, address water resource management and develop irrigation.

In recognition of the heavy dependence of the Afghan economy on the ability of the population to seek work in Pakistan, Iran and elsewhere, the strategy noted that, by 2010, the Government would reach agreements with its neighbours 'to enable Afghans to seek work in the region and send remittances home'.

The strategy did not anticipate significant private sector investment in the manufacturing sector and looked to small and medium sized enterprises as the primary elements in the non-farm economy. The creation of access to electricity for a majority of these was seen as an important objective, either through arrangements with Afghanistan's neighbours or through hydropower generated within the country. Hope was nonetheless expressed that international investment could be attracted into the extraction and processing of Afghanistan's mineral (iron, copper, coal, hydrocarbons and quarry materials) and gemstone deposits, as well as into a trans-Afghanistan pipeline to bring gas from Turkmenistan to Pakistan and, possibly, India. Important potential was also seen in Afghanistan's role as a transit country for goods travelling between the Central Asian Republics and the Indian subcontinent. To facilitate this, the Government envisaged that the major highway system would be completed by the end of 2008.

Significant emphasis was placed on the need to address the very high level of poverty, the serious health indicators and the limited access to clean water and sanitation. The rapid urbanization process was seen as a concern in this context. The strategy recognized that economic growth would not automatically benefit the poorest in the sector. It therefore proposed specific initiatives to provide a safety net.

The strategy outlined the many constraints to progress, including insecurity, the opium trade, corruption, the low revenue base, the very limited capacity of the government bureaucracy, the severe shortage of skills, and 'a pervasive culture of impunity... due to the lack of an independent judiciary and professional law enforcement'.

It thus noted that:

> ...the legal and regulatory framework necessary for Government to function effectively, ensure the rule of law and protect our citizens is still nascent or absent.

While the Government has passed new laws designed to protect the rights of citizens, our ability to enforce these laws is compromised. Our different government branch members lack legislative, oversight and representational experience. Our sub-national administrative structure is especially weak, which inhibits coordination across Government at the provincial and district levels and lowers our accountability to the vast majority of our population, who live in rural areas. Too many of these sub-national governance structures remain under the influence of illicit power holders.

The document commented that 'control over arms and money enables power holders to seize land, levy tributes and control access to credit and markets' and added that 'the poor have no effective rights to land or other assets'. It further stated that 'in the justice sector, the sale of judicial access and favourable decisions to the highest bidder fundamentally undermines the security and basic rights of citizens, especially the poor, women and children' and added that 'state and non-state actors who violate the law are emboldened by this state of impunity'.

In recognition of the enormous difficulties that returning refugees were facing in recovering their land, the strategy identified the registration of entitlement to land as a major objective in both rural and urban areas, together with measures to ensure that the judicial system could handle disputes fairly.

To address competence and corruption in the government service, the strategy envisaged that 'a clear and transparent national appointments mechanism will be established... for all senior level appointments' and that 'merit-based appointments, vetting procedures and performance-based reviews will be undertaken for the civil services at all levels of government'. To improve the skills of civil servants, the strategy anticipated that the Government would offer on the job training, special courses and intensive study abroad.

To improve skills within the wider economy, the strategy included plans to 'provide the less educated with vocational skills to fill demands for construction, infrastructure building and maintenance of assets', and to orientate the higher education system towards managerial and professional skills. Literacy and numeracy were also seen as key targets.

On counter-narcotics, the document stressed the continuing use of simultaneous strategies, including law enforcement, the use of eradication 'as appropriate', regional cooperation and alternative livelihoods.

The Government costed the implementation of the Interim Afghanistan National Development Strategy at $19.829 billion over five years. In presenting this to donors, it set out a system for reviewing progress through a body known as the Joint Coordination and Monitoring Board. It added that information and analysis in support of the strategy would be sought from 'sub-national monitoring and coordination mechanisms, including Community and Provincial Development Councils, NGOs, Provincial Reconstruction Teams, the private sector, civil society and research units'.

It further stated that, in preparation for the full Afghanistan National Development Strategy, the government planned to consult with a wide range of actors, including 'line ministries, the National Assembly, sub-national administrative units, UN agencies, NGOs, civil society representatives, communities and the private sector'. Through this process, the government noted, it would seek to gain ' a much better understanding of demographic, economic, political and security-related realities at the sub-national level'.

This consultative mechanism complemented a system which had been in place since 2002, under which the Government linked with international donors, the UN and NGOs through sector-based Consultative Groups. Prior to this, coordination was organized through Secretariats placed in each Ministry. However, the effectiveness of the Consultative Groups was variable according to the sector and the degree of responsibility taken by the lead agency. The Groups were headed by lead agencies which were, in most cases, UN bodies. Certainly, a need for greater coherence between the programmes of individual donors is often identified as a major priority in Afghanistan. Whether this is simply a reflection of the fact that the USA is acting independently of the wider donor community, or there is also a relative failure of the other donors to communicate sufficiently, is difficult to determine.

Several donors agreed to take on specific responsibilities, including a major role in helping build up the capacity of the Afghan state. The UK, in particular, opted to allocate a significant proportion of its funding to the Afghan Government, both directly and via the Afghanistan Reconstruction Trust Fund. Individual donors took responsibility for specific areas of reform. Thus, the UK took on counter-narcotics, Germany police training, Japan disarmament and Italy judicial reform.

Some donors also took a hands-on approach, moving beyond their traditional grant-giving role to play an active part in, for example, building the capacity of specific ministries. Many deployed advisers, but the overall benefit of their contributions was less than optimum. Each donor government brought in its particular tradition of governance and the donor community did not make as much effort as it could have to agree on common systems and principles to impart to the Afghan Government. Further, there were weaknesses within the Afghan Government arising from the historical system of patronage, the high prevalence of corruption and the tendency for ministers to use their ministries as part of the complex power play in which they were continually engaged. The receptivity to new approaches was therefore limited.

The Afghan Government commented, in 2007, that it planned to make greater use of advisers from its neighbours, taking the view that the systems in operation within Afghanistan's hinterland were relatively similar to those in use in Afghanistan. It also noted that the cost of these advisers was very much less than that of advisers from the USA or Europe.

Donors have come together periodically to review progress in Afghanistan. The regular donor meetings which took place before 2001, in the form of the Afghanistan Support Group, were replaced in November 2001 by the Afghanistan Reconstruction Steering Group. At the Tokyo Conference of January 2002, it was decided to establish an Implementation Group, to bring together the Afghan Government, donors, the UN, the international financial institutions and NGOs. This replaced the Afghanistan Programming Body, which had been the highest decision-making structure within the previous Strategic Framework Process. However, the Afghanistan Support Group continued to meet until the end 2002, when it was formally disbanded. The Afghanistan Reconstruction Steering

Group and the Implementation Group were combined, in March 2003, under a new body, the Afghanistan Development Forum.[47] As has been noted above, a donor conference was organized in Berlin, from 31 March to 1 April 2004, at which $8 billion was pledged for the following three years. A further major review was undertaken in London in January 2006, when the Afghanistan Compact was drawn up. Through this, the Afghan Government and international donors each agreed to carry out specific actions by agreed dates in order to give greater impetus to the reform process.

It is important, in considering the role of the UN following the Bonn Agreement, to recall the fact that it was, in many respects, acting as the de facto government of Afghanistan for many years. It did so to the extent that it was overseeing the delivery of education, health care, water supply, sanitation, support to agriculture and the rehabilitation of roads. Although it would consult the Afghan Government on policy and seek to complement the capacity to implement services that the government still retained, it was the major provider. Certainly, much of the policy formulation fell to the UN rather than the Government.

The emergence of an internationally-recognised government following the Bonn Agreement placed the UN in a situation where it needed to work with the Government to support a new policy making process while continuing to oversee the delivery of services, pending a build up of the Government's own capacity.

However, the UN was not in a strong position to do this, organizationally, during the initial months. In September 2001, the UN Security Council had decided that the UN would take the lead role in supporting the transition to a democratically-elected government. To this end, it was agreed to replace the UN Office for the Coordination of Humanitarian Affairs (UNOCHA) with a new structure known as the UN Assistance Mission for Afghanistan (UNAMA). Initial proposals that UNAMA should have a management role in relation to the other UN agencies were soon set aside in favour of the traditional 'facilitative coordination role'. However, discussions as to the exact role that UNAMA should play dragged on and it was not until March 2002 that UNAMA was in being.[48]

UNAMA was established as two distinct entities, which were referred to as Pillars[49], each headed by a Deputy Special

Representative of the UN Secretary General and accountable to the Special Representative. Pillar 1 (political) was responsible for:

- monitoring, analyzing and reporting on the overall political and human rights situation and the status of implementation of the Bonn Agreement
- maintaining contact with Afghan leaders, political parties and civil society groups
- performing 'good offices' in such areas as confidence building and governance
- providing information and guidance on political issues for other UNAMA activities
- investigating human rights violations and, where necessary, recommending corrective action.

Pillar 2 (assistance) was given the task of supporting the Afghan Government to draw up a National Development Framework and coordinating international assistance to ensure that it was consistent with that framework.

UNOCHA was therefore in a process of winding up its affairs when it should have been playing an instrumental role in supporting a difficult transition. It certainly did not want to take decisions which could pre-empt the role that its successor might want to play. This meant that major agencies such as UNHCR, UNICEF and the World Food Programme were developing large programmes without, until March 2002, the strategic oversight that a fully mandated UN coordinating body might provide. It also meant that the new government did not have an effective planning partner, although it was aware of the fact that UNOCHA was, to a degree, operating on the basis of business as usual. By the spring of 2002, the Government was already accusing the UN of running a parallel government. It also expressed its concern over the existence of other apparent parallel governments within the US embassy, the UN and the NGO communities, and it called for the international community to support and respect its wish to be placed firmly in the driving seat, at least with regard to the formulation of policy. The UN, in response, set up the succession of consultative mechanisms, referred to above, to facilitate a partnership process between the

Government, the UN, the donor community and NGOs. However, these mechanisms certainly did not make the government feel that it was in the driving seat.

The UN was responsive to the Government's concern, as was the donor community. Over the following months, a determined effort was made to accord greater weight to the government. This was facilitated by the publication of the National Development Framework, which created a clear strategy for future government policy, and by the creation of the Afghanistan Reconstruction Trust Fund and other trust funds. The willingness of some donors to allocate funds to the Government, directly or through the trust funds, gave it enough resources to, at least, pay its staff and embark on some major initiatives such as the National Solidarity Fund and the Basic Package of Health Care. However, the overall capacity of the Government to deliver services remained weak.

The situation was not helped by the fact that there were so many new actors. Before the Bonn Agreement, the UN could see the big picture and work with the government and NGOs to reflect on the best use of limited resources and also agree on an implementation process. Now, the US Ambassador was orchestrating outcomes behind the scenes and the US military had arrived in force. ISAF had also been set up to provide a degree of security in Kabul. The World Bank and the Asian Development Bank were new on the scene and were major players. The donor community became active participants, rather than simply providing funds, as they took responsibility for certain capacity building programmes. New NGOs arrived to respond to the serious drought conditions but did not always coordinate with those that had already been working in Afghanistan for a long time. The UN no longer had the mandate to pull all these actors together for the greater good, and yet the Government was not yet in a position to do so. Thus, while there was progress on many fronts, there was also a high degree of chaos.

UNAMA also had to take on major tasks which had not fallen to its predecessor. In particular, it was called upon to organize the electoral and constitutional processes including the Loya Jirga, the drafting of the constitution, the Constitutional Loya Jirga, the presidential elections and the parliamentary elections. In addition, it was asked to oversee the Disarmament, Demobilisation and Reintegration (DDR) and the Disarmament of Illegal Armed Groups (DIAG) programme processes. This required a substantial increase in the number of UN international staff, which had reached 670 in total by the middle of 2002, thus increasing the highly visible international presence.[50]

These were major organizational undertakings, for which the UN was under-resourced. The elections proved to be well organized, but both the DDR and the DIAG processes were of limited effectiveness. Whether this was a failing of the UN or a consequence of complex power dynamics over which it had no control is difficult to say.

However, it was, to a significant degree, business as usual for specialist UN agencies such as UNHCR, WFP, WHO and UNICEF, which continued to be the dominant players in their particular spheres of refugee and internally displaced persons support, food assistance, health care and education.

UN Habitat and the UN Office for Project Services (UNOPS), on the other hand, took on quite new roles as contractors for the Government and for others providing funds, such as the World Bank, UNDP and international donors.

It may now be useful to reflect on the progress made up to January 2008 in implementing the Afghan Government's development strategy, as outlined in the three development plans.

In considering, first, the re-integration of returning refugees, it could reasonably be argued that the process of refugee return during the early part of 2002 was premature. The Government was certainly in no position to support those who returned and international agencies could do no more than provide very limited assistance. Returnees therefore had to rely on their own resources, for the most part, to re-establish their lives. While the arrival of international personnel, on a large scale, provided employment opportunities in construction work to bring office premises and residences up to an adequate standard, this was not sufficient to meet the high level of demand for employment. It did, however, lead to a rapid expansion in the population of Kabul from less than a million in 2002 to over 4 million in 2007. At the same time, families typically found themselves having to send some family members back to Pakistan or Iran to look for work.

It is not clear why Afghans returned in such large numbers at the beginning of 2002. Certainly, the international media presented a highly optimistic picture of the situation in Afghanistan, and many of the international personnel who established themselves in Kabul appeared to believe the rhetoric, for which there was no real justification. It is therefore possible that Afghans living in Pakistan were induced, by this prevailing optimism, into believing that there would be peace, security and plenty of jobs to be had as reconstruction assistance poured in. However, it is also possible that Afghans were coming under pressure, in the form of police harassment and a more hostile political climate, from Pakistan and Iran, such that they felt that their continued presence in their host countries was time limited. There may also have been the usual pattern that exists in immediate post-conflict situations of families seeking to get back quickly in order to secure the limited employment opportunities that exist or to stop others claiming their property.

Whatever the motives, it would appear from studies conducted by the Afghanistan Research and Evaluation Unit, the World Bank and others that returning refugees did not find a land flowing with milk and honey but a situation of continued impoverishment. Thus, although per capita GDP increased from $145 in 2001 to $293 in 2006, the population at large remains at an economic level at which it is highly susceptible to shocks.

This links with the question of how effective the programmes to improve livelihoods have been. While the population at large does not appear to have seen a significant improvement in income, there has been some progress, at least, through the rural development programmes implemented under the National Solidarity Programme and through various additional programmes aimed to strengthen the agriculture sector. However, the expansion of the private sector on which all three of the Afghan Government's development programmes have depended has been extremely slow to materialize.

This has been due, in large part, to the presence of the ongoing insurgency and to the risk that personnel and premises could be targeted. The investment climate is not, therefore, conducive to economic growth. Further, the absence of an effective rule of law, and the corresponding lack of a reliable system for dispute resolution, deters potential investors. The companies that do exist complain that they share an unfair burden of the taxes and that bureaucratic regulations continue to represent a time-consuming and costly, in requiring bribes, constraint on their operations. A key question is whether more private sector organizations in the principal donor countries could have been better encouraged, through risk guarantees provided by their governments, to invest in a rebuilding of the Afghan infrastructure.

The principal success story in terms of international investment is in the telecommunications sector, where Roshan and others have built up a mobile phone network which covers large areas of the country. As a result, communication across the country and internationally is now relatively easy, whether by phone or email.

However, investment in oil, gas and the extraction of minerals is at an early stage in that surveys have been conducted and the legislative framework is now in place. Thus, the US Geological Survey has carried out a thorough study of Afghanistan's gas and oil fields. Further, expressions of interest have been received from some potential investors. The one tangible outcome has been agreement reached between the Afghan Government and the State-owned Chinese company, China Metallurgical Group, to extract Afghanistan's copper deposits at Aynaq, to the south of Kabul. The extraction process is provisionally scheduled to commence in 2013, after work to establish the necessary power and transport infrastructure has been completed.

The proposal, drawn up as early as 1996, to construct a Trans-Afghanistan Pipeline to take gas from Turkmenistan's Dawlatabad gas field to Pakistan and India, has suffered a chequered history, as a result of many variables. At the time of writing, it seems unlikely to come to fruition.

The few attempts to establish factories have suffered from the fact that Afghanistan is not competitive in relation to its neighbours, particularly China, Iran, India and Pakistan, in producing manufactured goods. Further, the policy of the Afghan Government, that no trade barriers should be in place, has left Afghanistan exposed to the effects of external competition. Some firms also report that they have suffered from the absence of a rule of law, resulting in attacks on personnel or premises, or threats of such action.

The safety net programmes set up have not been on a sufficient scale to provide for the population. Labour migration to Pakistan or Iran continues, therefore, to represent the principle safety net for families in difficulties. This is particularly the case in the insurgency-affected areas of southern Afghanistan, where it is difficult for the NGOs operating National Emergency Employment Programme projects, or distributing food aid or other emergency assistance, to operate. However, the continuing pressure imposed on Afghans by the authorities in both Pakistan and Iran is making it increasingly difficult for households to rely on labour migration as a source of income. 2007 saw large-scale deportations from Iran. The situation for Afghans in Pakistan is not significantly better, with enforced camp closures and increased police harassment of unregistered Afghans. The population has therefore faced considerable difficulties in its efforts to survive. The construction boom which has been stimulated by the arrival of the international community in large numbers since 2001, and by the funds in circulation from the growing drugs trade, has provided an important source of short-term employment. It is, however, the pattern that those working on construction sites are only able to secure work on an intermittent, rather than continuing, basis. The annual opium harvest also provides a source of seasonal labour.

However, the inflation in property prices, which has arisen as a consequence of the international presence, the investment by drug barons and the increase in the population, has had a considerable impact on the ability of the population to afford accommodation. This has inevitably squeezed the funds which are available for food. The Afghan economy is, therefore, highly polarized, with a small elite living in relative comfort while the broad mass of the population remain highly impoverished.

One consequence of the return of refugees has been a pronounced urbanization process. Kabul, for example, has seen an increase from less than a million in 2001 to over 4 million in 2007. Other cities have also seen large increases.

Progress in building up the education sector has been significant, with the number of children attending school increasing from a million in 2002 to 6 million in 2007. However, this apparent improvement has to be set against the more limited progress in bringing the quality of the teaching, and of school premises and materials, up to a reasonable standard. Further, there are significant regional differences. The presence of the insurgency in the southern provinces, accompanied by threats against parents who send their children to school, has resulted in a much lower level of attendance than in the north. This process has been accelerated by the murders of some teachers in the wake of threats that they should stop teaching or face the consequences. The proportion of girls who attend school in the southern provinces is, in some areas, less than 10 per cent, as compared with 50 per cent in Kabul and Herat. Arson attacks on schools have also been a problem although efforts to establish local security committees, made up of parents, to protect schools would appear to have been successful: the number of such attacks showed a steady decline over the 2005–6 period, in spite of an overall increase in terrorist activity.

Urban development has been given very much less attention. The Ministry of Urban Development has had almost no capacity, and responsibility for building up the urban infrastructure has largely fallen to the municipalities, with support from UN Habitat, the World Bank and NGOs. Notwithstanding these inputs, the pace of population growth in the urban areas has far outstripped any improvements in drainage, waste disposal or access to water supply or sanitation.

Reconstruction of the main highway system, including the ring road, has been accorded extremely high priority. Iran was the first to take the initiative, in this regard, in rebuilding the road from the border, at Islam Qala, to Herat. This was completed in December 2005. Iran has also undertaken improvements to the road from Herat to the Turkmen border and to many roads within the city. In addition, it has constructed a bridge over the river Helmand to connect Milak, in Iran, to Zaranj, the provincial capital of Afghanistan's Nimroz Province. Other interventions by Iran include the planned construction of a railway line to link iron ore reserves in Herat to an iron ore processing unit in eastern Iran.

The US Government has funded work on the Kabul to Kandahar highway, to lay a new tarmac surface on the stretch that had not already been completed by the Taliban. However, this was built too quickly, in order to meet a deadline of October 2004 set by President Bush, and it had to be substantially resurfaced the following year. At the beginning of 2008, US- and Saudi-funded contractors were still working on the highway from Kandahar to Herat, in the face of considerable difficulties arising from the insurgency and other security-related constraints.

Similar problems are being encountered by the Indian Government, which is seeking to construct a road from Zaranj, on the Iranian border in southwest Afghanistan, to the Kandahar to Herat highway. This would link with a transport corridor on the Iranian side of the border, which leads to the port of Chabahar on the Indian Ocean. India is seeking to use this route from Chabahar to Torghundi, on the Turkmen border, to facilitate its own trade with Afghanistan and the Central Asian Republics. India has no choice but to use this circuitous route while Pakistan refuses to allow Indian goods to transit its territory. The effective blockade imposed by Pakistan currently inhibits exports from India to Afghanistan, which have to travel largely by air.

This road was originally scheduled to have been completed by the end of 2006, but only a quarter had been finished by that time. Attacks on project sites and on personnel have compounded an adverse climate, with extremely high temperatures and a desert terrain, in which dust storms and encroaching dunes impede construction work.

India has gained political ground, relative to Pakistan, through its aid to Afghanistan. This has been helped by the fact that President Karzai studied in India and that the Northern Alliance elements within the Government are deeply suspicious of Pakistan, seeing India and Iran as important counterweights. Indian aid is valued at $650 million and has, in addition to the road project, included reconstruction of the Salma Dam, in Herat Province, and the supply of planes and buses.

The Asian Development Bank has also faced attacks on its project sites, in working on the road from Kandahar to Spin Boldak. However, its efforts to reconstruct the stretch of the ring road from Bala Murghab, in north-west Afghanistan, to Pul-i-Khumri, to the north of the Salang Pass, are proving to be relatively straightforward.

The World Bank has already completed another stretch of the ring road, from Kabul to Pul-i-Khumri, including the Salang Pass, together with an extension to Kunduz, on the northern border. It is now working to extend this further, to reach Faizabad in the northeastern province of Badakshan.

The European Commission funded the successful reconstruction of the highway from Kabul to Jalalabad and this has linked with the road from Jalalabad to the Pakistan border, which Pakistan completed in September 2006.

Through this and other means, Pakistan has aimed to achieve an economic foothold in the country. In so doing, it has been able to build on the fact that the border areas of Afghanistan are closely linked, through trade, to Pakistan and that many make frequent use of the Pakistani rupee as a medium of exchange. There is also smuggling across the border on an enormous scale, benefiting from the Afghan Transit Trade Agreement of 1965, which allows certain goods to transit from Pakistan to Afghanistan duty free. These goods are then smuggled back into Pakistan where they are sold at local Bara markets, benefiting from the absence of duty. Pakistan is also a major source of goods, legally supplied, for the Afghan market and exports very considerably more than it imports from Afghanistan.

Italy is currently funding work to improve the road from Kabul to Bamyan, in central Afghanistan. This is scheduled for completion at the end of 2010.

Progress in building secondary roads is less easy to establish. While there are isolated reports of particular stretches being improved, it is difficult to build up a comprehensive picture. Among the more important sections of road which are scheduled to be improved are the road from Dara-e-Suf to Bamyan and the road from Bamyan to Yakawlang. The Asian Development Bank is funding both of these roads to link the Hazarajat with the wider economy.

In seeking to implement the road-building element of the National Development Framework there was a regrettable conflict between the perceived need to demonstrate fast delivery of results and the desirability of providing employment to as many Afghans as possible. The achievement of the latter objective was rendered more difficult by a severe shortage of personnel with the necessary technical skills within the population. In the event, a significant proportion of the workforce was brought in from Pakistan, India, China, Turkey and Korea. There was also a preference for capital- rather than labour-intensive methods because of the highly insecure operating conditions. However, these strategies to maximize the speed and effectiveness of the process were undermined by shortcomings, on the part of the major US contractors, in supervising the implementation of sub-contracts entered into with other companies for the actual construction work.

The provision of access to electricity is another area in which there is a clear tangible output. Herat has benefited particularly, in that Iran has linked the city up to its own grid and this has been supplemented by additional supplies from Turkmenistan. Iran has actively invested in the economy of western Afghanistan, including the trading and manufacturing sectors, in order to build up a sphere of influence. As a result of this and other economic interventions, the economy of Herat has grown enormously, although it is currently seeing a downturn, precipitated, possibly, by strains within the Iranian economy. It would appear that Iranian investment has helped it gain a political hold in western Afghanistan, not only in Herat but also in the provinces of Farah and Nimroz

Some locations on the Pakistan border have been similarly linked to the Pakistan grid, although on a much smaller scale. Kabul will have to wait until 2009, when a programme initiated by the Asian Development Bank will bring an electricity supply from Tajikistan. In the meantime, the capital has experienced some improvement to its supply as a result of work undertaken to the Sarobi Power Station and other sources. The supply nonetheless remains extremely limited and the population continues to largely rely on generators. Kandahar also has to survive on a limited supply while work to pumps at the Kajaki Dam, to the north, remains constrained by the ongoing insurgency.

In considering security sector reform, the picture is extremely complex and progress highly constrained. The Afghan National Army (ANA) has been a relative success story in that it has proved to be reasonably effective in carrying out military operations, both independently of international forces and with their support. It is, however, recognized that considerably more investment needs to be put into it, both in terms of training and in the provision of equipment, if it is to be able to defend the country in the long term. The USA has recently committed additional funding to this end. The Afghan Minister of Defence has expressed the hope that the ANA would reach its planned complement of 64,000 by the end of 2008. A high attrition rate during the initial period has been partly reversed by improved pay and conditions. However, there is also a reluctance to serve away from home areas, particularly if there are language differences. Dari-speaking soldiers from northern Afghanistan are therefore resistant to operating in the Pashto-speaking areas of the south. Serving soldiers and potential recruits will all be aware of the fact that the army has suffered particularly high casualties in combat against the insurgency in the south.

Work to build up an effective police force has been more problematic in that it has been very much undermined by a long-standing tradition of patronage and corruption. The recruitment of police has tended to be a gift of the local Chief of Police, with the result that a district or provincial police force will be, to all intents and purposes, a fiefdom or militia of the local chief. The function of the police is thus, very often, to provide protection for vested interests, including those linked to the opium trade. Payments to facilitate this protection role are normally made to the Chief of Police or, if the need is smaller in scale, to those lower down the hierarchy. It is said to be common for the Chief of Police to take a cut from the salaries of his men, before these are paid.

The Government has made determined efforts to overcome this tradition by changing Chiefs of Police, but these efforts have often foundered on the fact that Chiefs of Police may have strong political links with the major power holders, including those in the Afghan cabinet. They may also have links with key people in the Ministry of the Interior, and this has made it necessary to make changes to both the personnel and structure of the Ministry.

Further, ousted Chiefs of Police are in a position to undermine the work of their successors or to take revenge in some way. The murder of five staff of Medecins Sans Frontieres in Badghis in June 2004 was thought to be a consequence of the removal of a particular Chief of Police and his wish to demonstrate that he remained a powerful figure.

In seeking to build a professional, centrally accountable, police force in the face of this tradition, the Afghan Government has looked to the international community to provide training on the basis of internationally accepted norms and standards. Germany has thus re-established the Kabul Police Academy as a source of high quality police officers, and the first class of 210 students graduated in August 2005. The USA has supplemented this by providing short courses for the police rank and file, with additional courses offered to build up literacy levels.

However, the skills inculcated are geared to a situation in which police can arrest, charge and take to court those who are suspected of criminal activity. This is not the current situation in Afghanistan, where the judiciary are not adequately trained in legal codes and procedures and tend to make decisions on highly subjective grounds. Further, there is not a comprehensive network of courts across the country, with many having fallen into disrepair.

The police also tend not to be trusted by the population because they are seen to have links with local power holders and militia and will often be the perpetrators of criminal activity themselves. The individual citizen therefore feels unprotected from abuse at the hands of power holders. A climate of impunity thus continues to prevail.

In the rural areas, people will normally look to traditional dispute resolution structures, such as Jirgas or Shuras, rather than the police or the courts, if they want to make a charge against another individual. Those arrested by the police will often seek to settle the matter immediately through a bribe.

Trained police therefore find themselves working on sentry duty, to protect buildings or individuals, rather than pursuing criminals. They do not, therefore, necessarily retain the information that they have learned on their training. Those involved in the training process nonetheless feel that some progress is being made, albeit gradually, but an assessment undertaken by the US Government in 2006 concluded that the police would not be fully capable of operating as a professional body before 2010, at the earliest. The present indications are that this target will be far from being met.

Many police have also been used as a supplementary army, engaged to fight against the insurgency in southern Afghanistan. Considerable numbers have been killed in action. This pattern has been accentuated by the creation of what is termed an Auxiliary Police Force, through which pre-existing tribal militia, known traditionally as Lashkar, have been provided with short training courses, equipped with uniforms and weapons, and paid salaries. Their purpose is to help tribal elders defend themselves against attacks by insurgents but they can also be called upon to participate in offensives by international forces.

Reform of the judiciary has been the responsibility of the Italian Government, alongside the Afghan Government, since 2001. Italy has undertaken useful work in codifying the existing laws and in providing some limited training to judges. However, it has not made any headway in addressing the complex organizational structure that relates to the judicial system. It thus remains unclear where the responsibilities lie as between the Ministry of Justice, the Supreme Court and the office of the Attorney General. The Government has made important changes to the Supreme Court to replace the more conservative elements with those of a more technocratic approach. Some limited work has also been undertaken, largely by the international community, to bring courthouses back into a state of repair.

A further element in the security sector reform process is that of the disarmament of the country's many militia. The Disarmament, Demobilisation and Reintegration (DDR) programme was set up in 2002 and has been successful in removing much of the heavy weaponry held by the militia who were on the payroll of the Ministry of Defence. However, it has proved difficult to reduce, in any sustainable manner, the number of small arms in circulation. Further, the DDR programme did not address the existence of many other militia forces which were not linked to the Ministry of Defence. The Demobilisation of Illegal Armed Groups (DIAG) programme was set up for this purpose, but it was subsequently submitted to a review process because of the limited progress made.

Public Administration Reform has, like the reform of the police, come up against the major obstacle of patronage. Many ministries started as the effective fiefdoms of their ministers and President Karzai has made some progress in addressing this through the appointment of technocrats to ministerial positions. However, the efforts of these can be undermined if those lower down the hierarchy remain linked to the previous leadership and block progress.

The Public Administration Reform process has also favoured some ministries over others. The Ministries of Finance, Interior, Defence, Health and Education, together with the Ministry of Rural Rehabilitation and Development, have received significant inputs from the international community, both in the direct provision of resources and in the deployment of advisers. The Asian

Development Bank has also provided a significant degree of support to capacity-building programmes within the Afghan Government. However, many ministries, as is noted above, continue to remain as almost-empty shells in which a minister and a few assistants seek to determine policy but have no staff to take these policies forward.

The US Government has recently allocated additional funding to support capacity building in other ministries, but it is far from clear that it will be able to overcome the serious obstacles created by patronage, corruption, bureaucratic inertia and the low skill base. Further, as noted above, the severe depletion of Government staff, which goes back to the early purges of the Soviet-backed Government and continued during the periods of the Mujahidin and Taliban Governments, has reduced the professional and other skills base of the civil service to a very low level. This has placed a high premium on the relatively small number of Afghans in the country who have been able to complete higher education courses and who have achieved a reasonable standard in English language and computer studies. As has been previously noted, in order to attract and retain these people, the Government has been compelled to offer higher salaries to key individuals. Chris Johson comments: 'Faced with an impossible gap between government salaries and salaries in the international sector, a number of ministries created what was, in effect, a parallel structure, with a few highly paid staff on special contracts'.[51]

One positive outcome is that the aid community, in providing employment for many thousands of Afghans over more than a decade prior to 2001, has trained up a significant number of skilled personnel. While some of these have been among those who have sought asylum in the West, in response to pressures from the Mujahidin or the Taliban, many are presently supporting the governance-building process. A few have become ministers. Yet they are facing serious obstacles in the form of traditions of patronage, entrenched positions and conservative opinions.

It is difficult to know whether donors could have done better in their efforts to build up the capacity of the Afghan government. Certainly, many governments provided technical experts and governance advisers on a large scale, and they clearly had enormous difficulties making progress because of the low education and skill base of most civil servants, compounded by the fact that the ethos of the civil service was radically different from that of the donor governments. Cross-cultural communication was also an issue. The need to save face would have prevented Afghans admitting weaknesses in the system. The complex dynamics between Afghan societal groups were a key inhibitor. Donor representatives tended to be task-focused and would have been frustrated at the high level of complexity involved. Some would have been arrogant. There were, therefore, no easy solutions but it could be argued that a reallocation of resources from the 'war on terror' to a strengthening of the state might have made progress somewhat faster.

The question of how best to build up a civil service that has effectively collapsed and which is undermined by corruption is, of course, not limited to Afghanistan, and yet there seem to be no clear solutions.

However, progress in building up the state infrastructure was also undermined by the fact that the USA was very much the dominant player in orchestrating outcomes in Afghanistan. Other donors felt that they were at the margins of the planning and decision-making processes. Communication between these other players was not helped by the decision at the Bonn meeting to give each donor nation responsibility for a specific area of work.

The situation was also not helped by the fact that, while each of these countries sought to take forward their respective programmes, the USA would, at times, take unilateral action which pulled the rug from under their feet. Thus, Japan's efforts to promote DDR were undermined by deals which the US government would strike with various power holders in pursuit of its strategic interests.

To conclude, there has been progress on many fronts, but it could have been very much greater if there had been a level of investment which was more commensurate with Afghanistan's needs. The relative absence of coherence within the donor community, with the USA tending to take unilateral action and other donors introducing systems which were not consistent with those of its partner donors, made a task which was already difficult almost impossible. This problem has been particularly prevalent with police training and judicial reform, compounding the serious obstacles to progress within the Afghan Government. The construction of a network of roads will, hopefully, strengthen the economy, but maintenance of these roads will present a serious problem. The planned arrival of electricity to Kabul during 2009 may also provide a boost to growth but, as has become apparent in Herat, the Afghan economy will not be immune to economic changes in the wider region and globally. Telecommunications continues to represent the major success story.

9

THE INTERFACE BETWEEN NGOs AND THE INTERNATIONAL MILITARY

In considering this question, it may be first useful to reflect on the nature of humanitarianism. The origins of humanitarianism lie in the creation of the Red Cross in 1863. The initiative came from a Swiss businessman, Henry Dunant, who was concerned that men, on both sides, were left to die due to lack of care after the Battle of Solferino in 1859. He proposed that national Red Cross Societies should be set up through which volunteers could be trained, in peacetime, to provide neutral and impartial help to relieve suffering in times of war. He also proposed that an international agreement should be drawn up, through which the status of medical services and the wounded would be recognized on the battlefield. This agreement, known as the Geneva Convention, was adopted in 1864.

The Geneva Conventions and their Additional Protocols protect people who do not take part in the fighting (civilians, medics, aid workers) and those who can no longer fight (the wounded or sick and prisoners of war). These legal provisions are part of International Humanitarian Law, a system of legal safeguards which govern the ways that wars may be fought and the promote the protection of individuals. They call for measures to be taken to prevent (or put an end to) acts that are known as 'grave breaches'; those responsible for breaches are to be punished. More than 190 states have signed up to the Conventions.

The International Committee of the Red Cross (ICRC), in its Mission Statement, asserts that it is 'an impartial, neutral and independent organization whose exclusively humanitarian mission is to protect the lives and dignity of victims of war and internal violence and to provide them with assistance'.

The principles of humanity, independence and impartiality codified in International Humanitarian Law are defined as follows in the Code of Conduct of the International Red Cross Movement and Non-Governmental Organisations in Disaster Relief (1994):

The primacy of the humanitarian imperative

The right to receive humanitarian assistance, and to offer it, is a fundamental humanitarian principle which should be enjoyed by all citizens of all countries.

The independence of humanitarian aid

Humanitarian aid is not a partisan or political act and should not be viewed as such. Aid will not be used to further a particular political or religious standpoint. Humanitarian NGOs (NGHAs) shall endeavour not to act as instruments of government foreign policy. NGHAs are agencies which act independently from governments.

Providing aid impartially

Aid is given regardless of the race, creed or nationality of the recipient and without adverse distinction of any kind. Aid priorities are calculated on the basis of need alone.

The applicability of these principles to Afghanistan has differed at each stage of the conflict since 1978. Thus, during the period of the Soviet military occupation, NGOs had a choice as to whether to work on both sides of the conflict or operate primarily in support of one of the parties. Many opted to work in solidarity with the Mujahidin while others sought to work on the basis of neutrality and impartiality to deliver basic services within the refugee camps, while accepting that these camps were bases for the Mujahidin insurgency.

However, NGOs did seek to work in conformity with humanitarian principles following the departure of Soviet troops in February

1989, although compromises were made to ensure continued access to beneficiary populations during the periods of the Mujahidin and Taliban Governments.

It may be useful now to reflect on how the NGO community operated prior to 2002.

As the anticipated withdrawal of Soviet troops approached, the aid community, building on the prevailing political view that the Soviet-backed government would collapse immediately thereafter, planned for the expected return of 6 million refugees to Pakistan and Iran. This was based on the reasonable assumption that the refugees would regard the departure of this secular government as justifying an end to the jihad which had led them to go into exile.

In response, the UN set up a new coordinating body in Geneva, with a sub office in Islamabad, known as the United Nations Office for the Coordination of Humanitarian and Economic Assistance Programmes Relating to Afghanistan. This sought to coordinate the responses of all the UN agencies to the anticipated return. These included the World Food Programme, UNHCR, Food and Agriculture Organisation (FAO), UNICEF, the World Health Organisation (WHO), UN Office for Project Services (UNOPS) and UN Habitat.

A huge logistical operation was established, based on the expectation that the refugees would return en masse and would need tents, plastic sheeting, food aid and medical care to sustain them over the initial period while they rebuilt their houses and got the land working again.

In the event, the Soviet-backed Government did not collapse and the resources set aside to support a mass return of refugees were left to be used more gradually, in support of programmes aimed both at those who had left and those who had remained behind.

At this stage, NGOs and the UN were expected to link with the various ministries of the Afghan Interim Government, based in Peshawar. There were, therefore, some interesting power dynamics in operation. The USA and Pakistan were pulling the strings of the Afghan Interim Government behind the scenes, including a strengthening of the AIG bureaucracy by US organizations, in particular. The AIG was, notionally, the point of reference for the UN but lacked the capacity to implement services inside Afghanistan.

The UN, therefore, took upon itself the role of overseeing the provision of direct services to the population and thus operated as a parallel government. Some useful work was done in, for example, drawing up health standards, with the World Health Organisation playing a key role.

However, the UN lacked the capacity to implement its policies and therefore relied on NGOs. International NGOs were the major implementers of services on the ground in the refugee camps but only to a limited degree inside Afghanistan. These had regard to the policies of the UN but drew up their own independent policies and programmes, based on their awareness of the situation in both the camps and inside Afghanistan. They tended to have much better understanding than the UN of local conditions in Afghanistan, a knowledge base which increased as they gained greater programme experience in Afghanistan.

The NGOs thus enjoyed considerable scope to respond to the situation, as they saw appropriate, and therefore possessed the power and flexibility to make a difference. They were not required to have regard to the development plans or policies of the Soviet-backed Government, or to act under the supervision of that government. Further, the Peshawar-based Afghan Interim Government (AIG) was regarded as having limited accountability to the Afghan population. Thus, while adherence to common health and education standards drawn up by the AIG was seen as important, NGOs operating to improve the rural infrastructure were not constrained by having to work in accordance with particular policy directives.

They also benefited from the fact that donors were willing to leave them free to determine the best use of resources, subject to reasonable narrative plans and reports. There was therefore a pragmatic, flexible approach by donor aid ministries, which had only limited representation in Islamabad and no presence in Kabul. Further, aid budgets were much smaller than they were to become during the post-2001 period. This made donors more willing to take risks.

NGOs had to recognize, nonetheless, that any funding which they received from the US Government was linked with political support for the Mujahidin. The USA regarded NGOs funded by it as de facto contractors, which were obliged to fully implement US Government policy. This contrasted with the European tradition of funding for NGOs, through which European donor governments respected the wish of organizations supported by them to maintain a high degree of independence. European benefactors, at this stage, were also more inclined, than the USA, to take a purely humanitarian view of the refugee situation in Pakistan and of needs in Afghanistan. The provision of funding for education, for example, was seen as an end in itself, based on the accepted universal need for education, rather than a means to another end, such as promoting particular values through the curriculum drawn up by the University of Nebraska at Omaha.

One of the early lessons learned by NGOs operating in this highly fragmented power-holding environment was that, in allocating resources, they were potentially strengthening the power bases and credibility of the commanders in whose areas of control they were working. They therefore needed to spend time, before embarking on projects, to inform themselves on local power dynamics. To do this, they needed to engage with community-based structures, whether Jirgas in the Pushtun areas or Shuras elsewhere. Such engagement was also of benefit in ensuring that the resources available were used as effectively as possible and with regard to local priorities. They also had to build relationships with local commanders and continually monitor shifting power relationships.

To access Afghanistan to the extent that they did, and reach the intended beneficiaries, NGOs needed to negotiate with multiple power holders en route. It was, therefore, common to provide resources to those whose territory they had to pass through.

They would thus negotiate access to beneficiary communities with those wielding power through the gun at the local level. They would also seek to establish, in advance, whether any local hostilities had broken out or, due to particular tensions, were at risk of breaking out. If there were local tensions, they would negotiate safe passage with the belligerents.

NGOs also relied on beneficiary communities to accord them protection. They were normally willing to do this because there were no other providers of aid in the vicinity, and NGOs were able to work for sufficiently long periods to build up relationships of trust with community representatives.

A further lesson was that the injection of resources on a large scale over a short period could have a potentially destabilizing effect. This lesson was learned very early on during the period after the Soviet withdrawal, when two large NGOs put considerable resources into the same valley in one of the eastern provinces. A consequence, arising from the limited knowledge that the NGOs held of local power dynamics, was that the resources benefited certain power holders more than others. A shift in the local balance of power, combined with jealousies and suspicions, produced open conflict in an area where the various factions had previously co-existed, albeit with underlying tensions. The NGO staff also found themselves physically threatened. As a result, the NGOs concerned had to withdraw, having barely started their programmes.

In response to this risk, there was a growing consensus that that it was important not to allocate too much aid at any one time. This led to a view that a long-term approach to programming should be taken, in which in-depth discussions with targeted communities would be followed by a phased programme of work over, say, a three-year period.

There was also a widely held view that NGOs and targeted communities should operate on the basis of what could be described as a business relationship, in which both the aid organization and the beneficiary community injected resources. For the most part, this involved the provision of free labour by communities.

However, in seeking to take forward such an approach, NGOs were constrained by the fact that much of the funding provided by donors for Afghanistan came from humanitarian aid budgets. These had six-month funding cycles, which were geared to the expectation held before the Soviet withdrawal that NGOs would be engaged in emergency programmes in support of refugee return.

UNOCHA, at this time, was struggling to find ways of accessing rural communities and to increase its implementation capacity. It was aware of the capacity of the existing NGO network but felt that this was not enough, nor did it wish to rely on the NGOs then operating to implement its programmes. It saw many of these as being resistant to any direct contractual relationships with the UN, instead preferring to adopt and act out their own policies. UNOCHA therefore encouraged the formation of new Afghan NGOs, to supplement the few that were then in existence. It hoped, perhaps naively, that this would result in rural communities in Afghanistan forming their own NGOs and implementing projects for their own benefit. In fact, most of the Afghan NGOs that were formed in response to the UN invitation were the creation of individual Afghan engineers, doctors and other professionals who saw an opportunity to receive relatively generous grants in return for a willingness to act as implementing partners of UN organizations.

This initiative by the UN had very negative consequences, for the most part, in that, apart from the dozen or so Afghan NGOs that had built up operational experience in the camps, the new and artificially-created members of the Afghan NGO community had no real track record in managing projects. This, in turn, made it particularly difficult for UN agencies, such as the World Food Programme, UNHCR and UN Office for Project Services, to ensure that the quality of outputs was of a sufficient standard. UN staff were also constrained, in accessing project sites, by the difficult security environment and had to impose increasingly stringent contractual requirements to provide a degree of leverage over the management of projects. These were largely focused on repairs to irrigation systems and flood protection structures, together with improvements to secondary roads through the construction of drainage systems such as culverts.

Regrettably, the quality of many of the funded projects was highly variable and was often very poor. This has created an abiding image of NGOs as, in many cases, providing very little of value and also as creating an opportunity for enterprising individuals to strengthen their own financial positions. The more established NGOs, which have been in a position to provide high quality work, have thus been tainted by association with what are often referred to as business-orientated NGOs, by virtue of the fact that they have operated from one short-term UN contract to another.

On the other hand, the Food and Agriculture Organisation (FAO) was particularly successful in distributing improved wheat seed, developed by the Swedish Committee for Afghanistan, in some of the border provinces, using Afghan NGOs.

During this period, a number of international NGOs decided to embark on a process of 'Afghanizing' their operations so as to create new, Afghan, NGOs out of the parent organizations. This resulted, for example, in the emergence of the Afghan Development Association out of the Salvation Army programme. They were supported in this by a few other NGOs, such as Norwegian Church Aid and the International Rescue Committee, which took on a capacity-building role to help Afghan NGOs build their organizational competence and skill base. However, these latter NGOs worked primarily with the Afghan NGOs that emerged out of international NGOs. Very few of the Afghan NGOs which came into being as a consequence of the UN initiative were seen as having the organizational ethos to justify a capacity-building process.

The Afghanization process also included an objective to minimize the expatriate presence within international NGOs so as to develop the capacity of Afghan staff. All expatriate staff had to be justified. This policy was particularly effective so that, by the end of the 1990s, the average international NGO was down to two or three expatriates. The senior management positions were therefore held by Afghans, and it was primarily Afghans who attended inter-agency meetings.

The level of power wielded by the UN and NGOs in Afghanistan was dictated by the resources at their disposal. They certainly operated as a parallel government in the sense that the actual Afghan Government was largely disregarded and policies and plans for the delivery of education, health care, water supply, veterinary care and agricultural support were drawn up in Islamabad or Peshawar. However, it might be more accurate to describe the function of the aid community at that time as a collective local authority in that it did not seek to cover governmental functions such as foreign policy, defence or security.

The UN and NGOs nonetheless remained minor players because, although UNOCHA benefited from a significant injection of funds at the end of 1988, the totality of their contribution to the Afghan economy was relatively small. Further, while the services that the UN and NGOs were providing in the camps were clearly crucial in ensuring that people had access to food, water, sanitation, education, health care, income-generation and vocational training, their impact on the ability of households, living in Afghanistan, to survive, was marginal. Those living in the urban areas benefited, to a degree, from the subsidies provided by the Soviet-backed Government on basic essentials such as wheat, flour or bread. The population of the rural areas also drew some benefit from these subsidies to the extent that they had opted to move into the cities, as those from the Panjshir Valley did, or had relatives in the cities who could provide them with resources. Others had links with relatives in Pakistan.

The aid community, in providing basic services in the camps, also made it possible for refugees in Pakistan to send some family members to Afghanistan for temporary periods to get their land working again, now that it was no longer being bombed by Soviet forces. Soviet bombing raids reduced in scale as the date of the 1989 withdrawal of Soviet forces approached. Many families had therefore been able to re-cultivate their land before 1989.

The resources available to the aid community were also infinitesimal in comparison to those provided by the Soviet Union to the PDPA Government, in the form of military supplies, advisers and financial contributions to the government's budget.

It would be interesting to reflect on whether, if the international community had been willing to inject large-scale resources into Afghanistan at that time, in support of a reconstruction process, the UN and NGOs would have enjoyed a significant degree of power. However, under such an eventuality, donors might have exercised greater control over aid policy and over project implementation. The degree of power and flexibility that NGOs enjoyed was, therefore, a consequence of their relative insignificance.

The potential power of NGOs was also constrained by the fact that they were continuing to deliver programmes in refugee camps in which the Mujahidin parties operated recruitment bases for the ongoing insurgency against the Soviet-backed Government in Afghanistan. These parties were in receipt of aid, in the form of arms supplies and other resources, from some elements of the donor community and this was on a much larger scale than the assistance allocated to the UN, ICRC and NGOs. The resources given to the Mujahidin parties were further enhanced by support from Pakistan's Inter-Services Intelligence as well as from Saudi Arabia. Substantial aid programmes were operated by Saudi and other Islamic NGOs at this stage. This was partly linked to political imperatives, although Islamic concepts of charity also played a major role.

Western NGOs were therefore caught up in a web of complex political dynamics of which they were often scarcely aware.

Certainly, a collective decision by NGOs to allocate resources to one refugee camp rather than another had political implications, in that individual Mujahidin parties had a dominant, or exclusive, presence in particular refugee camps. NGOs could not maintain a position of total neutrality, therefore, even though decisions were taken on humanitarian grounds with regard to the delivery of services to the population. Similarly, the World Food Programme, UNHCR and the Pakistan Government would have to take account of the networks operated by the Mujahidin parties in the camps, in distributing food and other assistance, even though they might make every effort to minimize the influence of these parties over the distribution process.

NGOs operating schools in the camps would also have been aware of the primary schools and, in some cases, secondary schools and universities, which were continuing to be operated by the Mujahidin parties and by the Afghan Interim Government. They would equally have been aware of the madrasahs organized by a multiplicity of Mujahidin parties, Islamic NGOs and Pakistan-based radical Islamic parties. Recruitment to these drew on the large number of orphans and on families for whom the material assistance provided by the madrasahs substantially helped to alleviate conditions of poverty.

Western NGOs also had to be mindful of the climate of fear generated by the more radical of the parties and so avoid operating programmes which these parties might regard as unacceptable. Programmes targeted specifically at women were particularly vulnerable unless these were clearly earmarked for widows and so were deserving of support under Islamic strictures. NGOs which were rumoured to be inculcating Western or liberal values came under particular scrutiny and many received threats, including death threats. The NGO, Shelter Now International, had all its premises burned to the ground in Nasirbagh camp when a Mullah preached that the organisation was seeking to convert women to Christianity. The environment was therefore highly politicized.

Thus, while the UN and NGOs had considerable scope to develop their programmes, with only limited regard to policies set by donors or the Afghan Interim Government, they remained very small players on the Afghan scene. A key exception was the World Food Programme, which was distributing significant quantities of wheat to some areas.

The period of the Mujahidin Government of 1992–6 was a relatively positive period for the delivery of aid. Although Kabul was difficult to access until 1995, it did prove possible for the UN and NGOs to undertake some effective, and often innovative, work in the capital over the period from then up until the Taliban takeover. This included the delivery of health care, education, water supply and sanitation. The ability of the municipality and some government ministries, notably the Ministry of Public Health, to still function made it possible for NGOs to link with the Government and work in accordance with policy guidelines, where these existed. UN Habitat worked hard to build up the capacity of the Kabul Municipality to provide waste disposal services and to help the Kabul Water Supply Authority to repair damaged infrastructure. Oxfam took on the ambitious project of working to restore the pumping system, but renewed insecurity slowed progress considerably. The aid community was also able to deliver relief supplies to ease the blockade of Kabul as the Taliban bombarded it with rockets over the winter of 1995–6.

NGOs thus worked with the state authorities to the extent that they could help build the capacity of key ministries and municipalities providing health care, education, water supply and sanitation facilities. In so doing, the aid community was operating within a policy context in which it was recognized that, in what were termed failed states or poorly performing countries, the UN, the International Committee of the Red Cross (ICRC) and NGOs were largely substituting for an absence of state capacity. In light of this, there was a consensus that it was important to help build what remained of the capacity of the Afghan State so as to enable it to deliver essential services to the population. Thus, for example, ICRC provided medicines to the health service, and the NGO, Healthnet International, provided training in Leishmaniasis control to government health service personnel. This policy was adhered to even when the British Government decided that it would not fund projects which, in any way, helped strengthen the Taliban Government. However, this capacity-building process was not regarded as a legitimization of the state. This was very much left to the diplomatic sphere, although the international community at large was not willing to accord recognition to either the Mujahidin Government or the Taliban Government.

Elsewhere in the country, the growing concentration of power under some relatively large fiefdoms created the opportunity for the UN and NGOs to establish programmes in new areas such as Herat, where health care, education, water supply, sanitation and agricultural support services were provided from 1993 onwards. They were also able to gain regular access to their beneficiaries in areas which had hitherto been insecure. The eastern provinces proved to be particularly easy to work in.

Herat offered considerable potential and this was further facilitated by Iran making it possible, although not always easy, for NGOs to enter western Afghanistan through its border. This followed an initiative in the summer of 1992 by the Iranian Government and UNHCR for NGOs to work in Iran, in support of Afghan refugees, and from Iran on reconstruction programmes in Afghanistan.

North-eastern Afghanistan, under Jamiat-e-Islami, was also readily accessible. However, the northern provinces, around Mazar-e Sharif, saw ongoing instability as a consequence of tensions between Dostam, Jamiat-e-Islami and Hisb-e-Wahdat. The delivery of aid, in consequence, was often truncated and remained relatively small in scale.

It is important to stress, in relation to the ease of access, that NGO staff should ideally be physically located on site if they are to deliver effective programmes. This is often achieved through the recruitment of local staff but these may need to be supported and overseen by technical and managerial personnel. The ability of the latter to regularly visit project locations, for the purpose of monitoring and evaluating progress, is often crucial to the effectiveness of programmes. However, the frequency of this access is constrained by considerations of cost and security. During the period of the Mujahidin government, when access might need to be negotiated with a multiplicity of power holders en route to the final destination, the complexities involved were the major constraint, while cost and security were certainly also significant factors. Over this period, the Afghan staff of NGOs were much less at risk than expatriates.

Although the previous fragmentation of power into small-scale, highly fluid and constantly shifting power-holding entities was now replaced by a consolidation into large, more stable blocs, it was still necessary to check out the security situation for the route in advance of any travel and to negotiate with the various power holders. It therefore remained important for NGOs to continue to present themselves as neutral and impartial. The professionalization process which had started in 1989 was now well advanced, and NGOs had a broader spread of staff, many of whom had no political links and were simply technocrats. Further, Afghans were far more in evidence at the managerial level and many international NGOs had only one or two expatriates.

The UN and NGOs, working with donors such as the European Commission, therefore had considerable scope to be creative in how they worked at this stage. This was possible because, with the brief exception of the 1995–6 period, there was still no government in Afghanistan setting a policy framework. The aid community was, therefore, the de facto government and local authority. While the absence of a governmental planning and policy-making process was, in some respects, problematic, it did make it possible to achieve a great deal with relatively small resources.

In part, this was the case because there were few enough organizations to make effective communication possible. This can be contrasted with the post-2001 period when there were simply too many actors on the scene. The fact that most NGOs operated from a particular locality of Peshawar and could attend coordination meetings within five minutes of their offices was an important plus. The Afghanization process which had started in 1990 now meant that a majority of NGO representatives at such meetings were Afghan managers who had a good knowledge of the areas in which they were working and were able to make reasonable judgements. Poaching of senior Afghans by other organizations was already in evidence, but it was not on anywhere near the scale that was evident after 2001. Further, the targeting of intellectuals for assassination, which had been a key element of the situation in 1990–1, was no longer a serious problem. Afghans working for NGOs could, therefore, operate in relative security and were not, as yet, coming under the pressures that they faced under the Taliban, which led many to leave for the West from 1998 onwards. They tended, therefore, to stay with their organizations for some time and provided important historical memory. Again, this can be contrasted with the fast turnover of staff which characterizes the post-2001 period.

The arrival of the Taliban also made it possible for NGOs to operate in Kandahar and the southern provinces on a reasonable scale for the first time. This enabled NGOs to, for example, embark on long-term community development projects in what had hitherto been inaccessible rural areas. The period from 1995 onwards saw an expansion of rural development programmes in the south on quite a large scale, often with funding from the European Commission. As a result of this growth in rural development over the 1992–8 period, when a serious drought hit the country, agricultural production saw a significant growth.

Although NGOs had to operate in accordance with the restrictions enforced by the Taliban, the security that the Taliban provided made access very much easier. Further, the Taliban were responsive to overtures by the World Health Organisation and NGOs operating in Kandahar that they should permit access to women and girls for the provision of health care, in spite of an initial ruling that this should not be allowed. This revised policy remained in place throughout their period in power, albeit with minor temporary setbacks in some areas. However, it did not prove possible for NGOs to negotiate successfully for women to have access to employment, and discussions over female access to education and training were only partially successful, resulting in agreements by some Taliban representatives, in some areas for certain periods, to permit education for girls at the local level and to allow the employment of female health workers, for example. This depended, in part, on how rigid individual representatives were during their tours of duty. It would thus happen that one Taliban Governor would be relatively relaxed about the existence of girls schools while his successor would be more hard line. The situation was also influenced by the degree of interest that local communities had in education for girls, their level of determination to insist on its continuation, and their negotiating power with the Taliban Governor.

It is important to stress, in this regard, that the role of NGOs, in resourcing and supporting the development of schools across the country throughout the periods of the Mujahidin and Taliban Governments, was crucial. NGOs, such as the Swedish Committee for Afghanistan, lent ongoing support to thousands of schools across the country. Teacher training courses were organized. UNICEF helped with school supplies. Thus, as refugees gradually returned, particularly after 1992, education was available to their children along with health care, access to clean water and agricultural support.

NGOs operating in Herat faced particular problems with the Taliban in relation to female education and employment. Not only did this mean that existing programmes had to be closed or significantly cut back, but it also seriously constrained discussion with the authorities. Thus, the regular meetings which agencies had held with Ismail Khan to discuss aid programming were replaced by an almost complete lack of interest on the part of the Taliban. This included a refusal to meet female aid workers, even those in charge of programmes. This was partly a reflection of the personalities involved within the local administration. While the Taliban in Kandahar had been willing to engage in dialogue with humanitarian agencies, the key figures in Herat had a much narrower vision. They had little understanding of what NGOs were and were disinclined to find out. NGOs also found themselves subjected to restrictions with regard to the dress and mobility of their staff. Women had to cover their heads and wear the traditional salwar kameez. They were also not allowed to drive. NGOs were aware of heightened tension in the city and of a climate of fear. Taliban searches of houses and offices, in their efforts to disarm the population, resulted in some brutality and professionals and others with liberal views felt at risk, as they had done under the PDPA Government.

The power of the UN and NGOs increased during this period in that they had much greater access to the country and greater resources at their disposal to deliver services. They also retained the power that they had developed during the 1989–92 period to determine their own priorities, methods of working and policies, albeit within guidelines and policies set by the UN and under the umbrella of the principal NGO coordinating body, the Agency Coordinating Body for Afghan Relief (ACBAR). Their ability to engage in long-term community development programming enormously increased their effectiveness. This meant that, for the first time in over a decade, the population of many areas was in receipt of quality services relating to health care, education, water supply, sanitation and agricultural support. While the scale of this could have been much greater, what was delivered made a difference.

Thus, the UN and NGOs went from being relatively small players on the Afghan scene, caught in a complex web of multiple power dynamics in which the USA, the Soviet Union, Pakistan, Iran, Saudi Arabia and others were embroiled, to being in a position to operate reasonably large programmes in significant areas of the country and to do so without feeling that they were party to some larger agenda. At the same time, they had to engage with local power holders and take account of their potential to impact on local power dynamics.

The donor community was helpful in providing relatively consistent funding from year to year and also in demonstrating flexibility between budget lines. This made it possible to use humanitarian and emergency budget lines for long-term work on areas such as health, education and rural development. It also made it relatively easy for agencies to plan some years ahead and to achieve a reasonable level of cash flow.

Following the Bonn Agreement of December 2001, NGOs found themselves caught up in a state-building process in which the USA was the dominant player. This inevitably meant that their image of neutrality and impartiality, which they had built up when there had been multiple power holders, was potentially under threat. However, given that, over the periods of the Mujahidin and Taliban governments, they had been working to build the limited capacity of the State bureaucracy to deliver, for example, health care, water supply and sanitation services, it would have been inconsistent for them to cease this when the post-Bonn government came into being. Further, a number of the key Afghan managers of NGOs during the pre-Bonn period now became ministers. There was, therefore, a wish to support these despite the feelings of disquiet arising from an association with the USA. In addition, the National Development Framework envisaged a clear role for NGOs, along with private sector organizations, to deliver services to the population under contract to the Afghan Government. NGOs, therefore, had to adjust to the fact that an internationally-recognized government was now in being and that they needed to work in accordance with government plans and through government structures.

Given the significant role that NGOs were already playing in the delivery of high-priority programmes, there was a strong case, at the beginning of 2002, for the Afghan Government to engage in discussions with NGOs as to how they might best support a process of transition. Through such talks, the Government would have hopefully identified the extent to which it saw a continued role for NGOs and, where it did not, to agree on a phased process through which responsibility for the delivery of basic services to the population was gradually transferred.

However, although the National Development Framework envisaged that the government would contract out services to the private sector and NGOs, the Afghan Government saw NGOs as competitors for donor resources at a time when its own budget was extremely low. It is understandable that they drew this conclusion in that it was certainly the case that NGOs, collectively, benefited from significantly more resources after the Bonn Agreement than they had before, albeit for a relatively short period.

Much criticism has been made of NGOs in relation to the rush of international personnel and organisations into Kabul in the immediate aftermath of the Bonn Agreement. This is partly justified because the intervention coincided with and aggravated a period of serious drought. There was also significant media coverage of the fact that aid agencies were unable to access affected communities while US military operations were ongoing. This meant that a considerable number of NGOs were able to raise money on the back of drought appeals. This included the well-established NGOs, but it also brought new kids onto the block who had no experience of Afghanistan. Thus, the number of NGOs which were registered with the Ministry of Planning had increased from 250 in 1999 (of which 46 were international) to 1,005 (350 international) by November 2002.[52]

The NGOs that had been working in Afghanistan for many years were therefore in a situation where there were numerous new agencies which lacked the historical knowledge of how the aid community had operated. Many of them were therefore unaware of the community-based approach to programming which had underpinned much of the work of NGOs in the rural areas since the early 1990s. Their failure to respect the long-term relationships that NGOs had built with communities therefore had the effect of undermining the trust on which effective programming depended. The collective image of NGOs was further tarnished by an absence of cultural sensitivity on the part of a proportion of the new NGOs, together with a failure to appreciate the extreme conservatism of much of Afghan society, particularly in the rural areas. This insensitivity was, to a degree, reinforced by the over-optimistic image that the international community presented of the situation in Afghanistan after the US-led intervention. There was, therefore, a view that the Afghan population were pleased to have been 'liberated' and that it was not necessary to overcome their suspicions through painstaking negotiations. This, in turn, led to an impatience to deliver results which, by ignoring the need to first engage in in-depth discussions with potential beneficiaries, led to a sacrificing of quality in favour of quantity.

An expansion in the number of business-orientated Afghan NGOs also bred cynicism, with many Afghans knowing of individuals who had done well out of short-term contracts with the UN or the donor community.

The Government therefore had some grounds for criticizing the NGO sector, but there was also a tendency by ministers to scapegoat NGOs to divert attention from the inability of the Government to deliver services to the population during the early months. The consequent negative publicity put NGO staff at risk.

The British Government and the European Commission responded to Afghan Government representations on this question and took strong policy positions in favour of directing as much funding as possible through the Government. As a result, funding for NGOs, from these two major sources, was significantly cut back. This meant that long-standing NGO programmes ceased to be funded before the government had built up its own capacity to replace those programmes.

The availability of funding for NGO programmes was also influenced, from 2006 onwards, by the fact that many donors were contributing to either the US-led coalition forces or to the International Security Assistance Force (ISAF) and tended to allocate their reconstruction assistance to the areas where their forces were concentrated. Thus, the UK earmarked a major part of its assistance to Helmand, where British forces had responsibility for security as part of ISAF. Germany was similarly focused on the northern province of Kunduz, in the allocation of reconstruction support, because it was operating a Provincial Reconstruction Team there, under the ISAF umbrella. New Zealand prioritized the central province of Bamyan for the same reason. USAID allocated more than half its aid to four southern provinces where the counter-insurgency and counter-terrorism operations of US-led coalition forces were concentrated.

The NGO community was therefore already facing some major adjustments, both external and internal, when a new threat emerged in the form of military involvement in the delivery of assistance to the population.

It is standard practice in counter-insurgency operations for the military to seek to provide benefits to the immediate population. This has three primary purposes: first, to detach the population from the insurgents; second, to protect the forces engaged in the operations from hostile attack by the surrounding population, referred to as 'force protection'; third, to gain intelligence on the movements of the insurgents. In order to achieve these objectives, the military engage in what are called 'hearts and minds' operations.

In Afghanistan, the benefits provided have tended to take the form of the construction of schools, the digging of wells, the provision of medical care by the army medics, and the distribution of items such as pens, sweets and hats to children. In addition, a few larger reconstruction projects have been undertaken, such as the construction of local dams.

These 'hearts and minds' operations were initially structured through civil-military entities known as Joint Regional Teams, through which US civilians would oversee the administration of projects in support of military operations. At the end of 2002, the name was changed to Provincial Reconstruction Teams (PRTs), but the purpose did not change.

The US Army received significant funds from the Pentagon for such operations. Some of this was spent on projects such as those outlined above, which were normally contracted out to Afghan NGOs or private sector contractors. Others were disbursed through cash handouts to the population. It is not known whether local power holders were also beneficiaries of such handouts. The allocation of Pentagon funds is not transparent. In terms of outputs, the projects initiated by the US military made little impact on the reconstruction needs of the population. However, in terms of funds disbursed, they represented a sizeable amount.

Whether they won over the hearts and minds of the population is open to doubt. The projects only had limited value to the population, and these were offset by the major disincentives, already referred to, to cooperate with the international military.

NGOs were immediately concerned, when the US-led coalition forces started delivering aid, that this would blur the boundary between the operations of the aid community and that of the international military. This was particularly the case as many of the projects, such as school and well construction, were identical to projects which NGOs had carried out for many years. The image of neutrality and impartiality which NGOs had worked so hard to maintain over the preceding nine years was therefore irrevocably changed by their perceived association with US-led military operations and with a US-led state-building process.

This image was also very much undermined by the fact that it suited the US military to say that NGOs were on board. The US military would thus state that their primary purpose was to create secure zones so that NGOs could operate. To this end, they stated, they would make assessments of need and seek to coordinate inputs by NGOs. International Security Assistance Force (ISAF) spokespersons would also say this on occasion. In so doing, they sought to create a positive image of international forces coming in to create an environment in which reconstruction activity could take place. NGOs objected to the international military assessing needs, noting that they were already operating in the areas where the military planned to undertake assessments, and asserted that, if they were to enter areas as an actual or apparent consequence of assessments by the military, they would be associated with the military and thus lose their reputation for neutrality and impartiality. However, a limited number of NGOs did agree to operate as contractors of the US military. These included what have been referred to above as business-orientated Afghan NGOs.

In the meantime, it was presented as reasonable for the international military to deliver aid to areas that were, in the immediate term, too dangerous for NGOs to operate in. This was in spite of the fact that the international military would often set up projects where NGOs were already operating. They would, thereby, render these too dangerous for continued operations by NGOs.

However, it was not only the population of Afghanistan that the US military sought to impress. It was also important to be able to say to the US taxpayer that US soldiers were making it possible for aid to be delivered. This image was further enhanced by film footage of the US military delivering relief supplies by helicopter to areas affected by natural disasters such as flooding.

A further benefit of the image that the international military were seeking to promote, that they were creating the conditions for NGOs to provide for the population, was that this helped with the morale of international forces. It was very important for individual soldiers to be feeling that they were 'doing good', particularly as they were facing considerable obstacles in their military operations and were suffering heavy casualties. Similarly, the families of soldiers who died or were seriously injured needed to feel that it was for a good cause. It was easier to argue the case for reconstruction activity than the more nebulous objective of reducing the global terrorist threat, particularly when progress in the latter was far from evident.

NGOs therefore found themselves the unwitting agents of a public relations campaign targeted at the Afghan population, US taxpayers, international forces and the families of international forces.

Thus, when, from the middle of 2002 onwards, NGOs protested to the US military that their involvement in the delivery of aid was blurring the boundary between military and humanitarian operations, the US-led coalition forces listened but did nothing to change their practice.

NGO concerns were clearly put in a publication produced by Save the Children in 2004, under the title of 'Provincial Reconstruction Teams and Humanitarian-Military Relations in Afghanistan'. This study aimed to identify the progress that had been made, through negotiations with US-led coalition forces and NATO/ ISAF contributors, in order to persuade operators of Provincial Reconstruction Teams (PRTs) to focus exclusively on security and avoid actions which undermined NGO programmes.

Some progress was made, at least at the doctrinal level. ISAF, with the assistance of NGOs, produced a PRT handbook for forces serving under its umbrella. This outlined the humanitarian principles of NGOs, the history of their involvement in Afghanistan and the importance of long-term community-based approaches for their programming. It also stressed the need for NGOs to maintain their independence from international military forces when it stated that 'to preserve NGO principles of neutrality, impartiality and independence and retain access to populations in need, many NGOs will limit their interactions with PRTs'. The counter-insurgency manual of the US military[53] also stated that:

> Joint doctrine defines a non-governmental organization as a private, self-governing, not for profit organization dedicated to alleviating human suffering... Some NGOs maintain strict independence from governments and belligerents and do not want to be seen directly associating with military forces. Gaining the support of and coordinating operations with these NGOs can be difficult. Establishing basic awareness of these groups and their activities may be the most commanders can achieve. NGOs play important roles in resolving insurgencies, however. Many NGOs arrive before military forces and remain afterwards. They can support lasting stability. To the greatest extent possible, commanders try to complement and not override their capabilities. Building a complementary, trust-based relationship is vital.

British NGOs were also influential in a decision by the British-led Provincial Reconstruction Teams in Mazar-e Sharif and Helmand to fund projects geared to an improvement in the security situation.

But, in spite of this, statements continued to be made by representatives of the US military and ISAF, and by politicians from countries contributing forces, that the purpose of operations was to create an environment in which NGOs could work.

NGOs therefore had to plan on the basis that no differentiation was made by the insurgents, or by many within the population, between all the elements of the international presence, or the Afghans associated with that presence. NGOs had no special standing, in spite of their historical involvement in Afghanistan. This made it necessary for them to take certain measures to protect their staff. Primary among these was a strict control on the movement of staff in order to decrease the risk of exposure. No expatriate staff were kept in high risk areas. The areas of operations were also reduced. NGOs needed to allocate more resources to the maintenance of security and to be ever alert to risks to their programmes and staff. International staff were kept to a minimum although Afghan staff were very often equally at risk. This resulted in reduced access to programme areas, which inevitably led to a reduction in the effectiveness of projects. It was also difficult to comply with donor monitoring and evaluation requirements. In areas where expatriates would be clearly at risk and Afghan staff were also vulnerable, the latter would wear traditional dress and travel in ordinary cars or taxis rather than the highly visible agency vehicles. In some areas, only Afghans who were part of the local population would be employed and representatives of beneficiaries would be asked to travel with them to accord them greater security. Projects were delayed if the security situation deteriorated. Expatriates travelled by air between cities rather than overland.

The association with US-led military operations and with a US-led state-building process led NGO staff, both Afghan and expatriate, to be directly targeted as part of the insurgency. Thus, 24 NGO staff were killed in 2004. This increased to 31 in 2005[54] before falling slightly to 26 in 2006.[55] This contrasts markedly with the very small number, perhaps less than ten, who lost their lives in Afghanistan between 1989 and 2001.

The ability of NGOs to rely on the good will of the population to accord them a degree of protection was also reduced. This was due to a combination of factors. The deteriorating security situation made it more difficult to visit project areas and so nurture the long-term relationships which were crucial to the maintenance of trust. Further, NGOs were no longer the only providers of resources and, as their income from donor governments declined, the resources that they were able to offer were increasingly insignificant. The negative scapegoating of NGOs by the Afghan Government further dented the image of NGOs in the public eye.

It is difficult to be absolutely clear that the large number of murders of NGO staff since 2003 has been a consequence of the blurring of boundaries. However, these have mostly occurred in areas where international forces have been engaged in counter-insurgency operations. Further, beneficiary communities are reported, anecdotally, to have urged NGOs not to send international personnel to their villages lest it led to reprisals from the Taliban. NGOs have also found that they are losing their Afghan staff because their families are worried that the perceived association with the international military will put them at risk.

It is also of interest to note the comment, in May 2007, of the Deputy Director of the Voluntary Association for the Rehabilitation of Afghanistan (VARA), an Afghan NGO which has operated in southern Afghanistan for very many years. He thus noted that, when NATO forces monitored projects which they had contracted VARA to undertake, 'they come with tanks, with weapons, and this affects our staff badly'. He added that his agency had, in consequence, steadily reduced the scope of its programme over the previous two years so that it only operated in provincial capitals in the south. He noted that it had become impossible to deliver aid in outlying districts and that eight of his staff had been killed. He also noted that the Taliban had arrested his agency's engineers and taken their vehicles.[56]

As a consequence of the growing insurgency and of the operations of international military forces that this has provoked, NGOs have been compelled, by the insecurity of the operating environment, to suspend or close programmes in large areas of the south. This has left a vacuum which the international military have filled by contracting out to private companies, both Afghan and international, and to a few NGOs that have been willing to work for them. The situation in southern Afghanistan is therefore not dissimilar to Iraq, where the US Government has contracted out to US firms to undertake both large-scale infrastructure projects and to also work in areas traditionally carried out by NGOs such as water supply, health care and education.

The insecurity that has been generated by the pursuit of the 'war on terror' has, therefore, very clearly excluded the possibility of large-scale reconstruction assistance to the population, such as to seriously impact on their livelihoods.

The post-2001 period has also placed Afghanistan on the global stage so that developments, such that the US-led intervention in Iraq of March 2003, have had a ripple effect on Afghanistan.

This was well put in the International Committee of the Red

Cross Strategy for 2007–10, which noted that 'in recent years, the ICRC has been confronted with and has responded to a growing variety of crisis situations'. It adds that these include 'the emergence, following the 11 September attacks, of a confrontation of global dimensions that is being played out not only in Afghanistan, Iraq and other parts of the Middle East but also in Africa and Asia'. It goes on to say that 'the terrorist activity that has been one of the features of this confrontation, and measures taken to counter such activity, often have tragic consequences for the civilian population'. It also notes that 'when planning and conducting its operations and public communication, it must take into account the degree to which local, regional and global issues increasingly overlap'. It further states that 'problems of access to the field are a key challenge for humanitarian work', adding: 'An increasingly polarized world – or one that is perceived as such – and the fragmentation of non-State armed groups have tended to exacerbate these problems. Furthermore, humanitarian access is sometimes used for political or military ends. This can undermine the legitimacy of humanitarian action by calling into question its strictly humanitarian, neutral and independent character.'

A particularly stark example of this occurred in March 2003 when an ICRC member of staff, Ricardo Munguia, was shot dead as he returned to his base from a visit to a project in the southern Afghan province of Uruzgan. Prior to the murder, his killer had rung an associate to seek guidance as to what he should do with the foreigner that he had apprehended. He was advised to shoot him even though the killer had, according to some reports, benefited from an artificial leg provided by ICRC. There was, therefore, a total disregard for Ricardo Munguia as a person, and for the neutrality, impartiality and independence of ICRC. Mr Munguia simply had symbolic importance as a Westerner and as an aid worker, and this was seen to justify his execution.

ICRC also notes that, 'in recent years, humanitarian law has repeatedly been flouted and called into question' and adds that 'this has been illustrated in the high profile debates concerning people detained in connection with the "post 9/11" confrontation in facilities such as Abu Ghraib'. The objectification that was apparent in the murder of Ricardo Munguia is, therefore, also in evidence in detention centres operated by the international military.

ICRC similarly notes that global and regional issues impact on the local situation so that aid workers can be targeted in Afghanistan, as happened when a mob attacked an NGO office in eastern Afghanistan in February 2006, over developments such as the publication of cartoons in a Danish newspaper which were deemed to be offensive to Islam. This raises the question as to whether humanitarian agencies are in a position to negotiate humanitarian space when they are operating in a global political context.

The ODI paper, 'Humanitarian engagement with non-State armed actors: the parameters of negotiated armed access' comments that 'conflicts such as those in Afghanistan and Iraq are saturated with third states' strategic interests, politicizing the context and compromising humanitarian access conditions'. In noting that that the hard-line approach taken by some radical groups effectively precludes a process of negotiation, it adds: 'While it can be argued that violence inflicted by extremist groups in Iraq and Afghanistan is politically motivated, the deliberate targeting of humanitarian staff negates any potential positive outcome from engaging with this type of ANSA [Armed Non-State Actor].'

Afghanistan provides an unusual context in that many NGOs are actually working directly under contract to the Afghan Government, primarily to undertake rural development programmes and to implement the Government's Basic Package of Health Care Programme. In so doing, NGOs are clearly aligning themselves with the state-building process.

NGOs also have to take account of the fact that international actors in Afghanistan are taking very different approaches. The ODI paper, 'Humanitarian action and the "war on terror": a review of issues', notes: 'While the US broadly favours military options, the Europeans prefer the soft power technologies of human security: diplomacy, disarmament, social reconstruction, aid, poverty reduction and information and education programmes.' It comments that 'neither hard nor soft power seem to work particularly well'. It further reflects that 'aid transfers may buy the loyalty of States but not necessarily of their people'. In this context, NGOs are clearly within the 'soft power' domain.

This same paper provides a useful summation of the situation faced by humanitarian agencies at the present juncture:

> The challenge facing Western organizations is not only how to position themselves in relation to someone else's war or another society's culture but also how to do so in relation to their own. In navigating this fraught environment, it will be important to distinguish between the legitimacy and even legality of the multiple struggles being waged, the means by which they are being fought and their impact on civilians. In other words, humanitarianism will need to be clear precisely which of the many ethical and legal dilemmas are humanitarian in nature and which are not. In doing so, the traditional humanitarian principles of universality, impartiality and neutrality may prove to be just as valuable as before. Sustaining their perceived value within and outside of the humanitarian community will depend on achieving consensus that instrumentalising humanitarian action is likely to prove counter-productive and ineffective... It is notable that very few humanitarian organizations, either within the NGO community or the UN, have developed formal policy statements regarding their positions on the 'war on terror'. There remains, therefore, a need to invest in such a dialogue, in which the distinctiveness of the humanitarian agenda is asserted and its relationship with the political, military and developmental forms of international engagement clarified. Ensuring that the principles of humanitarian action are, and are perceived to be, truly universal in their aspiration and practice will be crucial.

10

CONCLUSIONS

In drawing comparisons between the British military interventions of the nineteenth century, that of the Soviet Union in December 1979 and the US military intervention of October 2001, one can identify many parallels as well as significant and subtle differences.

In so doing, it is also useful to reflect on the situation in Afghanistan as it was between these interventions, while recognizing that the period of Taliban conquests could also be regarded, according to some perspectives, as a military intervention.

Similarly, it is important to consider the specific role of humanitarian aid in relation to the provision of aid in pursuit of strategic interests.

Because of the enormous complexities of the issues involved, it may be easier to consider all these questions through a variety of lenses.

Legitimacy of the interventions

The British justified their interventions in the light of their assumed right to pursue their imperial ambitions. There was no attempt to disguise this as something else or to seek international sanction.

The Soviet Union, in contrast, sought to justify its intervention to the international community as an act of self-defence against the actions of 'imperialists', but it blocked any consideration of its legitimacy by the UN Security Council. However, the intervention was denounced by large sections of the international community and the arguments used by the Soviet Union, by way of justification, were regarded as simply masking a naked act of aggression.

In the case of the Taliban intervention, this was presented as a moral crusade, aimed to create an Islamic state, based on Shari'a Law, in which specific dress and behavioural norms would be strictly observed. The Taliban also declared that they sought to bring security to a country which had been brought to a state of chaos by the in-fighting of the Mujahidin. Their intervention was felt to be legitimate, on the terms in which they presented it, in the areas of southern Afghanistan which had suffered particularly from the internecine fighting of the Mujahidin. But in the north of the country, it was regarded as an invasion by a Pushtun force, in which elements within Pakistan had a strong role, of areas in which Tajiks, Uzbeks, Hazaras and Turkomans were the majority.

The USA also presented its intervention as a moral crusade in that it sought to overthrow a regime whose values it expressly criticized and to establish, in its place, a democratically-elected government. However, in seeking to legitimize it, it drew on Article 51 of the United Nations Charter, as the Soviet Union has also done, but identified the perpetrators of 'terror', globally, as the enemy against which it was seeking to defend itself.

Thus, while the insurgency engaged in by the Mujahidin against the Soviet forces was said to be backed by the 'imperialists', the insurgency operated by the Taliban was stated to be the product of a nebulous network of radical Islamic organizations operating world-wide.

Unlike the Soviet Union, the USA was able to secure international backing for its intervention through a vote of the UN Security Council. In so doing, it benefited enormously from the wave of international sympathy arising from the terrorist attacks on the World Trade Centre of 11 September. It was also able to build on legitimate concerns over the presence of training camps in Afghanistan, from which radical elements could provide military skills and encourage the use of terrorism against the USA and governments associated with the USA. In addition, it could exercise significant leverage within the UN, by virtue of its economic, military and political supremacy on the global stage, to ensure that it secured the necessary mandate.

Thus, while both the Soviet Union and the USA were acting on the basis of their own national strategic interests, the former was widely condemned while the latter achieved widespread support. It has to be said, however, that the Soviet Union sought to justify the intervention after the event, whereas the USA took steps to secure international support before it went in. Further, the Soviet Union, like the British, sent in a huge army, which took control of key strategic positions in order to establish its hold. In contrast, the USA made maximum use of air power and combined this with deals that its Special Forces made with Mujahidin forces on the ground, that these would engage in simultaneous offensives. The number of US troops with boots on the ground was therefore extremely small. The use of a limited US force was a consequence of a view taken, in the light of the Soviet experience, that a large force would generate significant popular resistance. It was, therefore, hoped that, by minimizing the visible international military presence and relying as much as possible on Afghan militia to drive out the Taliban, such resistance could be avoided.

In addition, the USA sought to legitimate their choice for the position of President through a process in which the international community, at the Bonn Conference, sanctioned his appointment as Interim President and this was subsequently ratified through nationwide elections. This contrasted with the Soviet intervention in which their nominee, as President, was installed by force, with the previous President being simultaneously killed under mysterious circumstances. The British had also brought their own nominee, for the position of Amir, to power on the back of their military intervention of 1839.

However, the Soviet Union did also seek to establish legitimacy for the Afghan government that it was supporting through Loya Jirgas and other consultative mechanisms, the key difference being that this was subsequent to Babrak Karmal's assumption of power rather than, as in the case of the US intervention, prior to Hamid Karzai taking on the role of Interim President.

It is important to stress, in this regard, that, in spite of the apparent legitimacy accorded to its intervention by the UN, the perception in the public mind in Afghanistan has been that the USA intervened in pursuit of its own interests.

The promotion of alternative value systems

During their interventions of the nineteenth century, the British did not actively set out to change the value systems of the Afghans although they may have hoped that, through limited efforts to improve the process of governance, they might achieve some shift in attitudes. It was Amir Amanullah, in the 1920s, who first made a significant effort to confront some of the more conservative attitudes with regard to the situation of women and girls. Daoud, when Prime Minister in 1953–63, repeated these efforts and took them further. However, he was careful to move cautiously.

Some of the Mujahidin parties, notably Hisb-e-Islami, also sought to transform society with a view to the creation of an Islamic state. This involved active steps to influence opinion through the organization of schools in the refugee camps, at primary, secondary and tertiary level. It also involved an ongoing process of recruitment in the camps.

Hisb-e-Islami may, in addition, have been among those groups or organizations who used intimidation, the threat of violence and, on occasion, actual violence against prominent liberals, intellectuals and those working for women's projects and organizations. By creating an intense climate of fear, particularly in Peshawar during the early 1990s, they brought about significant changes in behaviour and created a more conservative environment.

The PDPA were even more intolerant of dissent, to the point where they instituted purges, of fellow socialists of more moderate perspectives, within the Parcham faction of the party. Intellectuals, liberals and professionals outside the party were also targeted. The PDPA Government was, in addition, also impatient and insensitive, and often brutal, in its efforts to impose reforms relating to literacy, land reform and marriage on the population. The intelligence service became a powerful organ of the state during its rule and benefited from considerable support from the Soviet Union to this end. However, early efforts to create visible symbols of socialism, such as the widespread use of red paint and the use of a new flag, were soon replaced by references to Islam. The regime nonetheless continued to be associated with a foreign ideology and to be seen to have used force and brutality in seeking to promote this ideology.

The Mujahidin Government was too involved in in-fighting to have the capacity to promote its perspectives within the population. However, the political environment remained a conservative one. It was the Taliban who built on this conservative environment to enforce dress and behavioural codes on the population and to also ban female access to education and employment, while, at the same time, restricting their access to health care. They used force to this end, through the patrols of the Department for the Promotion of Virtue and the Prevention of Vice, and created a climate of fear in which intellectuals and professionals were intimidated into compliance. Large numbers went into exile under the pressure of these threats. The UN and NGOs suffered a loss of many of their key staff as a result.

The US-led intervention brought, with it, certain perspectives on the management of the economy. The National Development Framework, drawn up in the spring of 2002, included a strong emphasis on the creation of a framework within which the private sector could flourish. The arrival of the international community, en masse, also brought to Kabul a set of behavioural norms and attitudes which were at variance with the prevailing conservatism. These were, to an extent, reinforced through a mushrooming of TV, radio and print media outlets, which the international community actively supported. The availability of easy access to the internet, as a consequence of early investment by telecommunications companies, exposed the population to global thinking, drawing both on perspectives within the West and on those within the Islamic world. It also brought an exposure to pornography.

The Mujahidin parties, which played a prominent role within the government of President Karzai, expressed vociferous concerns over the influence of Western attitudes and used the power which they had in the parliament to actively challenge the media on some of the content of its programming. The growing power of the Taliban in the south of the country also influenced the overall political environment; President Karzai took steps to give greater weight to religious and conservative opinion in his efforts to erode their support base. Women felt intimidated into continuing to dress and behave in a conservative manner, even though they were now able to access employment and girls were able to attend school.

The international personnel living in Kabul took account of this environment in conditioning their own behaviour. However, the superficial liberalism that their presence manifested created the ever-present risk of a backlash from conservative elements. Thus, while the international community took a more subtle approach to the process of seeking to influence attitudes and values, than did the PDPA or the Taliban, its very presence was seen, by many, as an affront to traditional and Islamic sensibilities. The fact that the international community was also associated with a US-led state-building process, and thereby with the intervention in Iraq, activity in Guantanamo Bay and the behaviour of international forces, served to compound this.

In the cases of both the Soviet and US interventions, there has, therefore, been a wish to impose a societal vision, whether socialism, with loyalty to the ideal as the central element, or democracy, with an associated emphasis on personal freedom. In both cases, there was an injection of substantial resources into the media and the allocation of specialist advisers to this end. In the case of the US intervention, there was also a very significant investment in the electoral process. In both cases, also, the intervening powers were seeking to impose value systems which were at variance with those prevailing in the rural areas, in particular, but also in the cities.

During the period of Soviet occupation, the perceived affront to Islamic values was a key factor in the resistance. This was regarded as a primary reason for the exodus of refugees to Pakistan and Iran, on the grounds that Afghanistan had been invaded by a secular force. It thus provided a vehicle for the resistance through the declaration of a jihad. This made it possible to attract volunteers from other parts of the Islamic world and so sow the seeds for training facilities to be established in Afghanistan in support of radical causes elsewhere.

However, it could be argued that the role of Islam as a galvanizing force has been even greater during the post-2001 period. Thus, while the Soviet intervention created the conditions for a radicalization process, the US-led intervention in Iraq justified a global jihad against the US military presence in Afghanistan.

The influence of colonial attitudes

In considering the very interesting extract from the memorandum of the British official referred to in Chapter 2, particular patterns were evident which could be seen to denote what could tentatively be referred to as colonial attitudes.

First, there is an assumption on the part of the colonizing power that it has an absolute right to do what it wants with the country in which it is intervening militarily. This includes a further assumption that its own interests prevail over the interests of the population. In fact, the latter's interests are not even taken into account except in a manipulative sense – in that an assessment will be made as to how they can be persuaded to be compliant with the intervention. These attitudes inevitably lead the population to feel used, even violated. This creates a profound sense of humiliation which will often lead the individual to feel an overwhelming need to assert his or her own dignity. This need for dignity can be extremely powerful and, more likely than not, will prevail over any susceptibility to the 'gold' or other material benefits that may be offered.

Second, there is a tendency to objectify the population so that it takes on an image which is quite at variance with the reality. Thus, instead of engaging with the population to listen, learn, understand and show respect, the intervening power initially assumes that the population can be easily manipulated. However, as affronts to local sensibilities begin to result in a resort to violence, the intervening power comes to regard the population as containing 'terrorists' or 'fanatics'. The fear that this violence creates therefore reinforces stereotypes that other cultures are 'uncivilised' or 'barbaric'. This same fear also produces a tendency to behave in what is clearly a barbaric fashion towards the population through a resort to extreme violence, brutality and cruelty. This, in response, leads the population to also objectify the intervening power, to the point where they feel that any form of violence is justified. A cycle of violence thus ensues in which each side resorts to ever-greater brutality and cruelty. Further, the brutality of the intervening power increasingly mobilizes the population against them, so that those organizing acts of violence can retreat into the population and draw support. There is, therefore, a radicalization process in which hard-liners come to positions of leadership, thus justifying, to the intervening power, the importance of its intervention – to root out 'terrorism', restore order, combat 'fanaticism', and so on. This radicalization process increasingly permeates the population so that a critical mass of opposition is built up to the point where the intervening power no longer has the resources, or the political climate, to hold its dominant position.

Third, the objectification of the population as 'uncivilised' can generate a view that the intervening power has a duty to 'civilise' it. This can lead to an emphasis on education, which automatically includes the values of the intervening power. In providing education or other assumed benefits, the intervening power can then convince itself that it is bringing some benefit to the population. This is not only seen to justify the intervention, but it helps maintain the morale of the footsoldiers of the intervening power in that they can be made to feel that they are 'doing good'.

This combination of attitudes was very much in evidence during the British intervention in Afghanistan, with the possible exception of the provision of education, which was not a priority. In the case of the Soviet Union, there was already a recognition, at the time of the intervention, that the population needed to be appeased. However, once the Soviet forces had arrived, en masse, the objectification process seems to have prevailed. This was evident in the determination shown to crush the resistance, by depriving the population of its livelihood, and also by denying the resistance fighters the means to find shelter and food. At the same time, there were limited efforts to persuade the population of the benefits of socialism, through propaganda, while making simultaneous references to Islam. The Soviet Union had therefore already accepted that the population was resistant to its value systems. It was the PDPA which had assumed the right to impose these, rather than the Soviet Union.

In the case of the US-led intervention, in contrast, there was a very evident view that the intervening power had the right to impose its values on the population, particularly with regard to the situation of women. However, this was modified by perspectives within the wider international community which were more anchored in the realities of Afghan society. There was, nonetheless, an assumption that it was important to give priority to the creation of a democratic process, to the establishment of a 'free' media in which Western values might be disseminated and to a process of public administration reform. Similarly, there was a clear view that the government should aim to be 'lean and mean' and create an environment in which the private sector could flourish. This contrasted with the centralization model adopted by the PDPA in 1978–9.

In all three cases, there was a tendency for the leading representative of the intervening power to act as an effective viceroy. This was certainly the case with General Roberts in 1879, as it was with the Soviet Ambassador over the 1978–92 period, and as it has been with the US Ambassador since 2001.

Also evident is a tendency to objectify the population so that all Afghans are regarded as suspects when international forces are conducting house searches. There have been many reports of US forces failing to engage effectively with the population, with the result that they are said to feel considerable fear of their adversaries. This has manifested itself in episodes in which US troops, in particular, have simply 'lost it' and fired indiscriminately into crowds in the wake of terrorist attacks, or traffic accidents, in which they felt in an exposed position.

This pattern has been less in evidence amongst the troops of some of the other countries contributing to international forces in Afghanistan. A greater emphasis on engagement with the population in the training that soldiers receive in countries such as the UK, Canada or the Netherlands has served to reduce the propensity to objectify the population and, thereby, the intensity of the fear that is felt.

However, there has been an overwhelming view within the international community that it is 'doing good', by creating a democratic process and by seeking to build up the infrastructure of the Afghan state. This is seen to justify the US-led intervention. There is, therefore, a tendency to ignore or downplay the impact of the wider strategic interests of the USA on the situation and the human rights abuses committed in Guantanamo Bay, Bagram, Kandahar or other bases. These are seen as secondary to the fact that the international presence is seen, at one and the same time, as bringing benefits to Afghanistan and combatting terrorism, in order to 'make the world a safer place'.

There was also a view, during the early period after the US-led intervention, that Afghanistan had been 'liberated' from Taliban oppression. European governments that were keen to return their Afghan refugee populations thus appeared to delude themselves that they had created an environment to which refugees could safely return. This was in spite of clear indications that the law and order situation was far from conducive to a return of those who faced a high risk of violence from one or other power holder.

This focus on the need to return Afghan refugees as quickly as possible also led European governments to disregard the importance of labour migration, ignoring the fact that a high proportion of households in Afghanistan are dependent on their ability to send one or two sons to Pakistan or Iran to look for work. The large scale return of refugees, in the spring and summer of 2002, was thus presented as an indicator of the success of the Bonn Agreement, rather than a development of great concern in relation to the impact on the Afghan economy and on the ability of a fragile state infrastructure to cope.

The colonial attitudes demonstrated by the USA also influenced their approach to NGOs. Thus, NGOs, in seeking to engage with the population, were seen to be taking a soft approach to the population: in the eyes of the USA, it was important to show military muscle and, where appropriate, buy support from the population with the odd school or clinic.

The influence of traditional and religious values

The defence of traditional and Islamic values has been a central element in all the interventions, including that of the Taliban. Thus, Britain, the Soviet Union and the USA were seen to be bringing alien value systems with them, which threatened to undermine, weaken and potentially replace those of Islam and of Afghan rural society.

At the same time, Islam provided a rallying call for an anti-imperialist response to each intervention. It thus provided cohesion to an otherwise fragmented society, to enable confrontation of the invader.

In focusing on Islam as the element which binds the opponents of imperialism, it has been possible, in all three interventions by the major powers, to make claim to Islamic solidarity and, in the case of the Soviet and US interventions, also draw support from other Muslims outside Afghanistan. The Soviet intervention thus brought about the arrival of large numbers of volunteers from other parts of the Islamic world to fight alongside the Mujahidin. Many of these volunteers stayed behind to lend their support to the efforts of the Taliban to establish an Islamic state. Their presence in Afghanistan also provided an opportunity to build a network of radicals from across the world who were committed to the use of violence against governments that they perceived as corrupt, oppressive or over-associated with the West. The movement possessed, therefore, a strong anti-imperialist character, but it was nonetheless focused on the overthrow of specific governments within the Islamic world. Major issues of concern, such as the Israeli treatment of Palestinians and US support for Israel, strengthened the shared sense of injustice and lent solidarity to the movement. Following the US-led intervention in Afghanistan, the ability of the Taliban to build a new support base, both in Afghanistan and globally, was greatly enhanced by the additional US-led intervention in Iraq, in March 2003. The reference, by President Bush in 2001, to a 'crusade' against the Islamic world, although not repeated, has brought further cohesion to the movement.

In defending traditional and Islamic values, the resistance movements have also been able to mobilize support over perceived affronts to the honour of women. Thus, during the post-2001 period, the practice, by US soldiers, of bursting into houses and searching women's quarters has caused huge offence. Further, Western dress codes are deemed to be morally unacceptable, and the failure by some Western women to adopt a more conservative form of dress, akin to the looser clothing worn by women in Afghanistan, has helped fuel stereotypes of the West as 'decadent'.

In seeking to draw on Islam to create cohesion in response to perceived acts of imperialist aggression, the resistance movements, in relation to the Soviet and US-led interventions, at least, have sought to eradicate all traces of Western influence. In so doing, they have opted for what may be regarded as a puritanical position. This has manifested itself in restrictions on female access to employment and education, in particular, and in the enforcement of conservative dress codes. The strong emphasis on female honour has made it difficult for women to work alongside men or for girls to be educated alongside boys. Music, singing and dancing have also been greatly restricted.

Both the Mujahidin parties and the Taliban have, to varying degrees, behaved in a repressive manner in their efforts to enforce compliance with their decrees and with their advocated norms. This has created a climate of fear in which liberals and professionals have found themselves targeted.

The defence of Islam in the face of foreign interventions has also been seen to justify acts of violence, sometimes of a horrific nature. It is arguable that the extremity of this violence is a response, albeit excessive, to extreme violence perpetrated by the intervening power.

The significance of education

Education has been a sensitive issue for much of the past hundred years. It has been so because proposals to change it have often been within the context of exposure to foreign value systems, and because they have tended to provoke a backlash from tribal and religious leaders. Thus, Amir Amanullah took an initiative, in the late 1920s, to open a school for girls in Kabul, but he did this immediately following a tour of European capitals. The fact that this, combined with the simultaneous appearance of his wife and other women of the elite without the veil, brought about a resort to arms by tribal and religious leaders and his fall from power certainly influenced his successors to take a cautious approach. Thus when Muhammed Daoud, as Prime Minister, set out to remove the requirement for women to wear the veil and to also significantly increase the provision of education, he was careful to proceed at a modest pace, to draw support from a range of both Westen and Islamic countries and to ensure that the national army was strong enough to stand up against any opposition.

The question of education for girls has inevitably raised questions over the potential role of women outside the home. It has provoked defensive reactions from men, concerned to protect the honour of women within their families and also ensure that the traditional roles of women within the domestic sphere continues to be performed. It has also generated fears that the important role of women, as the primary vehicles for passing traditional and Islamic values from one generation to another, will be undermined if they are exposed to external and, particularly, non-Islamic values.

However, the 1950–78 period did see a rapid expansion in education provision and also in the tentative entry of women into the workforce in what are, globally, regarded as the more stereotypical roles of teachers, nurses, receptionists, administrators and air hostesses. It was also increasingly common for women to appear unveiled, in Kabul, at least, and, to a lesser extent, in other cities. It should, nonetheless, be noted that the number of children in school during the pre-1978 period was less than it is now. Having said that, the quality of education provided at that time may have been greater in that the good security conditions that then existed would have been conducive to the provision of uninterrupted teaching and of teacher training.

The PDPA coup of 1978 clearly involved a determination to change the education curriculum, so as to inculcate socialist values, and to do so quickly. The outreach programme which was embarked upon to bring greater literacy to the rural areas provoked strong reactions, not only because elders were humiliated in the process but also because the methods used were insensitive, were often brutal and immediately came to be associated with a foreign ideology, that of the Soviet Union.

The resistance movement therefore represented a defence against these efforts to impose a foreign ideology so that, when UN agencies and NGOs sought to operate schools in the refugee camps, they had to take on board the policies and attitudes of the Mujahidin parties, in determining the curriculum and in how they structured the classes. Girls and boys had to be segregated, for example. Some of the Mujahidin parties, notably Hisb-e-Islami, set up their own primary, secondary and tertiary education establishments. In addition, madrasahs emerged in increasing numbers, some linked to the Mujahidin parties, others to radical Islamic parties within Pakistan and yet others to Saudi NGOs and those of other Gulf states.

From these madrasahs emerged the Taliban, who were totally opposed to female education. However, it did prove possible for NGOs to negotiate the continued provision of education for girls with local Taliban representatives over certain periods.

It is important to stress, in this regard, that the role of NGOs in resourcing and supporting the development of schools across the country throughout the periods of the Mujahidin and Taliban Governments was crucial. However, the curriculum that was used was drawn up by the University of Omaha at Nebraska, in conjunction with the Afghan Interim Government, and caused some discomfort amongst NGOs because of its content, including a use of militaristic images.

With the emergence of the post-2001 Government, and its strong backing from the USA, education has again become a very high profile issue, particularly education for girls. The number of children in school, both boys and girls, is relatively high but progress has been slowed by a serious shortage of skilled teachers. Further, the propaganda value of education in justifying the US-led military intervention and in presenting the outcome as a success, partly to justify the return of Afghan refugees, has not been reflected in the level of investment. Education has also become a sensitive issue with the Taliban and other radical elements, which have burned down schools, intimidated teachers and parents, and murdered education personnel. Education has thus been seen as a vehicle for inculcating Western values into the population, and the involvement of the international military in the construction of schools, both for force protection and propaganda purposes, has resulted in many of these being burned down or otherwise destroyed.

Force versus engagement

The standard counter-insurgency doctrine involves a combination of force and efforts to win the support of the population, in the hope of weakening the support base of the insurgents. It is of interest, when considering the interventions of each of the three powers, to look at what proportion of effort was spent on the use of force compared with effort to engage with the population.

In the case of the British interventions, there was a prior assumption that the rulers and populations could be bought with gold or subsidies. In the case of the rulers, there was also a calculation as to how else they might be persuaded, failing an interest in material gain. Such considerations normally envisaged the use of threats, based on Britain's superior military capacity and on its ability to erode the ruler's support base by negotiating with tribes who were opposed to him. There was no real consideration given to the possibility of engaging with the population in order to listen, understand and show respect. In fact, the arrogance of the British contingent during the 1839–42 intervention and the consequent failure to pick up on signals as to how the population was responding to their presence, including affronts to cultural and Islamic sensibilities, was a major factor in their catastrophic retreat. Further, the use of brutality, as exemplified by the treatment of prisoners by Shah Shuja, Britain's protégé, was an important factor in alienating the population. It is also significant that Shah Shuja was returned to power by the British and could clearly be regarded as a 'puppet'.

The Soviet intervention differed from those of the British in that the PDPA regime of 1978–9, although sympathetic to Moscow, had emerged independently, albeit with a degree of support from the Soviet Union. Further, this regime had already opted for a maximum use of force in order to put down the resistance and had also demonstrated brutality in seeking to impose its reform programme on the rural population. The urban population had also been seriously alienated by the purges which the PDPA had carried out of moderate socialists within its own party, together with intellectuals, liberals and professionals within the wider society. The Soviet Union therefore found itself in a situation, prior to its military intervention, in which it was seeking to persuade the PDPA regime to reduce the use of force and to also reduce the scale of the purges of opponents. At the same time, it was proposing that the Government should seek to engage with elements within the rural society who might be persuaded to cooperate with the Government or, at least, maintain a position of independence from both sides. It also proposed that the Government should replace the visible symbols of socialism with references to Islam.

However, when the Soviet Union intervened and brought in a relatively moderate member of the PDPA to serve, effectively, as a 'puppet' under Soviet control, it then resorted to considerable brutality by laying waste whole valleys and driving out their populations. It was only during the rule of President Najibullah, from 1986 onwards, that any real attempt was made to engage with the population. The earlier efforts made by Babrak Karmal had no chance of succeeding in the immediate aftermath of the brutality of his predecessors, whereas Najibullah had a greater degree of success. However, this was never more than partial because he was always associated with a foreign presence even after the Soviet troops had left.

The US-led intervention also involved the maximum use of force, but it was international forces who were solely associated with the brutality that followed. The Karzai Government, although regarded as a 'puppet' of the USA, always maintained its distance from the excesses of international forces; President Karzai even criticized them at times. At the same time, it was the Government which sought to engage with both the population, at large, and with the insurgents. For the majority of the international forces which were in Afghanistan in 2002–5, their efforts to engage with the population were largely geared to the standard 'hearts and minds' approach relating to force protection and the gaining of intelligence. There was no real effort to listen, learn and understand. The assumption was therefore made that the population would be persuadable through material benefits. In making this assumption, the international forces failed to take into account the importance of Islam, of pan-Islamic sentiments and of human dignity in the face of the humiliation suffered in the searches of homes. As with the British interventions of the nineteenth century, cultural arrogance, combined with insensitive behaviour, led to perceived affronts to traditional and Islamic sensibilities and alienated the population. However, the brutality associated with searches and with air raids, with their consequent civilian casualties, was also an important component in the alienation. With the handover from the US-led coalition forces to the International Security Assistance Force in 2006, there was an attempt to engage more actively with the population but, as had happened with the Soviet intervention, the damage done, during the preceding years, to the image of the regime and its international backers, had been too great to easily reverse.

Human rights

All the interventions, including that of the Taliban, have involved human rights abuses, particularly if economic and social rights are included in the definition. All have involved the use of force against populations, and the number of deaths and injuries has been very considerable.

In considering the differences between the interventions, the use of force in order to punish populations was a particular characteristic of the British interventions. Thus, the murders of large numbers of civilians in response to the massacre of the retreating British contingent in 1842, and the hanging of suspects by General Roberts in 1879, were clearly punitive in nature.

With the Soviet intervention, it is important to differentiate their actions from those of the PDPA regime. The PDPA Government tortured and killed many thousands of fellow socialists, intellectuals, liberals and professionals in their purges and, although the Soviet Union encouraged the PDPA Government to significantly reduce the scale of its purges, the Soviet Union was party to the abuses perpetrated by financing, supporting and training the intelligence service, KHAD. The PDPA also demonstrated considerable ruthlessness in, for example, putting down the Herat rebellion and in the massacre of young men that it carried out in Kunar. Both responses were of a punitive nature and both were supported by the Soviet Union. However, one of the principal abuses perpetrated by the Soviet Union, apart from the many deaths and injuries from their bombardment, was the laying waste to large areas of agricultural land and property so that farmers could not secure a livelihood and had no choice but to leave.

Within the Mujahidin, Jamiat-e-Islami forces were widely reported to have been responsible for what has been termed the Afshar massacre when their forces launched a punitive offensive, in February 1993, against the Hazara neighbourhood of Afshar in western Kabul.

The Taliban were also reported to have engaged in massacres of a punitive nature against Hazara populations when they captured Mazar-e Sharif and the Hazarajat in 1998. This was, in part, a response to the murder, under horrific circumstances, of large numbers of Taliban fighters, by Uzbek militia, when the Hazara population of Mazar-e Sharif resisted an earlier attempt on the city. The Taliban's use of force to impose their behavioural and dress codes, as well as the bans imposed on female access to employment and health care, has also generated worldwide concern.

The US-led intervention created an environment in which the many militia in the country felt free to commit violence without fear that they would be held to account. A further massacre, by Uzbek militia, of Taliban fighters in the immediate aftermath of the intervention, was an early manifestation of this climate of impunity. The US Government also opted to create its own network of detention facilities to interrogate those who were suspected of links to Al-Qaida, the Taliban or other radical Islamic organizations. These detention facilities, at Guantanamo Bay, Bagram, Kandahar and elsewhere, have seriously tarnished the reputation of the USA, both within Afghanistan and globally, and undermined its efforts to build up the Afghan state in pursuit of its strategic interests. In the case of the US-led intervention, therefore, it is the USA which is most directly involved in the interrogation of suspects whereas, with the Soviet intervention, it was the Afghan Government.

Thus, while the Government of Hamid Karzai has been found, by the US Department of State, to be responsible for, among other human rights abuses, cases of arbitrary arrests, extra-judicial killings, torture and poor prison conditions, it is the USA which has come in for the greatest criticism on account of its treatment of prisoners in Guantanamo Bay and at the various detention centres in Afghanistan.

Those who have been arrested by the USA are not the intellectuals who were actively targeted by the PDPA, the Mujahidin and the Taliban. Rather, it is the rural population which finds itself at risk of arrest, torture and imprisonment during the post-2001 period, on account of its suspected sympathy for the Taliban, Al-Qaida, Hisb-e-Islami or other radical elements. As with the Soviet intervention, there has been a tendency to be over-suspicious, meaning that people have been taken in for questioning with initial evidence that they represent a threat to the Government that is, at best, tenuous.

Strategic interest versus humanitarianism

A central question in this book is whether the major powers that have intervened in Afghanistan achieved the strategic objectives which they pursued, and whether the use of aid was instrumental in their success or failure in this regard. A related question, in considering the US-led intervention, is whether the pursuit of strategic objectives has undermined the achievement of humanitarian objectives.

It could reasonably be argued that the British, in seeking to establish their presence in order to prevent Russia doing likewise, were able to secure a degree of public acquiescence through the provision of gold and subsidies. In imposing a 'puppet' government, through Shah Shuja, the use of their assistance clearly enabled him to remain in power. However, the benefit to the British of the initial willingness of the population to accept gold or other subsidies was, offset by public anger over affronts to traditional and Islamic values and over acts of brutality.

Thus, when the British faced growing manifestations of discontent towards the end of the first Anglo-Afghan War, their efforts to bribe the population through payments to those in leadership positions were of no effect. This clearly demonstrated that the need to assert dignity, in the face of assaults on personal honour and of acts of humiliation, is a more powerful driving force than the desire for material gain.

The experience of the Soviet Union was not dissimilar. Although it had invested significantly in the Afghan economy during the 25 years leading up to its military intervention, this was of no weight in comparison with the actions of the PDPA in seeking to impose socialist values on the population. Further, the insensitivity demonstrated, and the brutality used, by the PDPA Government seriously alienated the population. The subsequent violence committed by Soviet forces on the population accentuated this sense of alienation.

It also led to a large-scale exodus from both rural and urban areas, which placed much of the population in very different political environments, those of the refugee camps of Pakistan and the cities of Iran. They were therefore removed from any influence that the PDPA Government or the Soviet Union might exert through the media or through engagement with tribal or other leaders.

In addition, the PDPA Government lost its potential capacity to build a support base within the urban population through its purges of intellectuals, liberals and professionals. The absolute intolerance shown to anyone who did not share the PDPA vision therefore had a major impact. The Soviet Union may have hoped to establish a permanent military presence in Afghanistan, but it failed.

The USA may still have such hopes, but it may also fail. The insecurity that has been generated by the pursuit of the 'war on terror' has, therefore, very clearly excluded the possibility of large-scale reconstruction assistance to the population, such as to seriously impact on their livelihoods. Further, the delivery of aid has become identified with a US-led state-building process and with the international military presence, by virtue of the involvement of the international military in the initiation of strategic 'hearts and minds' aid projects. Aid has thus been tainted by association and this has made aid workers into what are seen as legitimate targets of terrorist attacks, along with government officials, members of the Afghan

National Army, police, religious figures demonstrating an allegiance to the government, and construction workers engaged in US-funded infrastructure projects. Completed aid projects are also seen as legitimate targets; schools, for example, have been burned down, in large numbers, because they are identified with the foreign presence and are thereby assumed to be inculcating Western values.

This raises the important question of the extent to which the provision of aid does influence public attitudes. A central flaw in the counter-insurgency approach of the international military is an assumption that the support of the population can be won through greater reconstruction assistance. This leads to an expectation that, if areas can be temporarily 'liberated', NGOs can come in to provide reconstruction assistance which will then encourage the population to withhold support for any renewed intervention by the insurgents. The view taken by a majority of NGOs, that it is not safe for them to operate in areas which have recently been retaken by international military forces, tends to be dismissed as a failure on their part, rather than a reasonable and considered response to the situation. This assumption, by the international military, that reconstruction assistance is the key to consolidating military gains also downplays the negative influences such as the impact of civilian deaths or affronts to sensibilities. The population is assumed to be easily 'bought', to be primarily influenced by material gain rather than personal honour and dignity.

The provision of aid also needs to be placed in the context of economic realities. In a situation in which the majority of the population is having to survive on the land, the level of investment in agriculture needs to be sufficiently large to make a difference. Alternatively, additional income-earning opportunities need to be made available through the creation of manufacturing or service-sector outlets. If aid is delivered on a relatively small scale, it may not make a sufficient difference to people's lives, even in the areas where it is delivered, for it to be felt to be significant. Further, it may not benefit the whole of the population in the areas concerned. In addition, there will be many areas where aid has not been provided at all. This may lead to perception that, overall, nothing much has been done.

There is, therefore, always the risk that the aid giver will overestimate the degree of difference that a project will make to people's lives, relative to the many other factors which condition their daily struggles to survive. Further, there is a tendency to assume that the population can live through agriculture alone whereas the reality, in Afghanistan, is that a high proportion of households have relied, for many decades, on being able to send one or more sons to Pakistan or Iran, or to one of the urban centres of Afghanistan, to look for work. The provision of support to the agriculture sector may therefore reduce the need to opt for labour migration as an economic strategy but, from the experience of the author, it is unlikely to be sufficient to totally remove that need.

To date, none of the three powers that have intervened have provided reconstruction assistance on the scale that would be required to make the population, at large, feel that their lives are clearly better. It does not, therefore, take much by way of negative influences for the population to feel that the benefits of aid are of little consequence. When these negative influences include ongoing acts of brutality, affronts to values, disrespectful behaviour, a failure to provide good security and a perception that the government is corrupt, aid pales into absolute insignificance.

Further, with both the Soviet and the US-led interventions, there was media-induced optimism, in the early stages, that reconstruction assistance would be delivered on a sufficient scale to make a real difference. Disillusionment soon followed when this failed to happen. It also led to anger over the existence of elites, within the government and amongst the plethora of international advisers, which were living in obvious affluence.

Experiences in Afghanistan suggest that humanitarianism can only function effectively when the interests of the major powers are not being played out, albeit with varying degrees of compromise. This indicates that aid can continue to be effective in countries which are not of strategic interest to these powers.

Pakistan's pursuit of its own strategic goals has added enormously to the risks that aid staff face in Afghanistan. Further, humanitarian agencies were not able to totally distance themselves from the activities of the Mujahidin parties in their midst as they sought to deliver services in the refugee camps in Pakistan. Nor were they able to adhere strictly to their humanitarian principles when operating in

Taliban-controlled areas. While they sought to negotiate a relaxation of the restrictions placed by the Taliban on female access to education, employment and health care, they had no choice but to compromise on their humanitarian principles in continuing to operate.

Conversely, the active pursuit of strategic and economic interests by the major powers can seriously undermine humanitarian effort and place aid organisations in a situation in which they are associated with the pursuit of these interests. Thus, the humanitarian agencies operating in Afghanistan since 2001 have totally failed in their efforts to dissociate themselves from the international military presence. Their image of neutrality and impartiality, which they carefully built up during the 1990s, has been completely lost. Instead, they are caught up in a situation in which there is no differentiation between one element and another, as far as the Taliban and other radical organisations are concerned, within what is perceived as a US-led state-building process. Thus, European military forces are not differentiated from US forces, aid workers are not differentiated from members of the Afghan Government, and the police are not differentiated from members of the Afghan National Army. All are associated with an international presence which is deemed to be unacceptable. Aid workers are thus seen as symbols of an imperialist process, much as they might perceive themselves as independent of that process. They thus draw on their humanitarian principles and their assessments of levels of humanitarian need, as well as their assessments of security risks, to take a nuanced position in relation to their own decisions to remain in Afghanistan or leave. There is no scope for nuances on the side of the resistance forces.

The creation of livelihoods

The vast majority of the population depend heavily on agriculture for their survival, although labour migration to Pakistan and Iran has long represented an important source of additional income. A number of initiatives during the 1950–78 period had the objective of increasing agricultural production. These included the US project to construct two dams in southern Afghanistan and the project initiated by China to improve irrigation in the Shomali Valley.

However, agricultural production suffered dramatically from the events which followed the 1978 coup, and a large part of the population had to opt for the food distribution programmes of the refugee camps in Pakistan, or look for work in Iran, Pakistan or the Gulf states.

The Soviet-backed government of 1978–92 was not able to do much more than provide a safety net, through subsidies on basic essentials, for those in the cities. The little investment that the Soviet Union made to the Afghan economy was largely geared to the export of natural gas, fertilizer and cement to the Soviet Republics of Central Asia. The contribution that was made to the creation of sustainable livelihoods was therefore very small. The obvious exception was the financial underpinning that the Soviet Union made to the army, the civil service and the PDPA itself. This ensured the employment of 250,000 people. However, with most of the rural areas under the control of the resistance, there was almost no investment in agriculture and, as has already been noted, agricultural production declined as a consequence of Soviet military operations.

With the greater access to the rural areas provided after 1992, UN organizations and NGOs were able to have a significant impact on agricultural production through programmes to provide improved seeds, repair flood production structures and vaccinate livestock. Incomes were also provided through UN and NGO programmes which delivered education, health care, water supply and sanitation services in both rural and urban areas. Further, many of these programmes benefited from an integrated rural development approach, in which NGOs would actively engage with beneficiary populations to agree on priorities and delivery mechanisms.

However, Kabul became increasingly impoverished as a consequence of the in-fighting between the Mujahidin groups. Particularly heavy fighting, which also involved Dostam's forces, in January 1994 led to a further exodus to refugee camps in Pakistan and also required the creation of camps for over 200,000 displaced people near Jalalabad. This was followed by the blockade instituted by the Taliban from 1995–6 in which the population suffered considerable privations.

Further, the offensives launched by the Taliban against Jamiat-e-Islami forces in the Shomali Valley, between 1996 and 2001, removed an important area of agricultural production from the market and also led to a large-scale influx of people into the capital. Kabul also lost its role as a trading post as the route to the north over the Salang Pass was now closed. In addition, civil servants were not being paid. Kabul was, therefore, a dead economy in which the population was dependent on food handouts.

The 1999–2002 period also saw a serious drought in large areas of the country. The World Food Programme (WFP) responded with large quantities of food assistance, which NGOs distributed from WFP warehouses in regional centres. The US-led intervention of October 2001 seriously disrupted the distribution process and also led to renewed displacement and the creation of new camps, in which the UN and NGOs worked to ensure food security.

Following the US-led intervention, the efforts of UN agencies and NGOs to support and strengthen agriculture were increasingly constrained by the adverse security situation. However, they were able to continue the integrated rural development approach through the Afghan Government's National Solidarity Programme, albeit in one-year cycles rather than the previous three facilitated by funding from the European Commission. The Government's National Emergency Employment Programme also provided a mechanism for safety net projects to be set up in the rural areas.

The large-scale return of refugees from Pakistan and Iran, under pressure from both countries, placed the economy under considerable strain. So long as Afghans were able to return to both countries to look for work, they could sustain their families. However, with the heightened pressures that Pakistan and Iran have placed on the Afghan populations during 2007, the situation, in terms of the ability of the Afghan economy to ensure adequate livelihoods for its population, looks very serious.

One consequence of the return of refugees has been a pronounced urbanization process. Kabul, for example, has seen an increase from less than a million in 2001 to over 4 million in 2007. Other cities have also seen large increases. While WFP, together with NGOs, have continued to operate safety net programmes, the population has faced considerable difficulties in its efforts to survive. The construction boom, which has been stimulated by the arrival of the international community, in large numbers, since 2001 and by the funds in circulation from the growing drugs trade, has provided an important source of short-term employment. It is, however, the pattern that those working on construction sites are only able to secure work on an intermittent, rather than continuing, basis. The annual opium harvest also provides a source of seasonal labour.

However, the inflation in property prices, which has arisen as a consequence of the international presence, the investment by drug barons and the increase in the population, has had a considerable impact on the ability of the population to afford accommodation. This has inevitably squeezed the funds which are available for food. The Afghan economy is, therefore, one that is highly polarized, with a small elite living in relative comfort while the broad mass of the population remain highly impoverished.

The adverse security created as a consequence of the US pursuit of the 'war on terror', among other factors, has served to discourage any significant level of investment by international companies. As a result, there has been no real emergence of a manufacturing sector to generate additional sources of livelihood. The economy has, therefore, remained dependent on a combination of agricultural production, informal trading and labour migration.

In conclusion, it could be stated that the US-led intervention has not had an obviously beneficial effect on livelihoods, although there are some exceptions, as in the case of the Afghan Government's National Solidarity Programme. It is also apparent, in looking back over the period since 1978, that it is the UN and NGOs, together with the Afghan Government since 2001, which have made the greatest impact on the capacity of the population to sustain itself.

Economic development

The period of greatest economic development was during the 1950–78 period. Thereafter, the disruption created by the policies of the PDPA Government, and the subsequent destruction of much of the agricultural base as a result of bombing raids, led to an ongoing decline in the economy. The 1995–9 period saw some improvement, with an expansion in agricultural production as a consequence of greater security and improved access to project areas for the UN and NGOs. However, a serious drought from 1999–2002 significantly reduced agricultural output. Agricultural production has improved again, since 2002, in many areas, albeit with some fluctuation due to climatic conditions and insecurity. However, the economy, although it has shown some growth, has not attracted much inward investment. The major exception is the telecommunications industry, which has grown enormously. The Kabul economy is nonetheless heavily dependent on the income that is derived from the significant international presence and from the drugs trade. The Herat economy is closely linked to that of Iran, and has appeared to be negatively affected by the downturn in the Iranian economy.

In neither the Soviet nor the US interventions has the economy grown to the extent expected from the resources injected. In part, this has been because a high proportion of the resources allocated have been spent on the international military deployment. It has also been because some of the aid allocated has been geared to the interests of the two countries. In the case of the Soviet Union, it benefited from highly concessional terms to access Afghan gas supplies. In the case of the USA, a significant percentage of the funds allocated by USAID were spent on US contractors. Much of the Soviet-provided infrastructure was damaged by sabotage and this has also been the case, albeit to a much lesser extent, with regard to US assistance.

Public administration reform

The process of building up the administrative capacity of the Afghan state made the greatest progress over the 1953–78 period. However, even at the end of this period, it was not able to pay its civil servants sufficiently high salaries to overturn a culture of corruption in which bribes were demanded for bureaucratic services rendered. The police force was particularly corrupt. Further, the operations of civil service remained heavily influenced by systems of patronage in which power holders in the provinces had their people within the government bureaucracy.

However, the capacity of the various ministries benefited from the enhanced investment in education from the 1950s onwards. The gains thus made in competence were then offset by the purges instituted by the PDPA. These set in motion a haemorrhaging of the civil service, which continued throughout the period of the Soviet military presence. It was accelerated further when the in-fighting between the Mujahidin in 1992–6 led to two major migrations of population and accelerated even faster when the Taliban placed a ban on the employment of women and began to intimidate and threaten intellectuals and professionals.

The efforts of the international community to again build up the state have therefore started from a low base. However, these efforts have been undermined by the continuing system of patronage and the culture of corruption. Further, it is difficult for government to recruit and retain good staff when higher wages can be secured with one or other of the international organizations in the capital.

A key parallel between the Soviet and US-led interventions has been the injection of advisers into government ministries. This has been in order to build up their capacity, but also with the objective of bringing the government administration into line with, in the case of the Soviet Union, its own systems, and, in the case of the USA, good practice in relation to global economic systems. The Soviet emphasis on state control of key elements of the infrastructure can therefore be contrasted with the strong emphasis in the present Afghan Government's development plan, which looks primarily to the private sector to deliver services and sees an important role of government as being to provide a facilitating environment for private sector investment. But just as the Soviet Union invested in the gas fields in northern Afghanistan and conducted surveys of oil deposits, so a US company has undertaken a further and more comprehensive survey of oil reserves.

However, the injection of advisers has been found, in both cases, to be of limited effectiveness. Further, the insecurity which has characterized much of the post-2001 period, combined with disillusionment, over corruption within the Government and other issues, has served as a major disincentive for professionals in the Afghan diaspora to return.

Another key parallel between the two interventions has been the high priority given to the provision of training to the national army and to the police. In both cases, the efforts with regard to the army, in terms of creating an effective force, were greater than with the police. The endemic corruption that has characterized the police for decades has foiled all efforts to reform it.

The effectiveness of aid

In considering whether aid is effective in alleviating poverty or in providing essential services to the population, there are two primary considerations: the adequacy of the level of engagement with beneficiaries and the ease of access to project locations. These considerations apply whether the aid is provided for humanitarian purposes or in pursuit of strategic objectives.

With regard to the level of engagement with beneficiaries, the experience of the past 18 years has been that programmes should ideally benefit from in-depth discussions with the representatives of targeted beneficiaries over a reasonably long period. This ensures that those in receipt of the assistance are fully involved in both the planning and delivery processes. It also minimizes suspicions that some are benefiting more than others if the discussion process is as transparent as possible. A related lesson is that if aid is provided on too large a scale over too short a period it can generate suspicions and create tensions within communities.

Over the 1989–2001 period, there was a marked shift away from emergency or 'quick impact' programming towards an integrated community development approach, with three-year funding cycles. Regrettably, the post-2001 period has seen a return to shorter funding cycles. This has been aggravated by the tendency of the international military to initiate short-term projects in pursuit of their 'hearts and minds' strategies.

During the period of the Mujahidin Government, when access might need to be negotiated with a multiplicity of power holders en route to the final destination, the complexities involved were the major constraint, while cost and security were certainly also significant factors. Over this period, the Afghan staff of NGOs were much less at risk than expatriates.

The complexities of negotiating with the Taliban were also considerable, but the security environment, during the period of the Taliban Government, was generally good, making access much easier than it was during the previous period and also than it has been since 2001.

The primary consideration since 2001 has been the risk that aid personnel will be killed as a consequence of targeted assassinations because they are associated with the state-building process. Afghan staff have been as much at risk as expatriates, if not at greater risk. The risks faced by NGOs are therefore much greater now than they were during the 1989–2001 period and this has affected the ability of technical and managerial staff to oversee the quality of the work undertaken, monitor progress and evaluate outcomes.

The acceptability of aid

Aid may be rejected if it is provided by a donor which is deemed to be unacceptable or if it is given in compensation for some harm done and is perceived to be insulting.

In the case of the British intervention of 1839–42, the Afghan population rejected the very presence of the British colony, because of its behaviour, even though this meant a potential loss of subsidies and other benefits. There was a similar rejection of the arrival of a British mission in 1879, manifested in the assassination of British representatives. Further, the hangings ordered by General Roberts, later that year, can be assumed to be one of the factors which led the British to conclude that it was better to do a deal with Abdur-Rahman than seek to remain in Afghanistan.

On the other hand, the aid provided by multiple donors between 1950 and 1978 was broadly welcomed, even though major initiatives such as the Helmand Valley Project did create some tensions between the Afghan and US governments. This was because it was not accompanied by any use of military force or by any major effort to replace traditional and Islamic values with alternative ones. Thus, while the reform programmes introduced by Daoud did seek to change Afghan society, his initiatives were carefully calibrated so as to minimize the risk of a backlash and, when it happened, to contain it. Similarly, the growth of educational establishments from the Soviet Union, the USA, France and Germany brought about subtle changes in attitudes within the urban population while leaving the rural population untouched.

The aid provided by the Soviet Union from 1979, in contrast, was largely allocated to the financial underpinning of an Afghan Government which had already alienated the population through its purges and its resort to force, brutality and culturally insensitive behaviour in seeking to impose its reforms. Contained within this underpinning was support to the Afghan army and intelligence services. Further, the Soviet Union included, in what it regarded as its official assistance to Afghanistan, the supply of Soviet troops and weaponry. This aid was therefore acceptable to the Government but not to the population.

It could be argued that the assistance received by the Taliban from elements within Pakistan was similarly geared to sustaining the movement although, given that the Taliban gave extremely low priority to public services, these resources were primarily used in support of the military efforts of the Taliban.

A similar prioritization of support to the infrastructure of the state is evident in the US-led intervention. Thus, the costs of operating the government administration are largely met by the international community, as are those of the Afghan National Army and Afghan National Police. A further large-scale allocation of resources has been committed to the electoral process on the basis of the view held by the US Government, in particular, that the establishment of democracy was an early priority.

The population has been seriously alienated by the actions of US forces and has come to view the Karzai Government in a negative light, in view of its perceived corruption. This has meant that the aid provided to the state-building process is seen as of no consequence, at best, and as reinforcing the view that the Government is backed by foreign powers, at worst.

The aid that might be more obviously beneficial to the population, such as the provision of education and health care and the reconstruction of the major highway system, is thereby tainted by association, leading to attacks on schools, teaching staff, pupils, health workers and personnel working on US-funded reconstruction projects.

Further, the efforts of international forces to compensate for civilian deaths, caused as an outcome of their military operations, through offers of schools or clinics are seen as insulting. On the few occasions that direct compensation is given to the families of those killed, this is often on such a small scale as to be derisory.

Aid therefore tends to be unacceptable when it is accompanied by force, brutality or by behaviour which is disrespectful, insulting to the dignity of the individual or culturally insensitive. The assumption consistently made by the international military, that the desire for material benefit will prevail over all other considerations, is thus deeply flawed.

Overall conclusions

The three major powers which intervened in Afghanistan proved to be unsuccessful in the pursuit of their strategic goals. Their inability to win the support of the Afghan population has been a major factor in their failure to achieve these goals. In fact, their tendency to inflame opinion has been an important characteristic of their interventions.

To seek to deliver aid as a means of winning hearts and minds is therefore ineffective. The provision of aid should, more appropriately, be the outcome of a sense of responsibility to address poverty and disadvantage. It should, therefore, be an end in itself rather than a means to another end.

ENDNOTES

1. 'Papers on Frontier Politics: Russia and Kabul: 1877–1878', from a collection of 26 confidential and other British Government memoranda: 1877–1885, compiled for General Sir James Browne. Property of Camellia plc, Linton Park, Kent.
2. Collection of letters from First Afghan War, held by Camellia plc. Linton Park, Kent.
3. Hopkirk, Peter, *The Great Game* (Oxford, 1991) p.237.
4. Hopkirk: *The Great Game*, p.238.
5. Hopkirk: *The Great Game*, p.238.
6. Hyman, Anthony, *Afghanistan under Soviet domination: 1964–83*, (London, 1984), p.148.
7. Nyrop, Richard F. and Seekins, Donald M., (eds.) *Afghanistan: A Country Study: The Economy* (Washington DC, 1986).
8. Nyrop and Seekins: *Afghanistan: A Country Study: The Economy*.
9. Nyrop and Seekins: *Afghanistan: A Country Study: The Economy*.
10. Hyman: *Afghanistan under Soviet domination: 1964–83*, p.120.
11. Hyman: *Afghanistan under Soviet domination: 1964–83*, p.155.
12. Hyman: *Afghanistan under Soviet domination: 1964–83*, p.108.
13. Hyman: *Afghanistan under Soviet domination: 1964–83*, p.111.
14. Hyman: *Afghanistan under Soviet domination: 1964–83*, p.165, incorporating quote from J. Erikson, 'Soviet Strategic Emplacement', *Asian Affairs*, February 1981.
15. Singleton, Dr Seth, 'The Soviet Invasion of Afghanistan', *Air University Review* (Ripon College, Wisconsin), March–April 1981.
16. Hyman: *Afghanistan under Soviet domination: 1964–83*, p.168.
17. Hyman: *Afghanistan under Soviet domination: 1964–83*, p.165.
18. Hyman: *Afghanistan under Soviet domination: 1964–83*, p.176.
19. Nyrop and Seekins: *Afghanistan: A Country Study: The Economy*.
20. Nyrop and Seekins: *Afghanistan: A Country Study: The Economy*.
21. Hyman: *Afghanistan under Soviet domination: 1964–83*, p.36.

22. Hyman: *Afghanistan under Soviet domination: 1964–83*, p.37.
23. Nyrop and Seekins: *Afghanistan: A Country Study: The Economy.*
24. Nyrop and Seekins: *Afghanistan: A Country Study: The Economy.*
25. Hyman: *Afghanistan under Soviet domination: 1964–83*, p.201.
26. Hyman: *Afghanistan under Soviet domination: 1964–83*, p.126.
27. Hyman: *Afghanistan under Soviet domination: 1964–83*, p.127.
28. Hyman: *Afghanistan under Soviet domination: 1964–83*, p.138.
29. 'Military Intervention in Afghanistan: Implications for British Foreign and Defence Policy', *Basic Papers – Occasional Papers on International Security Policy*, September 2002 , Number 40, ISSN 1353-0402.
30. Rebuilding America's Defenses: Strategy, Forces and Resources for a New Century : A Report of the Project for the New American Century, September 2000, p.i.
31. Rebuilding America's Defenses, p.i.
32. Rebuilding America's Defenses, p.ii.
33. Rebuilding America's Defenses, p.iii.
34. Rebuilding America's Defenses, p.iv.
35. Rebuilding America's Defenses, p.5.
36. Rebuilding America's Defenses, p.6.
37. Rebuilding America's Defenses, p.8.
38. Rebuilding America's Defenses, p.11.
39. Rebuilding America's Defenses, p.17.
40. Rebuilding America's Defenses, p.19.
41. '2006 Country Reports on Human Rights Practices' (US Department of State, 6 March 2007).
42. Human Rights Watch, press release issued on 16 February 2007.
43. Johnson, Chris, 'Afghanistan and the "war on terror"', *Humanitarian Action and the Global War on Terror: a review of trends and issues* (ODI).
44. Johnson: 'Afghanistan and the "war on terror"'.
45. Johnson: 'Afghanistan and the "war on terror"'.
46. Johnson: 'Afghanistan and the "war on terror"'.
47. Johnson: 'Afghanistan and the "war on terror"'.
48. Johnson: 'Afghanistan and the "war on terror"'.
49. Johnson: 'Afghanistan and the "war on terror"'.
50. Johnson: 'Afghanistan and the "war on terror"'.
51. Johnson: 'Afghanistan and the "war on terror"'.
52. Johnson: 'Afghanistan and the "war on terror"'.
53. 'Counterinsurgency' (Headquarters Department of the US Army, December 2006).
54. Afghan NGO Security Office, January 2006.
55. Agency Coordinating Body for Afghan Relief, March 2007.
56. Morajee, Rachel, *Christian Science Monitor*, 10 May 2007.

INDEX